OXFORD WORLD

THE OXFORD SH.

General Editor · Stanley Wells

The Oxford Shakespeare offers new and authoritative editions of Shakespeare's plays in which the early printings have been scrupulously re-examined and interpreted. An introductory essay provides all relevant background information together with an appraisal of critical views and of the play's effects in performance. The detailed commentaries pay particular attention to language and staging. Reprints of sources, music for songs, genealogical tables, maps, etc. are included where necessary; many of the volumes are illustrated, and all contain an index.

KENNETH MUIR, the editor of *Troilus and Cressida* in the Oxford Shakespeare, was Emeritus Professor and Honorary Senior Fellow in the University of Liverpool. He was also a Vice President of the International Shakespeare Association and a former editor of *Shakespeare Survey*. He edited four other Shakespeare plays, wrote twelve books on his works, and (in collaboration with Michael J. B. Allen) edited a facsimile of Shakespeare's quartos in a single volume.

THE OXFORD SHAKESPEARE

Currently available in paperback

The rest of the plays are forthcoming

OXFORD WORLD'S CLASSICS

WILLIAM SHAKESPEARE

Troilus and Cressida

Edited by
KENNETH MUIR

OXFORD
UNIVERSITY PRESS

OXFORD

UNIVERSITY PRESS

Great Clarendon Street, Oxford OX2 6DP

Oxford University Press is a department of the University of Oxford.
It furthers the University's objective of excellence in research, scholarship,
and education by publishing worldwide in

Oxford New York

Auckland Bangkok Buenos Aires Cape Town Chennai
Dar es Salaam Delhi Hong Kong Istanbul Karachi Kolkata
Kuala Lumpur Madrid Melbourne Mexico City Mumbai Nairobi
São Paulo Shanghai Singapore Taipei Tokyo Toronto

with an associated company in Berlin

Published in the United States
by Oxford University Press Inc., New York

First published by the Clarendon Press 1982
First published as a World's Classics paperback 1994
Reissued as an Oxford World's Classics paperback 1998
Reissued 2008

British Library Cataloguing in Publication Data

Data available

Library of Congress Cataloging in Publication Data
Shakespeare, William, 1564–1616.
Troilus and Cressida.
(Oxford world's classics)
Bibliography: p. Includes index. I. Muir, Kenneth.
II. Title. III. Series: Shakespeare, William, 1564–1616. Works. 1982.
PR2836.A2M84 1984 822.3'3 83–17483

ISBN 978–0–19–953653–5

3

Printed in Great Britain by
Clays Ltd, St Ives plc

PREFACE

THIS edition of *Troilus and Cressida* is indebted to a long line of previous editors, especially to the New Variorum edition of H. N. Hillebrand and the (Cambridge) edition of Alice Walker, although my interpretation of the play differs greatly from hers. My debt to Bonamy Dobrée is a more personal one since I had the privilege of discussing the play with him after he had seen a production by the York Settlement Community Players and while he was engaged on his edition. My greatest debt, however, is to the General Editor for his valuable suggestions and to Gary Taylor for letting me use a then unpublished article on the text of the play.

I should mention that the latest production of the play, by Terry Hands at the Aldwych Theatre (July 1981), was too late to be mentioned in the Introduction. According to a review in *The Times Literary Supplement*, it was 'seen from the perspective of Thersites'.

Mary Z. Maher's admirable doctoral thesis, *A Rhetorical Analysis of Troilus and Cressida* (University of Michigan, 1973), came to my attention too late for me to use.

KENNETH MUIR

University of Liverpool
September 1981

CONTENTS

INTRODUCTION

Troilus and Cressida has a number of unsolved, if not insoluble, problems. The exact date and place of the first performance are uncertain; we do not know whether it was ever publicly performed; we do not know for certain the nature of the manuscript which formed the copy for the Quarto (1609) or of the manuscript by which a copy of that edition was corrected for the First Folio (1623); and, more significantly, critics are as hopelessly divided as theatrical directors in their interpretation of the play.

Text

The play was entered in the Stationers' Register on 7 February 1603:[1]

m^r Robertes Entred for his copie in Full Court holden this day to print when he hath gotten sufficient aucthority for yt. The booke of Troilus and Cresseda as yt is acted by my lo: Chamb⟨er⟩lens Men   vj^d

Presumably Roberts did not obtain the necessary authority as he did not publish the play. Six years later, on 28 January 1609, there is another entry relating to the play:

Ri⟨chard⟩. Bonion   Entred for their Copy vnder thandes of m^r Segar
Henry Walleys   deputy to Sr George Bucke & m^r ward⟨en⟩. Lownes a booke called The history of Troylus & Cressida   vj^d

It was duly printed later that year, at first with the title-page shown in Fig. 1. (The Lord Chamberlain's Men had of course become the King's Majesty's servants.) While the edition was at press, the publishers were informed, or misinformed, that the play had not been seen at the Globe; they therefore prepared a cancel title-page altering the play's title and description (Fig. 2) and added an Epistle to the Reader implying that it was a sign of quality that the play had not been publicly acted. The rest of the title-page was

---

[1] S. Schoenbaum, *William Shakespeare: Records and Images* (New York and London, 1981), 216, 219.

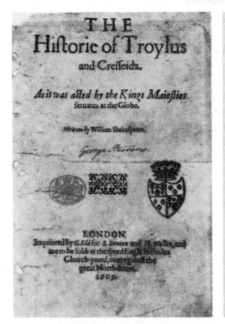

Fig. 1. Q^a

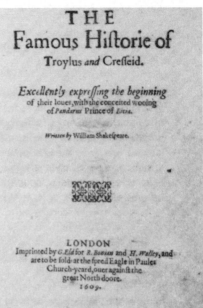

Fig. 2. Q^b

unchanged. The description of the play, calling attention to Pandarus' wooing – meaning presumably his wooing of Cressida on behalf of Troilus – is, to say the least, misleading. It supports the line taken in the Epistle that the play was comical. (The Epistle is printed and discussed in Appendix 1.)

Three copies of the first state (Q^a) survive, eleven of the second (Q^b), and one copy includes both title-pages and the Epistle. Altogether there are fifteen variants in the different copies and the Malone copy in the Bodleian Library contains twelve of the corrected readings. The corrections are of obvious misprints and need not have involved a reference to the manuscript.[1]

The next appearance of the play was in the First Folio. It had been intended that it should follow *Romeo and Juliet* and precede *Julius Caesar*. The printers began setting the play, using the Quarto text, but then it is thought that copyright difficulties with the publishers of the Quarto forced them to desist. *Timon of Athens* was inserted to fill some of the gap; but when the setting of the Folio was

[1] They are listed in the New Variorum, p. 323.

nearing completion the editors obtained a manuscript of the play, so that they could claim not to be simply reprinting the Quarto text. They therefore shoved the play after the last of the English Histories – *Henry VIII* – and before *Coriolanus*, but too late to include its title in the table of contents. They were able to add the Prologue, but the first page of the first scene was reset from the cancelled Folio page with numerous compositorial changes.[1] The next two pages were printed from the original setting. Thereafter – after 1.2.221– the printers consulted the manuscript, except for two other substantial passages where they had to rely on the Quarto text alone, the evidence for this being the absence of substantive variants.[2]

It is reasonably certain that the Folio text was set from a copy of the Quarto in which corrections had been made by comparison with the manuscript.[3] Some corrections were doubtless over-looked. The Quarto text is generally thought to be based on a private transcript of Shakespeare's foul papers, perhaps by the poet himself, and the Folio manuscript on the foul papers or a prompt-book based on them;[4] but Gary Taylor has recently argued that the Quarto derives from the foul papers, and the Folio from the prompt-book.[5] This would mean that the Folio text embodies some altera-tions by Shakespeare himself, not all of them improvements. The main thesis is convincing (although I cannot accept all the con-clusions that Taylor derives from it), and I have acted upon it in preparing my text.

There are more than five thousand differences between Q and F, mostly in spelling and punctuation, and these can 'be explained by the conscious or unconscious editing done by the F compositors';[6] but there are also about five hundred substantive differences. Both Q and F are good texts; and either could serve as control-text of a modern edition. F often corrects Q's errors and provides a large number of superior readings. With each variant one has to decide

---

[1] They are listed in the New Variorum, 324–7.

[2] K. Muir, 'A Note on the Text of *Troilus and Cressida*', *The Library*, 1 (1979), 168.

[3] Philip Williams, 'Shakespeare's *Troilus and Cressida*: the Relationship of Quarto and Folio', *Studies in Bibliography*, 3 (1950), 131–43.

[4] W. W. Greg, *The Shakespeare First Folio* (Oxford, 1955), 348, suggested that the company dispensed with a prompt-book as there was to be only a single perfor-mance.

[5] Gary Taylor, '*Troilus and Cressida*: Bibliography, Performance, and Interpreta-tion', *Shakespeare Studies*, 15 (1982), 99–136.

[6] New Variorum, 347.

whether F restored the true reading, introduced a genuine Shakespearian alteration, or committed an unauthorized 'improvement'. This edition takes Q as its control-text: it is assumed that its errors were due to the compositors, whereas those of F may be due to a variety of causes, not all authorial.

Two other points have to be borne in mind in attempting to establish a text of *Troilus and Cressida*. The Q text was set by two compositors with different habits and different foibles,[1] and the F text was likewise set by two or more compositors.[2] But even though we knew the errors to which these various compositors were prone, we could not be certain, in any particular instance, that they were not faithful to their copy. Another complication arises in those passages for which Q is the sole authority. Here one should be more willing to emend than elsewhere in the play, although the collator certainly overlooked some necessary corrections. He would be the more likely to do this because of the urgency of the task: if Hinman's calculations are sound, the play was set in nine working days. It follows that one has sometimes to emend even when the two texts correspond.[3]

The present edition, while taking Q as its control-text, is inevitably eclectic. Happily there is general agreement among modern editors in their choice of four hundred and forty variants; on another sixty they disagree, and in such cases we generally follow Q, unless there seem to be strong dramatic or literary grounds for departing from it. This leaves some eighty places where Q and F, whether agreeing or disagreeing with each other, provide readings so unsatisfactory that they have been emended in one way or another. The present edition, although conservative, introduces two emendations in lines which have been accepted without question by previous editors.[4] One or two passages, where lines have apparently dropped out, are beyond surgery,[5] and in several others we may suspect that a plausible F reading is further from what

[1] Philip Williams, 'Shakespeare's *Troilus and Cressida*'.

[2] Cf. Charlton Hinman, *The Printing and Proof-Reading of the First Folio of Shakespeare*, 2 vols. (Oxford, 1963), esp. ii. 326–40; Alice Walker, *Textual Problems of the First Folio* (Cambridge, 1953), esp. pp. 86–93; Gary Taylor, 'The Shrinking Compositor A of the First Folio', *Studies in Bibliography*, 34 (1981), 96–117.

[3] When the texts differ, one acts as a check of the other; when they are the same, this may conceal some careless collating.

[4] i.e. 2.2.119, 3.3.34.

[5] See 5.3.19–24, and Appendix 2d.

Shakespeare wrote than the unintelligible Q reading it replaces (e.g. *shrupd*).[1] One other textual matter should be mentioned here, although it will be discussed in another connection – the probability that there were alternative endings to the play, with or without Pandarus' closing speech, which, though spoken in character, forms a kind of epilogue.

Date

From the entry in the Stationers' Register we know that a version of the play existed in 1603, although this was not necessarily identical with the one that was published six years later. It used to be thought that some of the love passages belonged to the same period as *Romeo and Juliet*,[2] but there is little in the versification, the imagery, or the tone of the scenes to support such a theory. If the aubade in 4.2 recalls that of the earlier play, years rather than months may have lain between.

If, as will be argued in the section on Sources (pp. 12–19), Shakespeare had read *Seven Books* – the first instalment of Chapman's Homer – the play could not have been written before 1598. Although Shakespeare had exhibited knowledge of the Trojan story in *Lucrece*, it is noteworthy that he refers to Troilus and Cressida in *The Merchant of Venice* and to Cressida in *Henry V*, and that Troilus, Cressida, and Pandarus are mentioned in *Twelfth Night*. The tale of Troy figures prominently in *Hamlet* and allusively in *All's Well that Ends Well*.[3] *Troilus and Cressida*, moreover, seems closer in spirit to *Hamlet* and the 'problem' plays than to earlier comedies in which the heroines are all idealized. These considerations suggest that the play must be dated between 1598 and 1602.

The play has been associated with the War of the Theatres. There can be little doubt that the 'Prologue armed' (l. 23) is an allusion to the prologue in Jonson's *Poetaster* (1601), Shakespeare's 'gentleness' contrasting with, if not rebuking, Jonson's belligerence in the face of base detractors and illiterate apes

---

[1] See 4.5.193 n.

[2] F. G. Fleay, 'On the Composition of *Troylus and Cressida*', *New Shakspere Society's Transactions* (1874), 304–17.

[3] The virtuous Helena being contrasted with Helen of Troy; and the Clown has a song (1.3.66–75) about King Priam's joy, Helen.

(*Poetaster*, Prologue, l. 70). But since the Prologue is not included in the Quarto of *Troilus and Cressida*, it could have been added after the first performance. The rest of the play may therefore have been written before 1601.

In the Cambridge play *The Return from Parnassus*, Part 2 (1601), the actor Kemp complains that university dramatists

smell too much of that writer *Ovid*, and that writer *Metamorphosis*, and talke too much of *Proserpina & Iuppiter*. Why heres our fellow *Shakespeare* puts them all downe, I and *Ben Jonson* too. O that *Ben Jonson* is a pestilent fellow, he brought up *Horace* giving the Poets a pill, but our fellow *Shakespeare* hath given him a purge that made him beray his credit.[1]

It has not always been noticed that Kemp is here being satirized for his ignorance, as he is later satirized for his vanity, so that his abuse of Jonson is really a compliment by the authors. But presumably they believed that Shakespeare had somewhere satirized Jonson. It has been thought by many scholars[2] that the purge administered to Jonson must have been the curious portrait of Ajax in the second scene of *Troilus and Cressida* with its mention of 'humours' – which a contemporary audience might well associate with Jonson. Certainly the portrait bears little or no resemblance to the character when he appears later in the play; but the discrepancies may have been due to a change of plan during the composition of the play. Other scholars believe that the purge was Dekker's *Satiromastix* in which Jonson was indeed satirized, and which was performed by Shakespeare's company. The authors of *The Return from Parnassus* may have supposed that Shakespeare was the author. Marston, who was also involved in the War of the Theatres, is thought by some critics[3] to be portrayed as Thersites since his satires share the nastiness of Thersites' invective. But 'mastic jaws' (1.3.72) is not certainly a quibble on Marston's *Histriomastix*; nor, indeed, does the brief parody of a Troilus play by Marston necessarily refer to Shakespeare's, for there was a play by Dekker and Chettle called by Henslowe *Troyelles and Creasse* (7 April 1599), and the same play

[1] Ed. J. B. Leishman (1949), ll. 1766 ff., pp. 369–71.

[2] e.g. Robert Cartwright, *Shakspere and Jonson* (1864); F. G. Fleay, *Life of Shakespeare* (1886), p. 45; R. A. Small, *The Stage-Quarrel Between Ben Jonson and the So-Called Poetasters* (Breslau, 1899), pp. 168–9; William Elton, 'Shakespeare's Portrait of Ajax in *Troilus and Cressida*', *PMLA*, 63 (1948), 744–8.

[3] Fleay; Arthur Acheson, *Shakespeare's Sonnet Story 1592–1598* (1922), esp. pp. 494–510.

or a sequel entitled *Agamemnone* (26 May 1599).[1] Whether the fragmentary plot preserved in the Henslowe papers is of these, or of an earlier *Troye* (1596) is disputed. Either of these could be the object of Marston's parody. Although there is an obvious allusion to the War of the Theatres in *Hamlet* (2.2), the attempt to link *Troilus and Cressida* with the war is inconclusive.

Historical events have also been used to date the play, but with no greater success. Several critics have sought to show that Achilles is a portrait of the Earl of Essex.[2] They point out – and this is the one substantial piece of evidence – that Chapman had dedicated his *Seven Books* to Essex as 'the most honoured now living instance of the Achilleian virtues'. G. B. Harrison argued that the play was privately performed before an audience hostile to Essex, 'either in the summer of 1598 or else about two years later'.[3] John Dover Wilson, however, argued that the play was performed before an audience *friendly* to Essex, when he was sulking in the latter part of 1600, and that Shakespeare was urging him to make his peace with the Queen.[4] But, as Oscar J. Campbell aptly pointed out, 'to exhibit the efforts of the Greek chieftains to make Achilles join battle is certainly a curious way in which to tell Essex to do nothing'.[5] In the summer and autumn of 1600, moreover, Essex was continually beseeching the Queen for a renewal of her favour.[6] Essex was a friend of Southampton, Shakespeare's first patron, and, as late as 1599, there was a flattering reference to him in *Henry V* as 'the general of our gracious Empress' (Act 5, Prologue). If Achilles was in any sense intended as a portrait of Essex, the change of attitude is startling. It seems improbable, then, that Shakespeare was portraying Essex in the play; but there is no reason to doubt that *Troilus and Cressida* was first performed between 1599 and February 1603, and most critics favour the latter part of this period. The 'Dido' speeches in *Hamlet* could be regarded as a substitute for the third part of a Trojan war trilogy, of which *Troilus and Cressida* was the first; but there is no evidence that

---

[1] *Henslowe's Diary*, ed. R. A. Foakes and R. T. Rickert (Cambridge, 1961), 106, 121.

[2] New Variorum, 377–81.

[3] TLS (1930), 974.

[4] *The Essential Shakespeare* (Cambridge, 1932), 101–2.

[5] *Comicall Satyre and Shakespeare's 'Troilus and Cressida'* (San Marino, 1938), 223.

[6] Ibid., 220.

Shakespeare ever intended to write a sequel or sequels to the play.[1]

Most critics believe that the play was privately performed at one of the Inns of Court. The evidence for this is the scrapping of the original title-page of the Quarto, the added Epistle, the prevalence of debates and discussions, some legal terminology, and the epilogue which, it is thought, would be inappropriate for a performance at the Globe. A private performance would explain the publishers' claim that the play had 'never been clapper-clawed with the palms of the vulgar' nor 'sullied with the smoky breath of the multitude'. Nevertheless Bonian and Walley may have been mistaken in thinking that the play had not been acted publicly; or the Epistle may have been written after a private, but before a public, performance.

As we have seen, Pandarus at one time seems to have made his final appearance in 5.3 and the play ended with Troilus' couplet

> Strike a free march to Troy! With comfort go;
> Hope of revenge shall hide our inward woe.

Shakespeare could have changed his mind during the composition of the play, but it is more natural to suppose that there were alternative endings, one with the epilogue, the other without. One theory, propounded by Nevill Coghill and others,[2] is that Shakespeare converted what had been a predominantly tragic play, culminating in Hector's murder, into a comical satire for the Inns of Court audience, mainly by the addition of the Prologue and epilogue. Recently, however, Gary Taylor has argued that Shakespeare converted the play as originally performed privately to a Globe play by the omission of the epilogue and the dismissal of Pandarus in the earlier scene.[3] This theory is linked with the view that the Quarto text is derived from foul papers, and that the absence of the duplicated lines from 5.3 and the presence of the epilogue is what one would expect if the private performance preceded the public one. The objection that there is no evidence that the epilogue was marked for deletion Taylor counters by saying that we are bound to delete either the epilogue or the lines in

---

[1] 'Two months hence' in the epilogue refers to Pandarus' approaching death, rather than to a sequel to the play.

[2] *Shakespeare's Professional Skills* (1964), 78–97.

[3] *'Troilus and Cressida'*, 102–4.

5.3 and by suggesting that 'the last page of the promptbook would have contained the approval of the Master of the Revels; the page would therefore certainly have been retained, even if all the dialogue on it were intended for omission'.

Stage history

After the hypothetical adaptation of the play for performance at the Globe, there is no record of a revival in England until the present century, except for performances of Dryden's adaptation (1679), of which there were four productions in the first half of the eighteenth century. Dryden was very proud of one scene he added to the play, a quarrel between Troilus and Hector about the exchange of Cressida and Antenor. Dryden felt that Shakespeare's Troilus submits too easily to the King's decision; but the more he is allowed to argue, the less effective the scene becomes. There is a more serious alteration in the last act, in which Cressida, on her father's advice, pretends to accept Diomed's addresses so as to get an opportunity of escaping from the Greek camp. Troilus believes her to be unfaithful and she commits suicide. This absurd scene, in the middle of the battlefield, completely destroys the point of the traditional Cressida story. Dryden seems not to have realized that for Cressida to promise Diomed sexual satisfaction which she has no intention of giving makes her not 'purest, whitest innocence', but morally inferior to Shakespeare's heroine. Dryden simplified Shakespeare's language and eliminated all the characteristic imagery. The war plot is reduced to a shred. Ulysses' speech on degree is reduced to nineteen lines, three of them Shakespeare's and the others paraphrased:

> Then everything resolves to brutal force,
> And headlong force is led by hoodwinked will.
> For wild ambition, like a ravenous wolf,
> Spurred on by will, and seconded by power,
> Must make an universal prey of all,
> And last devour itself.

After Dryden's adaptation, designed to achieve a greater unity of action, we have to skip two centuries to reach the next performance of Shakespeare's play.[1] This was at Munich in 1898,

[1] Kenneth Muir, 'Three Shakespeare Adaptations', *Proceedings of the Leeds Philosophical and Literary Society*, 8 (1958), 233–8.

where it was played as a travesty of Homer with an all-male cast. Other performances followed in Germany: in Berlin in 1899, and again in 1904, when many of the audience left before the end. Between 1902 and 1925 there were productions at Stuttgart, Leipzig, Essen, Frankfurt, Munich, Vienna, Zurich, Prague, Budapest and Paris.[1]

Meanwhile the play had at last been revived in England. This was a 'costume recital' by a mixture of professional and amateur actors in London on 1 June 1907, directed by Charles Fry at the Great Queen Street Theatre. *The Times'* reviewer commented that the play was 'better left unacted' (3 June). Five years later, on 10 December 1912, it was produced by William Poel at King's Hall, Covent Garden. There were numerous cuts caused by Poel's squeamishness and pacifism; Aeneas, Paris and Thersites were played by women; and a gifted amateur, Edith Evans, as Cressida, exhibited her genius for playing coquettes, which ten years later was to blaze triumphantly in the part of Millamant. The production was revived at Stratford-upon-Avon in the following year, with Ion Swinley replacing Esmé Percy in the role of Troilus. Swinley played the same part on 5 November 1923 at the Old Vic, in what was the first fully professional production in modern times, directed by Robert Atkins. The play itself was not yet appreciated. *The Times* thought that 'much of the play was dull and was bound to be dull' (6 November).

A more significant production had taken place at Cambridge in the previous year, when the Marlowe Society, directed by Frank Birch, staged it at the A.D.C. Theatre on 4 March: more significant, both because some of the cast and many members of the audience were veterans who responded enthusiastically to the tone of the play, and because it was the beginning of a kind of campaign to establish it in the modern theatre. George Rylands, who played Diomedes in this production, revived the play with the Marlowe Society in 1940, 1948 and (with John Barton) in 1956. Anthony Quayle, who played Hector in Birch's 1932 production at the Festival Theatre, Cambridge, took the part again in his own production at Stratford in 1948, and played Pandarus there in Glen Byam Shaw's production (1954). John Barton assisted Peter Hall in another Stratford production (1960), which was revived at the Edinburgh Festival and at the Aldwych in 1962; he directed

[1] New Variorum, 505 ff.

the play himself in 1968 and, assisted by Barry Kyle, again in 1976.

Yet it took a long time for the play itself to win favour with the dramatic critics, who in this respect lagged behind audiences and academic critics. The only Stratford production between the wars was directed by Ben Iden Payne (1936).[1] Despite an impressive cast, the critics' verdict was generally hostile – 'dull and poor', 'loose and splattery', 'a museum piece'. That it was far from being a museum piece was demonstrated by a modern-dress production in September 1938, directed by Michael Mac Owan at the Westminster Theatre. During the battle scenes in the last act, the words jarred with modern weapons and costumes; but the rest of the play made a formidable impact in the days of the Munich agreement. Similarly the Marlowe Society production of March 1940 seemed uncannily relevant in the period of the phoney war. Tyrone Guthrie's 'Edwardian' production at the Old Vic in 1956 had the curious effect of trivializing the love plot and glamourizing the war plot.

Perhaps the most satisfying production till now was the Hall–Barton one (1960–2). There were some complaints of the sandpit in which the action took place, but only one critic now spoke of the interminable speeches, the 'arid wastes' of the dialogue. The directors had made the play 'not merely a collection of beautiful speeches, but a planned, architected, coherent and powerful drama'.[2] As *The Times* said, 'The essential soundness of the production lies in its gradual isolation of Hector and Achilles, symbols of the conflict between chivalry and brutal opportunism to which the ruin of Troilus by the faithless Cressida is secondary' (27 July 1960). After more than three and a half centuries the play had come into its own. The cast included a fine Hector (Derek Godfrey), a superb Pandarus (Max Adrian), and a good Ulysses (Eric Porter). Troilus (Denholm Elliott) was outclassed by a brilliant Cressida (Dorothy Tutin), described as 'sweltering with concupiscence', and 'a wisp of rippling carnality that is almost unbearably alluring'. There was no doubt of the effectiveness of the performance, although one suspects that Shakespeare did not intend her to be quite so obviously a daughter of the game.

---

[1] For productions within living memory, I have relied partly on my own, and partly on the scrapbooks in the Shakespeare Centre, Stratford-upon-Avon.

[2] See previous note, and '*Troilus and Cressida* on the English Stage' by Michael E. Kimberley (unpublished MA thesis, University of Birmingham, 1968).

Barton's later productions at Stratford exaggerated the cynical side of the play, as though Thersites were Shakespeare's chief spokesman, whose satirical invective provided an objective account of the other characters. Barton was accused of reducing 'the various moods to garish nihilism'. Achilles (Alan Howard) was apparently the effeminate partner in his relationship with a very masculine Patroclus. Gareth Lloyd Evans complained of the 'perversity of the conception and of the ineptitude of a great deal of the execution'.[1] This referred to the 1968 production. That of 1976 was 'saner, cooler, more balanced', but too many of the performances were either 'stereotyped or dull'. Agamemnon absurdly appeared wearing a straw hat and carrying a frying-pan. The best performance was that of Francesca Annis as Cressida, less obviously sensual and more sympathetic than most of her predecessors.

In the United States the play was first performed in 1916, but this, like most other American productions, was on a university campus. A professional production in New York in 1932 was badly acted and ill received. There was a better production in 1948 by the Veterans' Theatre Workshop in Boston. In Joseph Papp's production in Central Park, New York (1965), to judge by the preface he wrote two years later, Troilus was blamed for giving up Cressida without a struggle, for doubting her fidelity, and for advertising, like a pander, the attractive qualities of the Greek warriors, so that she 'cynically accepts the role of harlot conferred upon her by Troilus'.[2]

No attempt has been made here to provide a comprehensive stage history of the play.[3] For that we must wait for the forthcoming book by Joseph G. Price and Jeanne T. Newlin.

Sources

Shakespeare was doubtless acquainted with the outlines of the tale of Troy from an early age. He would know of the rape of Helen, the

---

[1] 'The Reason Why: The Royal Shakespeare Season 1968 Reviewed', *Shakespeare Survey 22* (Cambridge, 1969), 135–44; p. 143.

[2] *The Festival Shakespeare: Troilus and Cressida*, ed. B. Beckerman and J. Papp, with an essay on the direction of the play by Joseph Papp (New York and London, 1967), p. 60.

[3] See Jeanne T. Newlin, 'The Modernity of *Troilus and Cressida*', *Harvard Library Bulletin*, 17 (1969), 353–73.

wrath of Achilles, the death of Hector, the fox-like cunning of Ulysses, the wooden horse, and the escape of Aeneas. It is possible that at the Stratford Grammar School, as at others, pupils were asked to compose speeches for and against the restoration of Helen to her husband. A few years later when Shakespeare wrote *Lucrece*, his account of the picture on which his heroine gazed after the rape includes sketches of the leading characters on both sides of the war: Helen, 'the strumpet that began this stir', fond Paris, sly Ulysses, the blunt rage of Ajax, the golden words of Nestor, bold Hector, Troy's brave hope, and Hecuba, who exemplified 'Time's ruin, beauty's wrack'.

It is, of course, possible that Shakespeare was acquainted with one or other of the lost plays on the Trojan War and that he was influenced by them, either directly or by his wish to avoid a duplication of their treatments. But nearly all the characteristics and incidents of his play can be traced to extant sources. Any dramatist who chose to write on the fall of Troy would be more sympathetic to the defeated than to the victors, especially as he would be more familiar with Virgil than with Homer, and as Trojan refugees were thought to have come to Britain; and anyone who chose to write on Cressida could not easily rehabilitate the leprous whore into which Chaucer's charming heroine had been transformed. So the difference between Shakespeare's Cressida and Chaucer's cannot be taken to mean that *Troilus and Criseyde* was not the main source of the love-plot.[1] No one doubts that Shakespeare had read what was rightly regarded as the greatest poem in the language; and the comparative absence of close verbal parallels probably means that Shakespeare relied on his memory, as he did not with North and Holinshed.

Since R. A. Small wrote in 1899, there have been many discussions about the influence of Chaucer's poem on Shakespeare's play – in the Variorum edition (1953), by myself (1957), by Muriel C. Bradbrook (1958), Robert Kimborough (1964), Geoffrey Bullough (1966) and Ann Thompson (1978), the last being the most comprehensive.[2] Most of the incidents in the love

---

[1] See New Variorum, 449: 'Therefore the burden of proof is on those who question his connection with a poem which everyone knew to be the authoritative treatment of the Cressida story.'

[2] pp. 447–9; *Shakespeare's Sources*, 78–96; 'What Shakespeare Did to Chaucer's *Troilus and Criseyde*', *Shakespeare Quarterly*, 9, pp. 311–19; *Shakespeare's 'Troilus and Cressida' and its Setting*; *Narrative and Dramatic Sources of Shakespeare*, vol. 6, esp. pp. 94–5; *Shakespeare's Chaucer: A Study in Literary Origins*.

scenes were selected or developed from incidents in the poem. Troilus' fear of 'swooning destruction' was doubtless suggested by his namesake's actual swoon; his description of his state of mind in the first scene recalls the effect of his passion on Chaucer's hero; and his words in 5.6

> Fate, hear me what I say:
> I reck not though thou end my life today

seem to be based on Chaucer's

> Myn own death in armes will I sech;
> I retch not how sone be the day.
>
> (v. 1718–19)

Everyone notices the difference of tone between the two works. This is due to a number of causes. One has been mentioned already – the debasement of Cressida's character during the two centuries since the poem was written. Then the speeding up of the action leads to her seduction by Diomedes only a few hours after her parting from Troilus, and the abandonment of the conventions of courtly love gives a different tone to the secrecy of the affair. Chaucer's explicitly religious frame of reference, as Ann Thompson points out, was deliberately omitted by Shakespeare who 'leaves his characters in the disorder of mortality'.[1] What was possible in a narrative poem, written about pagans for a Christian audience, would have been absurdly anachronistic in a play.

Shakespeare's Troilus is not very different from Chaucer's; but his Cressida, though not a widow, is more knowing, more crafty, more self-possessed and more sensual than Criseyde, and she is unprotected by the excuses and evasions of the narrative form. Shakespeare's Troilus, unlike Chaucer's, has ocular proof of her infidelity. Most critics have exaggerated the differences between Pandarus and the much younger Pandare. The impression we get of Shakespeare's character is coloured by the epilogue in which he stands outside the play, in Elizabethan London – a speech which was probably omitted at the Globe – and by his address to the maidens in the audience after he has despatched the lovers to bed. This comes just after the symbolic scene in which the characters assume for a moment their legendary roles. Apart from this, Pandarus, sentimental and silly as he is, is not drawn as unsympatheti-

---

[1] *Shakespeare's Chaucer*, 155.

cally as we are usually told. He is not, like his namesake, an unsuccessful lover; he is genuinely fond of his niece, and even fonder of Troilus. He wants them both to be happy, unlike his critics who are vaguely disapproving. There is no suggestion that he is rewarded for his pains. Moreover he does not trick Cressida into an assignation, as Pandare does, and his bawdy jokes are harmless. Indeed, his badinage is very similar to that of his namesake after the lovers have spent the night together:

> And ner he com, and seyde, 'how stont it now
> This mery morwe, nece, how can ye fare?'
> Criseyde answerde, 'never the bet for yow,
> Fox that ye beene, god yeve your herte care!
> God helpe me so, ye caused al this fare,
> Trow I,' quod she, 'for alle your wordes whyte;
> O! who-so seeth yow knoweth yow ful lyte!'
>
> With that she gan hir face for to wrye
> With the shete, and wex for shame al reed;
> And Pandarus gan under for to prye,
> And seyde, 'nece, if that I shal ben deed,
> Have here a sword, and smyteth of myn heed.'
> With that his arm al sodeynly he thriste
> Under hir nekke, and at the laste hir kiste.
>
> (iii. 1562–75)

It is difficult to agree with Ann Thompson who regards the teasing in the play more indelicate because Troilus is present.

In Chaucer's poem Diomed is a noble warrior who wins Criseyde by his long and eloquent wooing; in the play his attitude to Cressida is one of lustful contempt, although his sardonic remarks on Helen as a war aim show him willing to animadvert on the sexual morals of others.

The main outlines of the love plot are therefore derived from Chaucer, although three of the characters are considerably altered. There is some slight evidence that Shakespeare had also read Henryson's sequel which was included in sixteenth-century editions of Chaucer, and which was largely responsible for the Elizabethan attitude to Cressida.[1]

For the war plot Shakespeare read more widely, at least four sources having been determined: Chapman's translation of *Seven*

---

[1] Kenneth Muir, *The Sources of Shakespeare's Plays* (1977), 143.

Books of the *Iliad*; Caxton's *Recuyell of the Historyes of Troye*; Lydgate's *Troye Booke*; and Ovid's *Metamorphoses*, either in the original or in Golding's translation. Chapman's translation would have provided the basic facts about the anarchy in the Greek camp and the character of Thersites:

> A man of tongue whose ravenlike voice a tuneles jarring kept,
> Who in his ranke minde coppy had of unregarded wordes
> That rashly and beyond al rule usde to oppugne the Lords,
> But what soever came from him was laught at mightilie.
> The filthiest Greeke that came to Troy, he had a goggle eye;
> Starcke-lame he was of eyther foote; his shoulders were contract
> Into his brest and crookt withall; his head was sharpe compact
> And here and there it had a hayre.   (ii. 206–13)

Shakespeare omits the Homeric motive for Achilles' refusal to fight – his justifiable resentment – and substitutes (from Caxton) his promise to Polyxena. He invents the manipulation of the lottery and the choice of Ajax to fight with Hector so as to arouse Achilles. Although there is a brief debate in Troy, in which Antenor proposes the return of Helen to her husband (vii. 293 ff.), the debate in the play is influenced more by the account given by Caxton of a debate that took place before the siege began. Hector and Helenus argue for the return of Helen, Paris and Troilus for her retention. Hector's initial speech in the play follows closely the arguments used by him in Caxton's account, and Troilus sneers at Helenus as a cowardly priest. Homer describes the rousing of Achilles caused by the death of Patroclus and, although this was not in the part of Book xviii translated by Chapman in *Achilles Shield*, it was one of the best-known incidents of the Trojan war.

It is not always possible to tell whether Shakespeare was following Caxton or Lydgate since the two accounts, derived from Guido delle Colonne's, have much in common. In some cases we can be sure that Caxton was the source – the names of the gates of Troy in the Prologue, the mention of the sagittary (in Lydgate this is merely an archer), the spelling of Polyxena, Hector's use of the term 'cousin-german' about Ajax, and the embrace following their combat. But Shakespeare apparently consulted Lydgate for the longer character sketches provided by him, for Guido's statement, quoted only by Lydgate, of the rapid transfer of Cressida's affections –

> Longe or it was nyght
> How Cryseyde forsoke hir owne knyght
> And gave hir herte unto Dyomede[1] –

and for the episode of the knight in sumptuous armour, pursued by Hector just before his fatal meeting with Achilles.

Many details are derived either from Caxton or Lydgate (e.g. Diomed's capture of Troilus' horse, the name of Hector's horse), but used 'With such a careless force and forceless care' that it is clear that Shakespeare felt at perfect liberty to vary them. Caxton, for example, provided him with the roll-call of names in 5.5, but they are used with little relation to his narrative. Achilles returns to the battle after the death of Policeus; Shakespeare, remembering the Homeric account, links the return to the death of Patroclus, but adds from Caxton or Lydgate the havoc wrought by Hector on the Myrmidons as a cause of Achilles' wrath. He takes the details of the murder of Hector from the Caxton–Lydgate account of the death of Troilus:[2]

And afore that Achiles entryd in to the bataylle he assemblid his Myron-dones and prayd hem that they wolde entende to none other thynge but to enclose Troyllus and to holde hym wyth oute sleyynge tyll he cam ... And as he was all allone amonge hem and had no man to socoure hym they slewe his horse and hurte hym in many places and araced of his heed his helme and his coyffe of yron. And he deffended hym the beste wyse he cowde. Than cam on Achilles whan he sawe Troyllus alle naked, and ran upon hym in a rage and smote of his heed and caste hit under the feet of the horse and toke the body and bonde hit to the taylle of his horse and so drewe hit after hym thurgh oute the ooste.

This has the effect of blackening Achilles' character, and so does his arrogant behaviour when he meets Hector in 4.5. Shakespeare alters the tone of the reception of Cressida by the Greeks –[3]

The comming of Briseyda pleased much to all the Greeks, and they came thither and feasted her, and demaunded of her tidinges of Troy ... Then all the greatest that were there, promised her to keepe her and hold her, as deere as their daughter –

and he omits her bitter reproaches of her father for his treachery:

[1] Lydgate, iii. 4434.
[2] Caxton, iii. xxii (New Variorum, 447).
[3] Ibid., iii. xv (New Variorum, 438).

'Certes it was not only the God Apollo that thus abused thee; but it was a company of devils'.[1]

Shakespeare confused, or fused, two different Ajaxes. According to Lydgate, Oyleus Ajax was

> of his speche rude and reckles.
> Ful many worde in ydell him asterte,
> And but a coward was he of his herte.

Another Ajax, Thelamonyous, was 'discrete and vertuous', a good musician, and a noble knight:

> No man more orped nor hardyer for to fyght,
> Nor desyrous for to have vyctory,
> Devoyde of pompe, hatynge all vaynglorye.[2]

The Ajax who is backward in fighting (2.1) is modelled on Oyleus; the Ajax who fights with Hector in 4.5 is modelled on Thelamonyous. The fusion was probably deliberate as Lydgate juxtaposes the two sketches. But, as Bullough argues,[3] Shakespeare also incorporates the character depicted in Ovid's *Metamorphoses* (xiii. 1–441), where Ulysses speaks of Ajax's 'blockish wit' and contrasts the functions of the intelligent soldier such as himself with the brainless fighter such as Ajax, as Shakespeare's Ulysses does in 1.3. Nor is this all. Fleay pointed out that the 'character of Ajax' spoken by Alexander reads like a parody of Jonson's character of Crites in *Cynthia's Revels*.[4] The style of the two portraits is similar, but this does not mean that we should accept Dekker's view that Crites was a self-portrait, or that Ajax is Shakespeare's satirical portrait of Jonson. These conflicting impressions (to use Morgann's phrase) do not in this case make the character of Ajax three-dimensional. They present the actor with an impossible problem, which he can solve only by omission. The discrepancies in Ajax's character in both texts could be used to support the view either that Shakespeare changed his mind during the course of composition, or else that the play underwent some hasty revision before its first performance.

Two other books may have contributed something to the play. Shakespeare had been acquainted with Elyot's *The Governor* for

---

[1] Ibid., III. xv (New Variorum, 437).
[2] Lydgate, ii. 4571 ff.
[3] Bullough, *Narrative and Dramatic Sources*, vol. 6, p. 88.
[4] Fleay, *Life of Shakespeare*, 45.

most of his working life, and the bee speech in *Henry V* (1.2.187–204) was derived from the second chapter of that book. In the same chapter Elyot refers to the way Ulysses and Nestor had overcome the sedition in the Greek camp; and in the first chapter he rehearses some of the arguments used by Shakespeare's Ulysses in the third scene of the play.

The other book is Robert Greene's *Euphues his Censure to Philautus*, in which, as in the play, Hector during a truce walks with Achilles, and Ulysses with Troilus; and in which there is a discussion on the restoration of Helen to Menelaus. She is called, as in the play, a gem, a pearl, and a piece; and the Trojans are said to be ignorant of moral philosophy.[1]

⋅*Interpretation*

'A disillusioned Shakespeare turns his back upon his former ideals and the world's ancient ideals of heroism and romance, and questions them.'
E. K. Chambers (1907)

'The work of a man whose soul is poisoned with filth.'
Agnes Mure Mackenzie (1924)

'As a whole it must be admitted to be an ugly, inconsistent and unpleasant performance.'   John Bailey (1929)

Here, chosen at random, are three verdicts on *Troilus and Cressida*, written in the early years of this century.[2] Although they must seem peculiar to readers today, they could be matched by many criticisms in the nineteenth century. It was often assumed, in mitigation of Shakespeare's artistic failure, that he was going through a period of gloom and cynicism as a result of his unfortunate experience with the Dark Lady of the Sonnets – despite the fact that he seems to have written *As You Like It* and *Twelfth Night* after that hypothetical experience – or else he was sharing what

---

[1] *Euphues his Censure* (1587), in *The Life and Complete Works in Prose and Verse of Robert Greene*, ed. Alexander B. Grosart, 15 vols. (1881–6), vol. 6; Kenneth Muir, *The Sources of Shakespeare's Plays*, 150. This book also provides a longer discussion of the sources of the play. There are longer ones still in Geoffrey Bullough's volume (see p. 13, n. 2 above), in Robert K. Presson's *Shakespeare's 'Troilus and Cressida' and the Legends of Troy* (Madison, 1953), and in Robert T. Kimbrough's *Shakespeare's 'Troilus and Cressida' and its Setting* (Cambridge, Mass., 1964).

[2] *Troilus and Cressida*, the Red Letter Shakespeare (1907), repr. in *Shakespeare: A Survey* (1925, repr. 1964), p. 150; *The Women in Shakespeare's Plays* (Garden City, 1924), p. 199; *Shakespeare* (1929), p. 156.

Chambers called 'the disenchantment of the Elizabethans' in the last years of the old Queen's reign. Any popular dramatist is bound to have his finger on the pulse of his audience, and although *Troilus and Cressida* may not have been greatly liked Shakespeare may have thought it would appeal to the taste of the intellectuals to whom it was originally addressed. No doubt he was influenced by the spirit of the age, which was nevertheless more varied than Chambers implied. In any case, the idea that Shakespeare wrote comedies when he was cheerful, tragedies when he felt gloomy, and satires when he was feeling cynical or indignant, is as absurd as the contrary view that he merely followed the fashion. The mood of *Troilus and Cressida* was largely dictated by the subject.

A dramatic poet has to 'make his mind a thoroughfare for all thoughts',[1] so that every position he takes up embraces the possibility of its opposite. The conviction that love is not Time's fool, proclaimed in the Sonnets, coexists with the belief that it is subject to envious and calumniating Time; the belief that war is the 'royal occupation' can be followed in another mood by the views on war aims expressed by Diomedes as well as by Thersites, or even the anti-war beliefs of Erasmus; and Ulysses can be regarded as the voice of wisdom, or as the archetypal fox or a Machiavel. *Troilus and Cressida*, indeed, is unique even among Shakespeare's works in its changes of viewpoint from scene to scene. In the first scene, for example, every reader and every member of an audience looks at the situation through the eyes of Troilus, in the second through the eyes of Cressida, in the third through the eyes of Ulysses, in the fourth through the eyes of Thersites, and in the fifth through the eyes of Hector. Yet Pandarus, Thersites and Ulysses have all been regarded by some critics as expressing the poet's own view of the action. 'Of all Shakespeare's characters', A. L. Rowse confidently declared, 'Ulysses is the one who most completely expresses his creator's views; indeed he hardly speaks anything else.'[2]

That there is an element of satire in *Troilus and Cressida* can hardly be disputed; but it is difficult to see any resemblance between the play and the comical satires of Jonson (such as *Poetaster* and *Cynthia's Revels*) or those of Dekker and Marston. As only Marston among the dramatists had written formal satires, the banning of satire cannot be said to have driven the satirists

---

[1] John Keats, *Letters*, ed. Hyder E. Rollins, 2 vols. (1958), ii. 213.
[2] *William Shakespeare* (1963), 342.

into the theatre, as Oscar J. Campbell argued.[1] To support his notion that Troilus was satirized as an embodiment of lust, Campbell gave some strange interpretations of a number of crucial speeches. The lovers, we are told, are 'two virtuosi in sensuality'. Troilus' first speech in 3.2 'exhibits him, at least in prospect, as an expert in sensuality'. He

is beset with the sexual gourmet's anxiety lest the morsel which he is about to devour will be so ravishing that thereafter he will lose his sense of nice distinctions in sexual experience.

He displays 'the educated sensuality of an Italianate English roué'. On the speech which begins 'O that I thought it could be in a woman' Campbell comments:

On the surface, he seems to be merely appealing for fidelity. But that wish . . . is his response to a fear that she will never be able to satisfy the demands of his discriminating, if voracious, sensuality.

The scene on the following morning is described as 'the fretful dialogue of two sated sensualists'. Even Troilus' reasonable fear that Cressida will catch cold is held against him, and Cressida's grief at their separation is described as 'the hypocritical posturing of a wanton putting on an ill-conceived display of feeling'. The audience, we are assured, would have laughed at Troilus' speech in which he tells Cressida that he loves her 'in so strained a purity' because of the atmosphere of a brothel in which it is spoken, and laughed again at his speech after he has witnessed Cressida's unfaithfulness, when he 'forces his logical machine to perform feats of prestidigitation that make it creak ridiculously'. All these comments can be refuted; and it is abundantly clear from the speeches of Pandarus and the lovers at the end of 3.2 that Troilus was depicted as the constant lover who had fixed his affections on one who was to prove faithless. Troilus is foolish, but not a libertine. His idealization of Helen, as well as of Cressida, is fraught with tragic consequences. Although, no doubt, we should accept Ulysses' assessment of him as a natural successor to Hector as the Trojan leader – especially as it comes from Aeneas[2] – the Victorian idea that he emerges at the end, recovered from his unworthy and effeminate passion, as manly and heroic, should be

---

[1] *Comicall Satyre*, 211–17.
[2] Richard C. Harrier, 'Troilus Divided', in *Studies in English Renaissance Drama in Memory of Karl Julius Holzknecht*, ed. J. W. Bennett *et al.* (New York, 1959), 149.

qualified by Hector's word for him – savage. Yet, it must be added, in a total war Hector's chivalry is anachronistic, as Caxton makes clear:

This was the cause wherefore the Troyans missed to have the victorie, to the which they might never after attaine, nor come: for fortune was to them contrary: and therefore Virgile saith: *Non est misericordia in bello*, that is to say, that there is no mercy in battaile. A man ought not to be too mercifull, but take the victory when he may get it.[1]

The delusions of the sexual instinct, however comic to the outsider, are not comic to the sufferer. Some members of a modern audience, brainwashed by Brecht, will be properly alienated spectators; others will tend to identify, or at least to sympathize, with Troilus, as they will with Hector. It is notable that Troilus' great speeches of disillusionment (5.2.135–74), which Campbell supposes were punctuated with bawdy laughter from the original private audience, are not, as most of that masterly scene, interrupted by the satirical jeers of Thersites. Troilus is allowed his tragic moment, as he is again after the murder of Hector. Nor should we laugh – nor do we laugh – when he and Cressida make their vows, despite the fact that these are undercut by our awareness of what is to come.

It should never be forgotten that Thersites is the most despicable character in the *Iliad* and that Shakespeare's portrait belongs to an unbroken tradition. This means that when modern directors assume that Shakespeare chose Thersites as his chief spokesman, they are compelled either to take liberties with the text, or else to allow Troilus and Hector to arouse at least intermittent sympathy. Thersites is a Fool, licensed to be scathing about everyone and everything. Whenever he appears he provokes laughter as well as disgust by the colourful violence of his invective – which Shakespeare must have enjoyed writing.

There is plenty of black comedy in the play, especially in the war scenes. Ajax's absurd vanity is a proper object for ridicule, and Aeneas' failure to recognize the god-like Agamemnon was an incident inserted by Shakespeare in order to cut him down to size. However much Thersites' character-sketches are discounted, it is clear, if one compares Menelaus, Nestor, Diomedes, Achilles and Patroclus with their Homeric counterparts, that Shakespeare was

---

[1] Caxton, III. xi (New Variorum, 434).

subjecting the glory and heroism of the *Iliad* to a less than sympathetic scrutiny. What, he seems to be asking, was the Trojan war, after seven years of indecisive battles, really like, when stripped of the glamour of poetry? As Heine says:

Whereas the classical Greek poets seek to glorify reality, and soar into the ideal, [Shakespeare] presses more into the depth of things; the keen-whetted shovel of his intelligence digs into the quiet earth of appearances, disclosing to our eyes their hidden roots.[1]

As Audrey Yoder pointed out in *Animal Analogy in Shakespeare's Character Portrayal*, the satiric portraiture is mostly put into the mouth of Thersites, and

there is little doubt that satire implemented by animal characterization does play a great part in the depreciation of such characters as Achilles, Ajax, Patroclus, Menelaus, and Thersites, who receive the greatest amount of such characterization.[2]

However much we deplore Thersites, some of the mud he throws is bound to stick; and after we have heard Ajax compared to a bear, an elephant, a mongrel, an ass, a horse, and a peacock; after we have heard Achilles compared to a cur; after Menelaus has been described as worse than a herring without a roe or than the louse of a lazar – and some would remember that Cressida ended as a lazar – they cannot climb again on to their Homeric pedestals. The greater sympathy we feel for the Trojans is partly due to the fact that they are largely spared Thersites' satire. But they do not escape the criticism of the poet. Wilson Knight's chapter on the play, which pioneered its appreciation, is nevertheless flawed by its leniency to the Trojans:

The love of Troilus, the heroism of Hector, the symbolic romance which burns in the figure of Helen – these are placed beside the 'scurril jests' and lazy pride of Achilles, the block-headed stupidity of Ajax, the mockery of Thersites. The Trojan party stands for human beauty and worth, the Greek party for the bestial and stupid elements of man, the barren stagnancy of intellect divorced from action, and the criticism which exposes these things with jeers. The atmospheres of the two opposing camps are thus strongly contrasted, and the handing over of Cressida to the Greeks which is the pivot incident of the play, has thus a symbolic suggestion.[3]

---

[1] From *Shakespeares Mädchen und Frauen* (1839); quoted by Priscilla Martin in her *Casebook* (1976).

[2] New York, 1947, pp. 41–3.

[3] G. Wilson Knight, *The Wheel of Fire* (1930; rev. edn 1949), 47.

To this one can only reply that the one real intellectual in the Greek camp is Ulysses; that the level of debate in Troy is higher than that in the Greek camp; that the Greeks do act effectively in the end; that pride can be as 'emotional' as sexual desire and the pursuit of honour; that Achilles' motives for his actions are first his love for Polyxena and then his love for Patroclus; and that the suggestion that Shakespeare's two primary values were love and war, and that they exist in *Troilus and Cressida* 'in a world which questions their ultimate purpose and beauty' makes the mistake of trying to replace the idols Shakespeare was anxious to overturn. Whatever the views he normally held, in this play Hector and Priam, as well as Diomedes and Thersites, agree that Helen is an unsatisfactory war aim, and the one glimpse we have of her reveals her as an extremely silly woman. Troilus is as mistaken about her as he is about Cressida.

The debate in Troy between those who wish to relinquish Helen to Menelaus and those who wish to keep her in Troy, absorbing as it is, reveals some of the Trojan weaknesses. On the one side are prestige and aesthetic values[1] – beauty, honour; on the other, moral values. Hector demolishes the superficial arguments of Troilus and Paris and then throws his weight on their side:

> For 'tis a cause that hath no mean dependence
> Upon our joint and several dignities.
>
> (2.2.191–2)

His challenge to the Greeks, previously delivered, is a sign that although he fully realizes that Helen ought to be restored to her husband, he has decided, if he cannot persuade the warmongers, to act in defiance of the moral laws of nature and of nations, the more willingly because he is in love with glory. Troilus had argued that value was essentially subjective, a matter of taste. Hector had retorted that

---

[1] W. M. T. Nowottny, 'Opinion and Value in *Troilus and Cressida*', *Essays in Criticism*, 4 (1954), 282–96, says that Shakespeare 'has explored the antithesis between the values of the imagination and the values of organised society, and has shown that a society intent upon the preservation of its traditional form defeats itself', partly because 'it cuts itself off from that Protean power of imagination which can (in Milton's phrase) "create a soul under the ribs of death"'. Frank Kermode, however (*Essays in Criticism*, 5 (1955), 181–7), objected that Shakespeare was more critical of Troilus than Mrs Nowottny had argued.

> value dwells not in particular will:
> It holds his estimate and dignity
> As well wherein 'tis precious of itself
> As in the prizer.
>
> (2.2.52–5)

Troilus, unfit tọ hear moral philosophy, learns before the end of the play that his subjective valuation of Cressida is a recipe for disaster, as the volte-face of Hector ensures his own death and the destruction of Troy.

The other debate, in the Greek camp, is notable for two things: the grand statement of Tudor commonplaces on the interrelation of cosmic and political order, and the cynical undermining of the moral order by Ulysses' stratagem, relished by the 'wise' Nestor, to rig the ballot. The praise of a divinely sanctioned order – the last example in Shakespeare's works[1] – is put into the mouth of a fox; and, like all ideals enunciated in the play – fidelity, loyalty, chivalry, morality – it is violated in practice.

The tone of the play depends on the style, and here again the critics are divided. Van Doren said that the style was 'loud, brassy, and abandoned . . . tautology is on the rampage'.[2] Wyndham Lewis, admitting it was grand, complained of its disadvantages:

It transfigures everything at once, monotonously heightening it, so that it is impossible in the midst of its splendours to convey anything but the most elevated and dazzling perfections . . . With Ulysses, for example, the intention is to convey a feeling of craft and policy, and you would expect his utterance to be correspondingly circumspect, rather insinuating than grand.[3]

Other critics argue that the Latinate diction was intended by the poet to show up the empty pomposity of the speakers. Patricia Thomson, for example, writing of the 'rant and cant' in the play, compares one of Ajax's speeches (4.5.6–11) to Pistol's; complains that Agamemnon speaks '*too* nobly', that one does not know whether Ulysses' oratory is genuine or phoney, and that Troilus ends up as a 'terrible ranter'.[4] T. McAlindon makes similar

---

[1] Kenneth Muir, *The Singularity of Shakespeare* (1977), 61.

[2] Mark Van Doren, *Shakespeare* (New York, 1939), 202.

[3] *The Lion and the Fox* (New York and London, 1927).

[4] Patricia Thomson, 'Rant and Cant in *Troilus and Cressida*', *Essays and Studies*, NS 22 (1969), 33–56.

points.[1] He argues that Hector's speech to Ajax which puts an end to the duel (4.5.119 ff.) is 'merely bombastic' and that Shakespeare 'employed Latinate diction and neologisms to intensify' the dissonant effect of the play, the contrast between words and deeds. Ulysses, Agamemnon and Nestor 'suffer from the kinds of vicious surplusage to which professionally wise men are prone . . . pleonasmus . . . and macrologia'.

It is true that the first two speeches of Agamemnon and Nestor take fifty-five lines to enunciate the platitude that misfortunes are a test of character. Yet no critic has complained that Ulysses takes almost as many lines to inform Achilles that the man who rests on his laurels is soon forgotten. It should be stressed that as *Troilus and Cressida*, more than any other of Shakespeare's plays, is filled with debates and arguments, it was proper for him to make the speeches oratorical rather than self-revelatory. To use all the resources of rhetoric is what is expected in such circumstances. It is absurd to complain that politicians are talking after their kind. There seems little doubt, moreover, that Shakespeare was aiming at a style appropriate to a classical subject. When he wrote passages of Aeneas' tale to Dido, his model was Virgil as modified by Marlowe, but most Elizabethans would doubtless have accepted it as properly Virgilian. It is improbable that Shakespeare with his 'lesse Greeke' could have read Homer in the original – even Chapman relied heavily on a Latin translation – so that his impression of the style of the *Iliad* would be derived from the *Seven Books* and Chapman's style was excessively Latinate, his vocabulary including a number of words Shakespeare appears to have borrowed, and many others which would not seem out of place in *Troilus and Cressida*. A few examples must suffice: accost, authentic, depravation, distinction, emulous, expugnance, expulsure, imbecility, flexure, repugnant, repercussive, recureless, respective, responsive, stridulous, transportance. Some critics have complained of the inflated style of the 'Dido' speeches and have even ascribed to another hand the narrative of the bleeding sergeant in *Macbeth*. In both cases we can be certain that Shakespeare believed that the style used was appropriate to epic narration. It was, of course, the great age for coinages; and many of the words vomited by Marston in *Poetaster* have survived Jonson's scorn: retrograde, spurious, reciprocal,

[1] 'Language, Style, and Meaning in *Troilus and Cressida*', *PMLA*, 84 (1969), 29–43.

defunct, strenuous. Shakespeare was not given to boasting or he might have said 'They cannot touch me for coining: I am the King himself.'

The debate in the Greek camp and the debate in Troy are not the only important discussions in the course of the play. Almost as important is the conversation between Ulysses and Achilles, which, like the debate on the restoration of Helen, is concerned with the question of value. Ulysses argues that a man's value depends not on his personal qualities or on his integrity, but on what other people think of him. He uses the Platonic idea that other people act as a mirror.[1] This idea seems at first sight to be close to that expressed by Duke Vincentio at the beginning of *Measure for Measure*, when he chooses Angelo as his deputy:

> Thyself and thy belongings
> Are not thine own so proper as to waste
> Thyself upon thy virtues, they on thee.
> Heaven doth with us as we with torches do,
> Not light them for themselves; for if our virtues
> Did not go forth of us, 'twere all alike
> As if we had them not.
>
> (1.1.30–6)

Yet there is a fundamental difference. As the echo from the Gospels makes clear,[2] Vincentio is arguing for the use of one's talents, not for selfish reasons, but rather so as to let one's light shine before men for the glory of God. Ulysses, on the other hand, is arguing that our worth depends entirely on the opinion of others. The difference between the two positions is not merely the difference between Christian and pagan.

It should also be noted that the whole of Ulysses' argument is based on a lie. The Greeks do not actually prefer Ajax to Achilles: the ballot has been rigged precisely because the Greeks regard Achilles as their foremost warrior. Even the splendid speech on the power of Time is a cunning piece of persuasion rather than a solid philosophical statement. Yet its position in the play – Shakespeare deliberately violates the chronological order of events in order to stress the thematic significance of the speech – reminds us that love is subject to 'envious and calumniating time'. The words are

[1] See 3.3.95 n., and I. A. Richards, *Speculative Instruments* (Chicago and London, 1955), 198–213.
[2] Kenneth Muir, *The Sources of Shakespeare's Plays*, 7.

spoken just after the lovers have vowed eternal fidelity and just before they are separated for ever. When Troilus inveighs against injurious Time, Ulysses' sonorous commonplaces are still ringing in our ears. Claudius tells Laertes that Time qualifies the spark and flame of love; and it could be said that Cressida's frailty and the accidents of war accelerate what Ulysses regards as an inevitable process.

Time is a significant theme of *Troilus and Cressida*[1] which has been analysed by a number of critics, but it is a theme with which Shakespeare was obsessively concerned throughout his career.[2] It has been pointed out that the description of the painting of the Trojan war in *Lucrece* is juxtaposed with a long tirade by the heroine on Time in its two aspects, familiar to the Renaissance mind, as destroyer and revealer. Ulysses, for tactical reasons, is concerned to stress only its destructive powers. The main subject of Shakespeare's Sonnets is the unending war between Time and Beauty, between Time and Love. The early sonnets urge the poet's friend to marry so that he can hand down his beauty in his child; later in the sequence Shakespeare hopes to defeat Time by immortalizing his friend in his verse; and he distinguishes between sexual desire, which is subject to time, and love which is not time's fool.

In many of the sonnets the ravages of time are described:[3]

> When forty winters shall besiege thy brow
> And dig deep trenches in thy beauty's field ...

> For never-resting time leads summer on
> To hideous winter and confounds him there;
> Sap check'd with frost and lusty leaves quite gone,
> Beauty o'ersnow'd and bareness everywhere.

> Where wasteful Time debateth with Decay
> To change your day of youth to sullied night.

Time is a bloody and devouring tyrant. In several sonnets, imitated from the *Metamorphoses*, the inexorable march of time is compared to the encroaching waves of the ocean. What in Ovid is a statement

---

[1] G. Wilson Knight, *The Wheel of Fire*, 65 ff.; D. A. Traversi, '*Troilus and Cressida*', *Scrutiny*, 7 (1938), 301–19; Theodore Spencer, 'A Commentary on Shakespeare's *Troilus and Cressida*', *Studies in English Literature*, 16 (Tokyo, 1936), 1–43; L. C. Knights, '*Troilus and Cressida* Again', *Scrutiny*, 18 (1951), 144–57.

[2] Frederick Turner, *Shakespeare and the Nature of Time* (New York and Oxford, 1971).

[3] The quotations in this paragraph are from Sonnets 2, 5, 15, 60, and 116.

of the Pythagorean philosophy becomes in the Sonnets a threat to beauty and love:

> Time doth transfix the flourish set on youth,
> And delves the parallels in beauty's brow,
> Feeds on the rarities of nature's truth,
> And nothing stands but for his scythe to mow.

Shakespeare laments that beauty, no stronger than a flower, is less enduring than the lofty towers and the brass eternal which are both a slave to time. He was seeking desperately some way of defeating Time, some way of preventing its erosion of physical beauty, and if that is ultimately impossible, as of course it is, some way of preserving love despite the loss of beauty. Rosy lips and cheeks come within the compass of Time's sickle, but not, he vows, true love, manifested in the marriage of true minds. So Troilus wants at least to presume that a woman is able to

> feed for aye her lamp and flame of love; ...
> Outliving beauties outward, with a mind
> That doth renew swifter than blood decays!
> (3.2.150–3)

Cressida is spectacularly unable to meet these requirements, and how far Troilus' own love is of the kind to resist change is a moot point, which must now be considered.

Ever since Caroline Spurgeon counted up the images, it has been known that the iterative image of *Troilus and Cressida* is derived from cooking and eating. This was first pointed out by Walter Whiter at the end of the eighteenth century.[1] There are about eighty of these images and they appear throughout the play, in the war scenes as well as in the love scenes. The significance of this imagery is not difficult to interpret: sex is an appetite which can lead to surfeit and revulsion. From the first scene where Pandarus compares the wooing of Cressida to the making of a cake – grinding the corn, sifting the flour, leavening it, kneading it, heating the oven, etc. – to the scene in the final act where Hector is murdered, and Achilles refers to his 'half-supped sword, that frankly would have fed' (5.8.19), this imagery is omnipresent; and it occurs in several of the key speeches of the play. Just before Cressida

---

[1] *A Specimen of a Commentary on Shakespeare*, ed. Alan Over and Mary Bell (1967), 121.

surrenders, Troilus compares his prospective enjoyment of her to
a meal:

> Th'imaginary relish is so sweet
> That it enchants my sense. What will it be
> When that the wat'ry palate tastes indeed
> Love's thrice-repurèd nectar?
>
> (3.2.17–20)

Diomed speaks of Paris 'palating the taste' of Helen's dishonour,
and of Menelaus drinking up 'The lees and dregs of a flat tamed
piece' (4.1.60, 63). When Troilus bids farewell to Cressida on her
departure for the Greek camp, he declares that Time fumbles up his
many farewells into a loose adieu

> And scants us with a single famished kiss,
> Distasted with the salt of broken tears.
>
> (4.4.46–7)

Here *scants, famished, distasted, salt,* and perhaps even *broken* (suggested by broken meats) were derived from the kitchen. Kitchen
imagery is used too at the climax of Troilus' outburst on witnessing
the love-making of Diomedes and Cressida:

> The bonds of heaven are slipped, dissolved and loosed,
> And with another knot, five-finger-tied,
> The fractions of her faith, orts of her love,
> The fragments, scraps, the bits and greasy relics
> Of her o'er-eaten faith are given to Diomed.
>
> (5.2.154–8)

Here Troilus' disgust and revulsion expresses itself in terms of the
scraps and greasy relics collected from dirty plates after a meal.

Even in the two set speeches of Ulysses the same imagery makes
its appearance. In the debate in the third scene of the play, the
climax of the breakdown of order is when

> appetite, an universal wolf . . .
> Must make perforce an universal prey,
> And last eat up himself.
>
> (1.3.120–3)

Ulysses is thinking of envy as an appetite. Shakespeare would
know from Ovid that Envy feeds upon herself, and he may have
been aware that St Augustine compared the envious man to a

ravening wolf, for this idea was to be found in dictionaries of quotations. Thersites later remarks that lechery eats itself, and Agamemnon says that the proud man eats up himself. In Ulysses' other great speech, on the power of time, he describes Time as a personified figure with a wallet on his back:

> Wherein he puts alms for oblivion,
> A great-sized monster of ingratitude.
> Those scraps are good deeds past, which are devoured
> As fast as they are made, forgot as soon
> As done.

$$(3.3.145-50)$$

This imagery, therefore, links up the two plots of the play and, of course, the war is caused by the sexual infidelity of Helen, as Troilus' disillusionment is caused by Cressida's unfaithfulness. War and sex are the two areas of human experience which are most likely to be glamourized and idealized; and one theme of the play is the attack on idealization. Shakespeare is doing what Ibsen was to do in such plays as *A Doll's House* and *Ghosts*.

We must consider Troilus' love in relation both to this imagery and to the imagery of disease with which it is associated. In the first scene, in his fever of unsatisfied desire, he compares his heart to an open ulcer. He is depicted as young and inexperienced; and although it would be unfair to say that he regards Cressida merely as a sex-object, he is deluded by her appearance to credit her with imaginary virtues. In the assignation scene, Troilus compares himself to

> a strange soul upon the Stygian banks
> Staying for waftage,

$$(3.2.8-12)$$

so that he can 'wallow in the lily beds | Proposed for the deserver'. Critics who fasten on 'wallow' as an indication of swinish pleasures surely miss the point, since Shakespeare uses the word on only one other occasion, where 'wallow naked in December snow' (*Richard II*, 1.3.298) hardly suggests the hot-house atmosphere of a brothel. But to think of sexual consummation as though it were a post-mortem activity has some psychological interest. It is related to Troilus' next speech in which he fears either that he will die of excess of pleasure, or else that he is not sensitive enough to appreciate it to the full. The love-making is a kind of ordeal of which he is afraid – afraid almost of impotence.

> And all my powers do their bestowing lose,
> Like vassalage at unawares encountering
> The eye of majesty.

(ll. 35–7)

This attitude is hardly that of the libertine of Oscar Campbell's fancy. In the scene which follows Troilus drops into prose, either under the influence of Pandarus' banter, or attempting nervously to adopt the role of fashionable lover. Cressida, on the other hand, later rises from her normal element of prose to adopt the more romantic medium of verse. Both the lovers are fearful – Cressida that with her surrender she will lose her power, and Troilus that the sexual act will not be able fully to express the love of his imagination and heart. The 'monstruosity in love' is 'that the will is infinite and the execution confined; that the desire is boundless and the act a slave to limit'. Cressida's confession of love and her admission that she has concealed her feelings show that she has become infected with Troilus' sincerity; but he reveals, both by his comment 'Well know they what they speak that speak so wisely' and in the speech which follows, that he doubts whether Cressida matches up to his image of her. He claims, in words that once again destroy Oscar Campbell's thesis:

> I am as true as truth's simplicity,
> And simpler than the infancy of truth!

That Cressida speaks so wisely may lend additional point to her use of the proverbial:

> To be wise and love
> Exceeds man's might; that dwells with gods above.

At the end of the scene the three characters step out of the frame of the play and remind the audience of their roles in legend – as faithful lover, false lover, and pimp.[1]

Troilus' doubts about his valuation of Cressida are revealed again in his urgent pleas to her to remain true and in his overpraise of the accomplishments of the Greeks. Nevertheless, when he is confronted with her rapid defection he can hardly believe the evidence of his eyes: 'If beauty have a soul, this is not she' (5.2.136).

---

[1] L. C. Knights, TLS (1932), 408.

This is the most complex scene in all Shakespeare's works, and one which demands to the full the exercise of multi-consciousness.[1] In the centre Cressida and Diomedes are enacting their comedy of coquetry and seduction. Watching them Troilus enacts his tragedy of disillusionment, watched and monitored by Ulysses. The third observer is Thersites, who gives a running commentary on Cressida, and on Troilus' reactions to her conduct. Ulysses, who does not believe that love can be permanent, is amazed that anyone can be simpler than the infancy of truth, so as not to share his beliefs; and Thersites, who believes the worst of human nature, gloats over the confirmation of his cynical view. Yet the audience is compelled to be shocked by Cressida's fall, compelled to laugh at the ribald comments of Thersites, and compelled to share Troilus' agony. We are swung continually and sickeningly from one mood to another; and this happens even when the director accepts the gospel according to Thersites.

Troilus' beliefs are overthrown, and he is driven almost to madness:

> O madness of discourse,
> That cause sets up with and against itself!
> Bifold authority, where reason can revolt
> Without perdition, and loss assume all reason
> Without revolt! This is, and is not, Cressid.
> Within my soul there doth conduce a fight
> Of this strange nature, that a thing inseparate
> Divides more wider than the sky and earth;
> And yet the spacious breadth of this division
> Admits no orifex for a point as subtle
> As Ariachne's broken woof to enter.
>
> (ll. 140–50)

We can see now one important dramatic function of Ulysses' speech on anarchy and order in 1.3. It was necessary for him to build up a concept of order in the universe, with the stars in their courses and the people in a kingdom obeying divinely-ordained laws, so that when Troilus, with Ulysses at his elbow, watches Cressida's unfaithfulness, we should be reminded of that order which has been destroyed for the hero by the frailty of one woman. He could have said with Othello: 'When I love thee not | Chaos is come again' (3.3.92–3).

[1] S. L. Bethell, *Shakespeare and the Popular Dramatic Tradition* (1944), 98–105.

We have seen how the discourses of Ulysses on order and time are relevant to both plots; but the two plots are linked in more obvious ways. The war separates the lovers and precipitates Cressida's fall, and the rivals for her love are fighting on opposite sides. The physical beauty of Helen and Cressida raises in both plots the contrast between appearance and reality. The war aims of both sides are shown to be futile. In both camps passion usurps the place of reason. All the Greeks and most of the Trojans are motivated solely by self-interest – Pandarus is one of the few exceptions; and in both camps the chief spokesmen for sanity go against their own prescriptions.

Hector is an heroic figure, who shines by comparison with Henry V and Fortinbras, near to him in date. He arouses the admiration of his enemies during his visit to the Greek camp both for his prowess and his magnanimity. There is something admirable, but also foolish, in his attempt to follow the customs of chivalry in an unchivalrous age. He will not let his sword 'decline on the declined'. Nester compares him to Jupiter, 'dealing life'; and Troilus, in the baffled fury of disillusionment, complains that he lets the fallen Greeks 'rise and live'. Hector protests that this is fair play; but Troilus retorts that it is 'fool's play' and urges him to show no pity. Hector, despite the pleading of Andromache, the warnings of Cassandra, and the commands of Priam, goes out to fight: he has promised Achilles and his honour is at stake. His last chivalrous gesture, when he spares Achilles, is his last fatal mistake. The realities of war are brought home to us by the account of the wounds he inflicts on the Myrmidons, 'noseless, handless, hacked and chipped' – like broken statues – and by their slaying of Hector, an unarmed man surrounded by merciless thugs.[1]

Lydgate moralizes on Hector's cupidity in pursuing the cowardly Greek for his splendid armour. But this, surely, is not Shakespeare's point. He uses the episode as another example of the contrast between appearance and reality, the fair outside contrasted with the diseased body within. There is, as we have mentioned, a great deal of disease imagery in the play, from the 'open ulcer' of Troilus to the diseases bequeathed to the audience by Pandarus. Disease, too, is the main component of Thersites' invective. Leprosy was the punishment inflicted on Criseyde for her faithlessness, and was often confused by the Elizabethans with the pox. As Thersites

[1] The quotations in the paragraph are 4.5.189, 191; 5.3.42–3; and 5.5.34.

reminds us, the Neapolitan bone-ache is 'the curse depending on those who war for a placket', and, as Pandarus reminds us at the end, the penalty of promiscuity.

Although, as we have seen, most of the incidents of the war plot come from Caxton, this could be described as Shakespeare's feelings on first opening Chapman's Homer; he seems not to have altogether shared Keats's admiration. Possibly he found the dedication distasteful, partly because of its affected style and mock modesty, partly because Achilles was said to prefigure the Earl of Essex – as Shakespeare had said that Adonis and Helen had prefigured the recipient of the Sonnets – and mostly because the character described in the poem did not seem to exemplify one 'in whose unmatched vertues shyne the dignities of the soule and the whole excellence of royall humanitie'. To a modern reader Hector is a more admirable figure than the nominal hero, his slayer; and Elizabethans would start with a Virgilian prejudice on behalf of the defeated Trojans.

The fall of Troy was the great legendary secular disaster, the subject of three epics and ten dramatic masterpieces. Shakespeare was not writing a travesty of Homer, but attempting to provide a more realistic account of events. There are no gods or goddesses among his dramatis personae. Men are responsible for their own fates and they live in a fallen world, one that had suffered a 'terrible aboriginal calamity'.[1]

The old men in the *Iliad*, beholding Helen on the walls of Troy, were forced to say:

> What man can blame
> The Greekes and Troyans to endure, for so admir'd a Dame
> So many miseries, and so long? In her sweet countenance shine
> Lookes like the Goddesses.   (III. 167–70)

Shakespeare depicts Helen as supremely beautiful, but the reality of her character belies her appearance. Neither Hector nor Diomedes thinks her worth the cost of holding her, or fighting for her:

> For every false drop in her bawdy veins
> A Grecian's life hath sunk; for every scruple
> Of her contaminated carrion weight
> A Trojan hath been slain; since she could speak,
> She hath not given so many good words breath
> As for her Greeks and Trojans suffered death.

> (4.1.70–5)

[1] J. H. Newman, *Apologia pro Vita Sua*, ed. Martin J. Svaglic (Oxford, 1967), 218.

Achilles is deprived of all excuse for his behaviour. As the intelligence service discovers, he is having a treasonable correspondence with Hecuba and Polyxena. He is surly, boorish, spiteful, arrogant and boastful, so that his intelligent understanding of Ulysses comes as a surprise. Ulysses himself is an unsuccessful Machiavel, whose plot to persuade Achilles to fight is a complete failure; Diomedes is a cynical and vulgar lecher, Ajax a brainless buffoon, Patroclus a 'male varlet', Menelaus a stupid butt for jokes of cuckoldry, and Agamemnon a man who has the trappings of authority without the substance.

There is the same realism in the love plot. One could almost say that here too 'all the argument is a whore and a cuckold', for Troilus is cuckolded like Menelaus. Nevertheless we ought not to read into the Cressida of the first three acts the character she reveals in the last. We should not suppose that her words 'You men will never tarry' imply that she had had previous sexual experience; it is merely an example of the scraps of proverbial wisdom she has acquired. Such remarks as 'What folly I commit' and 'You smile and mock me as if I meant naughtily' do not mean that she regarded her relations with Troilus as sinful: she has merely picked up the attitudes of Trojan society. We may add that even Rosalind, Beatrice, and Portia enjoy bawdy jokes. Cressida's uninhibited behaviour on her arrival in the Greek camp may perhaps be ascribed to a reaction from the strain of being put on a pedestal. We should remember that Ulysses' famous summary of her character is mainly a dramatic device to prepare the audience, in the desperately short period at Shakespeare's disposal, for her seduction by Diomedes.

> Fie, fie upon her!
> There's language in her eye, her cheek, her lip,
> Nay, her foot speaks; her wanton spirits look out
> At every joint and motive of her body.
> O, these encounterers, so glib of tongue,
> That give accosting welcome ere it comes,
> And wide unclasp the tables of their thoughts
> To every tickling reader! Set them down
> For sluttish spoils of opportunity
> And daughters of the game.   (4.5.54–63)

It was Ulysses, however, who suggested that she should be kissed by all the Greek chiefs in turn, although he himself refuses, almost as though he were carrying out an experiment. The Greeks, more-over, separated from their wives for seven years, are the tickling readers of Ulysses' speech. It should not be held against Cressida that she is a woman of quick sense, witty and sensuous, and still less that she is here treated as a sex-object. Like Troilus, she had looked forward to their love-making as a consummation devoutly to be wished; and one of his speeches (3.2.16–27), which the new Puritans find distasteful, resembles that of the chaste Portia when Bassanio chooses the leaden casket. A clear distinction is drawn between his 'marriage' with Cressida, 'Tied with the bonds of heaven', and her union with Diomedes with its five-finger-tied knot of lechery. Even Thersites realizes that there is a difference. Diomedes is less civilized, less sensitive, and less 'romantic' than Troilus, and he proposes only the right true end of love; Cressida, therefore, would not be embarrassed by spiritual demands and ideals she could not satisfy. If she is not, as the young Bernard Shaw – then a virgin – asserted,[1] Shakespeare's 'first real woman', she is depicted more naturalistically than the earlier heroines and in some ways she is more modern than them.

We may return finally to the question of genre. The play has been called a history (Q), a comedy (Q), a tragedy (F), a comical satire (Campbell), a tragical satire (Muir), a problem comedy (W. W. Lawrence), a problem play (Tillyard), and a 'hybrid and hundred-faced and hydra-headed prodigy' (Swinburne). As Berowne says, 'Every godfather can give a name.' Shakespeare would not have bothered about a label and, in any case, he relished the mingling of genres. *Cymbeline* might have been justly described by Polonius as 'tragical-comical-historical-pastoral'. All the labels which have been attached to *Troilus and Cressida* apply only to parts of the play which, as Goethe declared,[2] exhibit Shakespeare's unfettered spirit. 'Comical satire' hardly describes the most memorable scenes in the play – the two great debates, the dialogue between Ulysses and Achilles, Troilus' disillusion-ment, and the murder of Hector; and the satirist of the play is himself satirized. On the other hand, the play does not quite answer to the eloquent account given by Brian Morris of its tragic struc-ture:

---

[1] Shaw's paper on *Troilus and Cressida*, given to the New Shakspere Society in 1884, appeared posthumously in *The Shaw Review*, 7 (1964).

[2] *Conversations with Eckermann* (Everyman edition, 1930), 123.

Troilus is the only character who is shown developing through his experiences and he must be regarded as the centre of the play. He has all the potentialities of greatness, his speech has the ennobling note of high tragedy, but his nature is to love 'not wisely but too well'.[1]

Certainly Troilus changes in the last scenes of the play, realism replacing idealism, revenge love. He has become a better warrior and fulfilled his potentiality as a leader, but in other respects he has deteriorated. To many critics Hector would be a more satisfactory tragic hero, his death concluding the play, as Troilus' does not. Of course most of the original audience, and many at the Globe, would know that Troilus, as well as Troy, was doomed.

The play in its present form is impossible to categorize in such a way as to satisfy most readers; but if, as Coghill argued,[2] the Prologue and epilogue were added for a special performance at one of the Inns of Court, six years after it was first produced at the Globe, or if, as Gary Taylor has more recently argued,[3] the Globe performance came after the private one, one version would be nearer to tragedy than the other version is to comedy. A modern director is at liberty to follow either of the Shakespearian versions; and the Trojans, including Cressida, can be presented with varying degrees of sympathy. It would not, however, be legitimate, in the interests of contemporary 'relevance', to offer Thersites as the fount of truth and wisdom.

The play has been more widely appreciated during the past thirty years than in the previous three and a half centuries. Few would regard it as one of the supreme plays, but only a great dramatic poet could have written it. It is, in a sense, Shakespeare's most intellectual play, 'a consciously philosophical play',[4] 'a play of ideas',[5] and for this reason it has a unique flavour, one that needs to be savoured if we are to experience the full range of Shakespeare's genius. As John Bayley says, Shakespeare is doing something quite different here from his other works.[6]

---

[1] *Shakespeare Quarterly*, 10 (1959), 481–91.
[2] *Shakespeare's Professional Skills*, 78–97.
[3] *'Troilus and Cressida'*.
[4] S. L. Bethell, *Shakespeare and the Popular Dramatic Tradition*, 98.
[5] Arthur Sewell, *Character and Society in Shakespeare* (Oxford, 1951), 128. But he goes on to say, I think mistakenly, that 'The characters are either mouthpieces in the presentation of ideas or else they are embodiments and illustrations or allegories of moments in the argument'.
[6] 'Time and the Trojans', *Essays in Criticism*, 25 (1975), 55–73; p. 73.

The nineteenth-century dislike of the tone of the play, expressed by Bradley as 'a spirit of bitterness and contempt',[1] was ascribed by Dowden to Shakespeare's mistake of writing comedy when he was in the depths and ought therefore to have been engaged on tragedy.[2] Brandes similarly remarked that it was written in the most despondent period of Shakespeare's life.[3] Even as late as 1933, John Dover Wilson complained of the note 'of disillusionment and cynicism, the air is cheerless and often unwholesome, the wit mirthless, the bad characters contemptible or detestable, the good ones unattractive'.[4] The implication is that the play reflects Shakespeare's own state of mind at the time he was writing the problem plays. Charles Williams likewise thought that the play reflected a crisis in Shakespeare's own life, and that Troilus' disillusionment was in some sense his own.[5] Even Una Ellis-Fermor's brilliant essay in *The Frontiers of Drama* is based on the assumption that

The idea of chaos, of disjunction, of ultimate formlessness and negation has by a supreme act of artistic mastery been given form ... The content of his thought is an implacable assertion of chaos as the ultimate fact of being; the presence of artistic form is a deeper, unconscious testimony to an order which is actually ultimate and against which the gates of hell shall not prevail.[6]

As I have said elsewhere,[7] I do not believe that Shakespeare's plays are so closely related to his life, and if they were I do not see how it could be demonstrated, as it could with Eliot and *The Waste Land*. I do not believe that Shakespeare ever asserted that life was meaningless. He was saying that men are often foolish and wicked, that women are often false, and that both act in defiance of their consciences, that the pursuit of self-interest is a danger to the state. He was certainly not saying that values were all illusions, but that men ignore them or violate them. The play shows how we are sometimes 'devils to ourselves' and that the world and the flesh

---

[1] *Shakespearean Tragedy* (1904), 185.

[2] *Shakspere, A Critical Study of his Mind and Art* (1875).

[3] *William Shakespeare, a Critical Study*, translated by William Archer, Mary Morison, and Diana White, 2 vols. (New York, 1898), ii. 206.

[4] *The Essential Shakespeare*, 116.

[5] *The English Poetic Mind* (Oxford, 1932), 60 ff.

[6] Una Ellis-Fermor, ' "Discord in the Spheres": The Universe of *Troilus and Cressida*', in *The Frontiers of Drama* (1945; rev. edn 1964), pp. 72–3.

[7] 'Troilus and Cressida', *Shakespeare Survey 8* (Cambridge, 1955), 28–39; p. 36.

make the best the victims of the worst. It is not a cynical play, but a sombre examination of a fallen world, which any contemporary preacher could have applauded.[1]

[1] Peter Alexander similarly wrote 'I regard the piece not as evidence of Shakespeare's cynicism but as his medicine for cynics' (TLS (1965), 220).

ABBREVIATIONS AND REFERENCES

IN the collations a reading is understood to derive from Q, or to be common to QF, unless otherwise stated. In readings common to QF we follow Q's spelling, capitalization, etc. Asides and indications of persons addressed have been added by successive editors, including the present one, and are not attributed individually. Acts and scenes are not marked in QF and were mostly added by Rowe, the remainder by Theobald and Capell. They have been retained in this edition only for ease of reference. In Act 5, as Alice Walker remarks, the 'fidgety changes from one part of the field to another slow down the action'. Changes in lineation are recorded in Appendix 3.

In the commentary, 'first occurrence' signifies that this is the first citation in *OED*. Quotations from the Bible are modernized from the Bishops' Bible (1568), the version (along with the Geneva Bible of 1560) best known to Shakespeare. References to other plays by Shakespeare are to Peter Alexander's edition.

The following abbreviations are used in the collations and commentary. The place of publication is London unless otherwise specified.

EDITIONS OF SHAKESPEARE

Q	*The Historie of Troylus and Cresseida*, 1609
F	The First Folio, 1623
F2	The Second Folio, 1632
F3	The Third Folio, 1663
F4	The Fourth Folio, 1685
Alexander	Peter Alexander, *Complete Works* (1951)
Baldwin	T. W. Baldwin, supplemental editor, *Troilus and Cressida*, New Variorum edition of Shakespeare (Philadelphia and London, 1953)
Bevington	David Bevington, *Complete Works* (Glenview, 1980)
Cambridge	W. G. Clark and W. A. Wright, *Works*, the Cambridge Shakespeare, 9 vols. (Cambridge, 1863–6)
Capell	Edward Capell, *Comedies, Histories and Tragedies*, 10 vols. (1767–8)
Collier	John Payne Collier, *Works*, 8 vols. (1842–4)
Collier 1853	John Payne Collier, *Plays* (1853)

Cowden Clarke	Charles and Mary Cowden Clarke, *Plays*, Cassell's Illustrated Shakespeare, 3 vols. (1864–8)
Craig	W. J. Craig, *Troilus and Cressida* (1905)
Deighton	K. Deighton, *Troilus and Cressida*, the Arden Shakespeare (1906)
Dobrée	Bonamy Dobrée, *Troilus and Cressida*, the Warwick Shakespeare (1938)
Dyce	Alexander Dyce, *Works*, 6 vols. (1857)
Dyce 1864	Alexander Dyce, *Works*, 9 vols. (1864–7)
Hanmer	Thomas Hanmer, *Works*, 6 vols. (Oxford, 1743–4)
Hudson	H. N. Hudson, *Works*, 11 vols. (Boston, 1851–6)
Hudson 1881	H. N. Hudson, *Works*, the Harvard edition, 20 vols. (Boston, 1880–1)
Johnson	Samuel Johnson, *Plays*, 8 vols. (1765)
Johnson and Steevens	Samuel Johnson and George Steevens, *Plays*, 10 vols. (1773)
Johnson and Steevens 1778	Samuel Johnson and George Steevens, *Plays*, 10 vols. (1778)
Johnson and Steevens 1785	Samuel Johnson, George Steevens, and Isaac Reed, *Plays*, 10 vols. (1785)
Kittredge	George Lyman Kittredge, *Complete Works* (Boston, 1936)
Knight	Charles Knight, *Works*, Pictorial Edition, 8 vols. (1838–43)
Malone	Edmond Malone, *Plays and Poems*, 10 vols. (1790)
New Variorum	Harold N. Hillebrand, supplemental editor T. W. Baldwin, *Troilus and Cressida*, New Variorum edition of Shakespeare (Philadelphia and London, 1953)
Pope	Alexander Pope, *Works*, 6 vols. (1723–5)
Pope 1728	Alexander Pope, *Works*, 10 vols. (1728)
Rann	Joseph Rann, *Dramatic Works*, 6 vols. (1786–94)
Riverside	G. Blakemore Evans, textual editor, *The Riverside Shakespeare* (Boston, 1974)
Rowe	Nicholas Rowe, *Works*, 6 vols. (1709)
Rowe 1709b	Nicholas Rowe, *Works*, 6 vols. (1709)
Rowe 1714	Nicholas Rowe, *Works*, 8 vols. (1714)
Seltzer	Daniel Seltzer, *Troilus and Cressida*, Signet Classic Shakespeare (New York, 1963)

Singer	S. W. Singer, *Dramatic Works* (second edition), 10 vols. (1856)
Sisson	Charles J. Sisson, *Complete Works* (1954)
Staunton	Howard Staunton, *Plays*, 3 vols. (1858–60)
Steevens	George Steevens and Isaac Reed, *Plays*, 15 vols. (1793)
Theobald	Lewis Theobald, *Works*, 7 vols. (1733)
Verity	A. W. Verity and Frank A. Marshall, *Troilus and Cressida*, in the Henry Irving Shakespeare, 8 vols. (New York and London, 1888–90)
Walker	Alice Walker, *Troilus and Cressida*, the New Shakespeare (Cambridge, 1957)
Warburton	William Warburton, *Works*, 8 vols. (1747)
White	Richard Grant White, *Works*, 12 vols. (Boston, 1857–66)
White 1883	Richard Grant White, *Comedies, Histories, Tragedies, and Poems*, the Riverside Shakespeare, 3 vols. (Boston, 1883)

OTHER WORKS

Anders	H. R. D. Anders, *Shakespeare's Books: A Dissertation on Shakespeare's Reading and the Immediate Sources of his Works* (Berlin, 1904)
Baldwin, *Small Latine*	T. W. Baldwin, *William Shakspere's 'Small Latine & Lesse Greeke'*, 2 vols. (Urbana, 1944)
Campbell, *Comicall Satyre*	O. J. Campbell, *Comicall Satyre and Shakespeare's 'Troilus and Cressida'* (San Marino, 1938)
Carter	Thomas Carter, *Shakespeare and Holy Scripture* (1905)
Caxton	William Caxton, trans., *The Recuyell of the Historyes of Troy ...*, ed. H. Oskar Sommer, 2 vols. (1894). References in the commentary are to volume and page of this edition.
Cercignani	Fausto Cercignani, *Shakespeare's Works and Elizabethan Pronunciation* (Oxford, 1981)
Chapman	*Chapman's Homer*, ed. Allardyce Nicoll, 2 vols. (1957). Quotations are from the *Seaven Books of the Iliades of Homere* (1598); Nicoll (i. 500–39) prints the first two books as well as the revised versions Chapman published in 1611 as part of his complete translation of the *Iliad*.
Chaucer	Geoffrey Chaucer, *Troilus and Criseyde*. Quotations are from Thomas Speght's edition, 1598.

43

Clarkson and Warren   Paul S. Clarkson and Clyde T. Warren, *The Law of Property in Shakespeare and the Elizabethan Drama* (Baltimore, 1942)

Colman   E. A. M. Colman, *The Dramatic Use of Bawdy in Shakespeare* (1974)

Cooper's *Thesaurus*   Thomas Cooper, *Thesaurus Linguae Romanae & Britannicae*, 1565

Cotgrave   Randle Cotgrave, *A Dictionarie of the French and English Tongues*, 1611

Davies, *Nosce Teipsum*   Sir John Davies, *Nosce Teipsum*, in *The Poems of Sir John Davies*, ed. R. Krueger (Oxford, 1975)

Greene, *Euphues his Censure*   Robert Greene, *Euphues his Censure to Philautus*, in vol. 6 of *The Life and Complete Works in Prose and Verse of Robert Greene*, ed. Alexander B. Grosart, 15 vols. (1881–6)

Greg, *Principles of Emendation*   W. W. Greg, *Principles of Emendation in Shakespeare*, Annual Shakespeare Lecture of the British Academy, 1928

Heath   Benjamin Heath, *A Revisal of Shakespear's Text* (1765)

Henryson   Robert Henryson, *The Testament of Cresseid*. First printed in 1593, this continuation of Chaucer's *Troilus and Criseyde* was included in Speght's Chaucer (1598)

Honigmann   E. A. J. Honigmann, *The Stability of Shakespeare's Text* (1965)

Hulme   Hilda M. Hulme, *Explorations in Shakespeare's Language: Some Problems of Word Meaning in the Dramatic Text* (1962, repr. 1977)

Jackson   Z. Jackson, *Shakespeare's Genius Justified* (1819)

Kellner   Leon Kellner, *Restoring Shakespeare* (New York, 1925)

Kinnear   Benjamin G. Kinnear, *Cruces Shakespearianae* (1883)

Lydgate   John Lydgate, *The Auncient Historie and onely trewe and syncere Cronicle of the warres betwixte the Grecians and the Troyans . . .* ; ed. Henry Bergen, *Lydgate's Troy Book*, EETS nos. 97 (1906), 103, 106 (1908), 126 (1935)

Mason   John Monck Mason, *Comments on the Plays of Beaumont and Fletcher, with an Appendix Containing some Further Observations on Shakespeare* (1798)

Mason, *Comments*   John Monck Mason, *Comments on the Last Edition of Shakespeare's Plays* (1785)

N. & Q.	*Notes and Queries*

Nares   Robert Nares, *A Glossary ... in the Works of English Authors, particularly Shakespeare* (1822)

Nashe   *The Works of Thomas Nashe*, ed. Ronald B. McKerrow, 5 vols. (1904–10; rev. edn, ed. F. P. Wilson, Oxford, 1958)

Noble   Richmond Noble, *Shakespeare's Biblical Knowledge and ᵀ of the Book of Common Prayer* (1935)

OED   *The Oxford English Dictionary, being a corrected re-issue .. of A New English Dictionary on Historical Principles*, 13 vols. (Oxford, 1933); and Supplements 1–2 (1972, 1976)

Onions   C. T. Onions, *A Shakespeare Glossary* (Oxford, 1911; rev. edn 1919; repr. with additions 1958)

Partridge   Eric Partridge, *Shakespeare's Bawdy: A Literary and Psychological Essay and a Comprehensive Glossary* (1947; rev. edn 1968)

Richards, *Speculative Instruments*   I. A. Richards, *Speculative Instruments* (Chicago and London, 1955). A section on *Troilus and Cressida* is reprinted in the Signet edition of the play, pp. 239–55.

Schmidt   Alexander Schmidt, *Shakespeare-Lexicon*, 2 vols. (Berlin and London, 1874–5)

Seymour   E. H. Seymour, *Remarks, Critical, Conjectural, and Explanatory, upon the plays of Shakespeare*, 2 vols. (1805)

Sisson, *New Readings*   C. J. Sisson, *New Readings in Shakespeare*, 2 vols. (Cambridge, 1956)

Spurgeon   Caroline Spurgeon, *Shakespeare's Imagery and What it Tells Us* (Cambridge, 1935)

Tannenbaum   Samuel A. Tannenbaum, 'Notes on "Troilus and Cressida"', *Shakespeare Association Bulletin*, 7 (1932), 72–81

Tannenbaum, *Critique*   Samuel A. Tannenbaum, 'A Critique of the Text of "Troilus and Cressida": Part II, The Folio Text', *Shakespeare Association Bulletin*, 9 (1934), 125–44, 198–214

Tilley   M. P. Tilley, *A Dictionary of the Proverbs in England in the Sixteenth and Seventeenth Centuries* (Ann Arbor, 1950)

Upton   John Upton, *Critical Observations on Shakespeare* (1746)

Walker, *Textual Problems*   Alice Walker, *Textual Problems of the First Folio: 'Richard III', 'King Lear', 'Troilus and Cressida', '2 Henry IV', 'Othello'* (Cambridge, 1953)

Acknowledgement

Photographs are reproduced by permission of the British Library.

Troilus and Cressida

THE PERSONS OF THE PLAY

Trojans

PRIAM, King of Troy
HECTOR
DEIPHOBUS
HELENUS, a priest
PARIS   } his sons
TROILUS
MARGARELON, a bastard
CASSANDRA, his daughter, a prophetess
ANDROMACHE, wife of Hector
AENEAS
ANTENOR   } Commanders.
PANDARUS, a lord
CRESSIDA, his niece
CALCHAS, her father, who has joined the Greeks
HELEN, former wife of Menelaus, now living as Paris' wife
ALEXANDER, servant of Cressida
Servants of Troilus and Paris
Soldiers
Attendants

Greeks

AGAMEMNON, Commander-in-Chief
MENELAUS, his brother
NESTOR
ULYSSES
ACHILLES
PATROCLUS, his friend
DIOMEDES
AJAX
THERSITES
MYRMIDONS, soldiers of Achilles
Servant of Diomedes
Soldiers

Troilus and Cressida

Prologue *Enter the Prologue in armour*

PROLOGUE

In Troy there lies the scene. From isles of Greece
The princes orgulous, their high blood chafed,
Have to the port of Athens sent their ships,
Fraught with the ministers and instruments
Of cruel war. Sixty and nine that wore
Their crownets regal, from th'Athenian bay
Put forth toward Phrygia, and their vow is made
To ransack Troy, within whose strong immures
The ravished Helen, Menelaus' queen,
With wanton Paris sleeps – and that's the quarrel.   10
To Tenedos they come,
And the deep-drawing barks do there disgorge
Their warlike fraughtage; now on Dardan plains
The fresh and yet-unbruisèd Greeks do pitch
Their brave pavilions. Priam's six-gated city –
Dardan, and Timbria, Hellas, Chetas, Troien,
And Antenorides – with massy staples

Prologue 0–31 *Enter ... Exit*] F; *not in* Q   12 barks] F2; Barke F1   17 Antenorides] THEO-
BALD; *Antenonidus* F

Prologue Walker (141) thought that 'the
deliberately elevated style' was 'intended
as a significant contrast to the unheroic
temper of the play'. But the Latinized style
is used throughout the play, especially in
the debates and in the battle-scenes of Act
5. Shakespeare, as in the 'Dido' speeches
of *Hamlet* (2.2.446 ff.) and in the account
of the battle in the second scene of *Macbeth*, was attempting to imitate the style
of classical epic.

2 **orgulous** proud. Used frequently by Caxton, obsolete by Shakespeare's day.
high proud, violent
chafed warmed

3 **port of Athens** Probably Piraeus, but
possibly 'the port which is Athens'.

4 **Fraught** laden

6 **crownets** coronets

7 **Phrygia** the country of which Troy was
the capital

8 **immures** walls (the only recorded use of
the word)

9 **ravished** carried away by force

11 **Tenedos** an island near Troy

12 **disgorge** The first use of eating imagery,
not noted afterwards. See Introduction,
p. 29.

13 **fraughtage** freight – not modernized to
'freightage' because of 'fraught' (4)
Dardan i.e. Dardanian, another name for
Trojan. Dardanus was the ancestor of the
Trojans.

14 **unbruisèd** i.e. not having fought

15 **pavilions** tents

16–17 **Dardan ... Antenorides** The gates
are so listed by Caxton (ii. 507).

51

And corresponsive and fulfilling bolts,
Sperr up the sons of Troy.
Now expectation, tickling skittish spirits   20
On one and other side, Trojan and Greek,
Sets all on hazard. And hither am I come,
A Prologue armed, but not in confidence
Of author's pen or actor's voice, but suited
In like condition as our argument,
To tell you, fair beholders, that our play
Leaps o'er the vaunt and firstlings of those broils,
Beginning in the middle; starting thence away
To what may be digested in a play.
Like or find fault; do as your pleasures are: 30
Now good or bad, 'tis but the chance of war.   *Exit*

1.1   *Enter Pandarus and Troilus*

TROILUS

Call here my varlet: I'll unarm again.
Why should I war without the walls of Troy
That find such cruel battle here within?
Each Trojan that is master of his heart,
Let him to field – Troilus, alas, hath none.
PANDARUS   Will this gear ne'er be mended?

---

19 Sperr] THEOBALD; Stirre F   25 condition] WALKER; conditions F   31 Exit] *not in* F
1.1.5 to field] to th'field *conj.* TANNENBAUM

---

18 **corresponsive** corresponding, i.e. equally
massy (first occurrence)
fulfilling complementary or suitable to.
The whole phrase probably means
'which fit tightly into their slots'.
19 **Sperr** Theobald's emendation, universally accepted, is supported by his
reference to Chaucer's *Troilus and
Criseyde*, v. 76, where *sperred* = shut. It
is an obsolete variant of *spar* (OED) and
here spelt to avoid confusion with
modern senses of 'spar'.
23 **armed** See Introduction, p. 5.
23–4 **in ... voice** confident of the value of
the play, or of the acting
24–5 **suited . . . as** 'dressed as' and
'appropriate to'
25 **condition** character. As Walker argues,
the singular is necessary since it refers to
the suitability of armour to the events of

the play.
25 **argument** (a) theme (b) quarrel
27 **vaunt** from the prefix *vaunt* (as in *vaunt-
courier*) and here meaning 'beginning' or
'preliminaries' (the only recorded use in
this sense). Perhaps influenced by *vaunt*
= brag.
28 **in the middle** *in medias res* (the Horatian
tag)
29 **digested** The usual word for reducing
material into dramatic form.
31 **Now . . . war** proverbial (Tilley C223)
1.1 In Troy
1 **Call here my varlet** (addressed to a servant, probably off stage)
again i.e. although he has just armed
5 **none** i.e. no heart (for fighting, because
he has lost it to Cressida)
6 **gear** business

TROILUS

The Greeks are strong, and skilful to their strength,
Fierce to their skill, and to their fierceness valiant;
But I am weaker than a woman's tear,
Tamer than sleep, fonder than ignorance,   10
Less valiant than the virgin in the night,
And skilless as unpractised infancy.

PANDARUS Well, I have told you enough of this. For my part
I'll not meddle nor make no farther. He that will have a
cake out of the wheat must tarry the grinding.

TROILUS Have I not tarried?

PANDARUS Ay, the grinding; but you must tarry the
boulting.

TROILUS Have I not tarried?

PANDARUS Ay, the boulting; but you must tarry the   20
leavening.

TROILUS Still have I tarried.

PANDARUS Ay, to the leavening; but here's yet in the word
hereafter, the kneading, the making of the cake, the heating of the oven, and the baking. Nay, you must stay the
cooling too, or you may chance to burn your lips.

TROILUS

Patience herself, what goddess e'er she be,
Doth lesser blench at suff'rance than I do;
At Priam's royal table do I sit,
And when fair Cressid comes into my thoughts –   30
So, traitor! When she comes? When is she thence?

PANDARUS Well, she looked yesternight fairer than ever I
saw her look, or any woman else.

---

15 must] must needes F   25 of] F *second setting; not in* Q. F *first setting*   26 you] F; yea Q
to] F; *not in* Q   31 So...thence?] ROWE (*subs.*); So traitor then she comes when she is thence QF

7, 8 **to** in addition to
10 **fonder** more foolish
14 **meddle nor make** have anything more to
    do with it; a common alliterative ex-
    pression (Tilley M852)
18 **boulting** sifting
23 **word** i.e. tarry. (It cannot be 'hereafter' as
    the word has not been used.)
25 **of** Although this word was inserted in the
    second setting of F, probably without
    reference to a manuscript, it seems desir-
    able after the previous 'of'.

27 **Patience** (not in the classical pantheon)
28 **lesser** The line means the opposite, i.e.
    that Patience flinches more than I do.
    suff'rance (a) long endurance (b) suffer-
    ing
31 **So ... thence** Most modern editors have
    reverted to the QF reading; but their ex-
    planations, when they give any, are un-
    convincing. Troilus calls himself a traitor
    because Cressida is never absent from his
    thoughts – an exaggeration characteris-
    tic of the speaker.

TROILUS

    I was about to tell thee – when my heart
    As wedgèd with a sigh, would rive in twain,
    Lest Hector or my father should perceive me
    I have, as when the sun doth light a-scorn,
    Buried this sigh in wrinkle of a smile:
    But sorrow that is couched in seeming gladness
    Is like that mirth fate turns to sudden sadness.   40

PANDARUS

    An her hair were not somewhat darker than Helen's –
    well, go to – there were no more comparison between the
    women. But, for my part, she is my kinswoman: I would
    not, as they term it, praise her, but I would somebody had
    heard her talk yesterday as I did. I will not dispraise your
    sister Cassandra's wit, but –

TROILUS

    O Pandarus! – I tell thee, Pandarus –
    When I do tell thee there my hopes lie drowned,
    Reply not in how many fathoms deep
    They lie indrenched. I tell thee I am mad   50
    In Cressid's love. Thou answer'st she is fair,
    Pourest in the open ulcer of my heart
    Her eyes, her hair, her cheek, her gait, her voice;
    Handlest in thy discourse – O that her hand,
    In whose comparison all whites are ink
    Writing their own reproach, to whose soft seizure

---

37 a-scorn] F; a scorne Q; a Storm ROWE   48 there] where *conj.* KEATS   52 heart$_\Lambda$]
THEOBALD; heart: Q; heart, F

---

35 **wedgèd** split, as with a wedge
36 **perceive** 'observe' or 'notice'
37 **a-scorn** in scorn or mockery, the smile
    being forced. Rowe's emendation, often
    accepted by editors, misses the point.
39–40 **But . . . sadness** Sorrow hidden in
    gladness is not really like mirth which is
    turned to sadness. Presumably the
    couplet means that in both cases ap-
    pearances are deceptive.
39 **couched** hidden
41 **darker** (and so less fashionable than the
    blonde Helen)
42 **go to** never mind
44 **I . . . praise her** Baldwin compares

4.1.77; but it may just mean 'I don't
want to sound prejudiced'.
46 **wit** intelligence
48 **there my hopes lie drowned** that it is
    there my hopes are drowned. Keats's con-
    jecture (recorded in the collations) was
    made in his copy of the 1808 Folio
    facsimile.
50 **indrenched** drowned. Used by Nashe in
    1593 (*OED*).
54 **Handlest in thy discourse** Troilus shifts
    from *Pourest* to *Handlest*, and this word
    reminds him of Cressida's hand.
    that her hand that hand of hers
56 **to** compared to

The cygnet's down is harsh, and spirit of sense
Hard as the palm of ploughman! This thou tell'st me –
As true thou tell'st me – when I say I love her;
But saying thus, instead of oil and balm   60
Thou lay'st in every gash that love hath given me
The knife that made it.

PANDARUS I speak no more than truth.

TROILUS Thou dost not speak so much.

PANDARUS Faith, I'll not meddle in it. Let her be as she is. If
she be fair, 'tis the better for her; an she be not, she has
the mends in her own hands.

TROILUS Good Pandarus, how now, Pandarus!

PANDARUS I have had my labour for my travail; ill thought
on of her, and ill thought on of you; gone between and   70
between, but small thanks for my labour.

TROILUS What, art thou angry, Pandarus? What, with me?

PANDARUS Because she's kin to me, therefore she's not so
fair as Helen; an she were not kin to me, she would be as
fair o' Friday as Helen is on Sunday. But what care I? I
care not an she were a blackamoor; 'tis all one to me.

TROILUS Say I she is not fair?

PANDARUS I do not care whether you do or no. She's a fool
to stay behind her father. Let her to the Greeks, and so I'll
tell her the next time I see her. For my part, I'll meddle nor   80
make no more i'th' matter.

TROILUS Pandarus –

PANDARUS Not I.

TROILUS Sweet Pandarus –

---

57 sense$_\Lambda$] F; sence: Q   59 As] And HUDSON 1881 (*conj.* W. S. WALKER)   69 travail] QF (trauell)
70 on of you] F; of you Q   74 not kin] F *second setting*; kin Q, F *first setting*   75 o' Friday] on
Friday F   care I] F; I Q

57 **spirit of sense** 'a delicate sense of touch'
or 'quintessence of sensibility'. Later
(3.3.106) Achilles calls the eye the 'most
pure spirit of sense'. According to Sir John
Davies, *Nosce Teipsum* (1124–8), spirits
of life ascend from the heart to the brain
and there 'the *spirits* of *sense* do make'.
These 'in Phantasies high court | Judge of
the forms of *Objects*' and report to the
heart. Shakespeare, however, does not
seem to make use of this idea.

66–7 **she has . . . hands** i.e. by the use of

cosmetics (Warburton) or other arts of
allurement. 'The mends in his own hands'
is a standard phrase (Tilley M872).

67 **mends** remedy

69 **I . . . travail** The pains I have taken are
my only reward.

75 **on Sunday** i.e. in her Sunday best

78–9 **She's . . . Greeks** The first reference to
her father's treachery.

80 **next time I see her** Perhaps implying that
Cressida does not live with her uncle.

PANDARUS Pray you, speak no more to me. I will leave all
    as I found it, and there an end.   *Exit*
      Sound alarum

TROILUS
    Peace, you ungracious clamours! Peace, rude sounds!
    Fools on both sides: Helen must needs be fair,
    When with your blood you daily paint her thus.
    I cannot fight upon this argument: 90
    It is too starved a subject for my sword.
    But Pandarus – O gods, how do you plague me!
    I cannot come to Cressid but by Pandar,
    And he's as tetchy to be wooed to woo
    As she is stubborn-chaste against all suit.
    Tell me, Apollo, for thy Daphne's love,
    What Cressid is, what Pandar, and what we?
    Her bed is India; there she lies, a pearl;
    Between our Ilium and where she resides
    Let it be called the wild and wand'ring flood;   100
    Ourself the merchant, and this sailing Pandar
    Our doubtful hope, our convoy and our bark.
      Alarum. Enter Aeneas

AENEAS
    How now, Prince Troilus! Wherefore not afield?

TROILUS
    Because not there. This woman's answer sorts,
    For womanish it is to be from thence.
    What news, Aeneas, from the field today?

---

92 do you] you do *conj.* WALKER   95 stubborn-chaste] THEOBALD; stubborne, chast QF   99
resides] F (recides); reides Q

87–91 **Peace . . . sword** Troilus' opinion of
  the war in this speech contrasts with his
  arguments for the retention of Helen in
  2.2.
89 **paint** daub, as though using blood as
  rouge
90 **I cannot fight upon this argument** an
  allusion to fighting on an empty stomach
  (Deighton)
91 **starved a subject** inadequate as a war-
  aim
94 **tetchy** to be fretful about being
94–5 **And . . . suit** Troilus is as mistaken
  about Pandarus, who is anxious to bring

the lovers together, as he is about
  Cressida.
96 **for thy Daphne's love** by your love for
  Daphne (who was as coy as Cressida
  seems)
98–102 **Her bed . . . bark** The first of several
  images relating to commerce.
98 **India** (regarded as an exotic source of
  wealth)
99 **Ilium** Priam's palace, as in Caxton. In
  later occurrences both Q and F sometimes
  use the alternative form 'Ilion'.
104 **sorts** is fitting; 'Because is a woman's
  reason' (Tilley B179)

AENEAS

That Paris is returnèd home, and hurt.

TROILUS

By whom, Aeneas?

AENEAS   Troilus, by Menelaus.

TROILUS

Let Paris bleed; 'tis but a scar to scorn;

Paris is gored with Menelaus' horn.   110

    Alarum

AENEAS

Hark what good sport is out of town today!

TROILUS

Better at home, if 'would I might' were 'may'.

But to the sport abroad: are you bound thither?

AENEAS

In all swift haste.

TROILUS   Come, go we then together.   *Exeunt*

1.2   *Enter Cressida and Alexander, her man*

CRESSIDA

Who were those went by?

ALEXANDER   Queen Hecuba and Helen.

CRESSIDA

And whither go they?

ALEXANDER   Up to the eastern tower,

Whose height commands as subject all the vale,

To see the battle. Hector, whose patience

Is as a virtue fixed, today was moved: 5

He chid Andromache and struck his armourer;

And, like as there were husbandry in war,

Before the sun rose he was harnessed light,

1.2.0.1 *Enter ... man*] THEOBALD (*subs.*); *Enter Cressid and her man* QF   6 chid] chides F

109 **scar** wound, cut (*OED sb.*³, 1)
110 **horn** (Menelaus having been cuckolded by Paris)
1.2 In Troy.
0.1 Perhaps Hecuba and Helen should pass over the stage before Cressida's entrance.
4–5 **patience . . . fixed** Theobald, Capell and others have argued that it was wrong to compare Hector's patience to a virtue, and so emended to 'the virtue'. But the meaning is simply 'Hector's patience

(being a virtue) is, as a virtue should be, fixed' (Deighton).
5 **moved** angry
7 **husbandry** economy (because of early rising)
8 **light** because he was fighting on foot. Warburton cites Fairfax's translation of Tasso (xi. 25) 'harness light | As footmen use'. Some editors, however, think that light = lightly, quickly.

57

And to the field goes he; where every flower
Did as a prophet weep what it foresaw   10
In Hector's wrath.

CRESSIDA   What was his cause of anger?

ALEXANDER

The noise goes, this: there is among the Greeks
A lord of Trojan blood, nephew to Hector –
They call him Ajax.

CRESSIDA   Good; and what of him?

ALEXANDER

They say he is a very man *per se*,
And stands alone.

CRESSIDA So do all men unless they are drunk, sick, or have
no legs.

ALEXANDER This man, lady, hath robbed many beasts of
their particular additions: he is as valiant as the lion,   20
churlish as the bear, slow as the elephant – a man into
whom nature hath so crowded humours that his valour
is crushed into folly, his folly sauced with discretion.
There is no man hath a virtue that he hath not a glimpse
of, nor any man an attaint but he carries some stain of it.
He is melancholy without cause, and merry against the
hair; he hath the joints of everything, but everything so
out of joint that he is a gouty Briareus, many hands and
no use, or a purblind Argus, all eyes and no sight.

CRESSIDA But how should this man, that makes me smile,   30
make Hector angry?

ALEXANDER They say he yesterday coped Hector in the

17 they] F; the Q   23 sauced] farced THEOBALD; forced WALKER   28 a] HANMER;   *not in* QF
29 purblind] purblinded F

10 **Did . . . weep** i.e. was wet with dew
12 **noise** rumour
13 **nephew** relation. Shakespeare followed
Lydgate (iii. 2046–8), Caxton, or Thomas
Cooper's *Thesaurus* in making Ajax the
son of Hesione, Priam's sister.
14 **Good** This presumably means 'so'; but it
may indicate that Cressida is thinking of
the usual quibble on Ajax/a jakes.
15 *per se* unique. Henryson, *Testament of
Cresseid*, l. 78, calls Cressida 'The floure
and A per se of Troie and Greece'. Compare Tilley A275.
19–29 **This man . . . sight** This character

sketch seems to have little resemblance to
the Ajax we meet later. This may be due
to a change of plan or to revision; but
many regard it as a topical allusion. See
Introduction, p. 6.
20 **additions** titles, or 'distinctive attributes'
(Onions)
25 **attaint** taint
26 **against the hair** against the grain. Tilley
H18: 'It goes against the hair.'
28 **Briareus** a giant with a hundred hands
29 **Argus** the hundred-eyed guardian of Io.
Tilley E254: 'As many eyes as Argus.'
32 **coped** fought with

battle and struck him down, the disdain and shame
whereof hath ever since kept Hector fasting and waking.

CRESSIDA Who comes here?

ALEXANDER Madam, your uncle Pandarus.

Enter Pandarus

CRESSIDA Hector's a gallant man.

ALEXANDER As may be in the world, lady.

PANDARUS What's that? What's that?

CRESSIDA Good morrow, uncle Pandarus. 40

PANDARUS Good morrow, cousin Cressid. What do you talk
of? Good morrow, Alexander. How do you, cousin? When
were you at Ilium?

CRESSIDA This morning, uncle.

PANDARUS What were you talking of when I came? Was
Hector armed and gone ere ye came to Ilium? Helen was
not up, was she?

CRESSIDA
Hector was gone; but Helen was not up.

PANDARUS E'en so: Hector was stirring early.

CRESSIDA
That were we talking of, and of his anger. 50

PANDARUS Was he angry?

CRESSIDA So he says here.

PANDARUS True, he was so; I know the cause too; he'll lay
about him today, I can tell them that. And there's Troilus
will not come far behind him; let them take heed of
Troilus, I can tell them that too.

CRESSIDA What, is he angry too?

PANDARUS Who, Troilus? Troilus is the better man of the
two.

CRESSIDA
O Jupiter! There's no comparison. 60

PANDARUS What, not between Troilus and Hector? Do you
know a man if you see him?

CRESSIDA
Ay, if I ever saw him before and knew him.

---

33 disdain] disdaind F   37 *Enter Pandarus*] F (*after l. 34*); *not in* Q

37 **Hector's a gallant man** Cressida is teasing
Pandarus by praising Hector while he
wants to interest her in Troilus.

41 **cousin** relation

54 **Troilus** (the first of many attempts to ad-
vertise Troilus, all of which Cressida
wittily evades)

PANDARUS Well, I say Troilus is Troilus.

CRESSIDA
Then you say as I say; for I am sure
He is not Hector.

PANDARUS No, nor Hector is not Troilus in some degrees.

CRESSIDA
'Tis just to each of them: he is himself.

PANDARUS Himself? Alas, poor Troilus! I would he were –

CRESSIDA So he is.   70

PANDARUS Condition I had gone barefoot to India.

CRESSIDA He is not Hector.

PANDARUS Himself? No, he's not himself. Would a were
himself! Well, the gods are above: time must friend or end.
Well, Troilus, well, I would my heart were in her body!
No, Hector is not a better man than Troilus.

CRESSIDA Excuse me.

PANDARUS He is elder.

CRESSIDA Pardon me, pardon me.

PANDARUS Th'other's not come to't. You shall tell me   80
another tale when th'other's come to't. Hector shall not
have his wit this year.

CRESSIDA
He shall not need it, if he have his own.

PANDARUS Nor his qualities.

CRESSIDA No matter.

PANDARUS Nor his beauty.

CRESSIDA 'Twould not become him; his own's better.

PANDARUS You have no judgement, niece. Helen herself
swore th'other day that Troilus for a brown favour –
⌈*aside*⌉ for so 'tis, I must confess – not brown neither –   90

CRESSIDA No, but brown.

PANDARUS Faith, to say truth, brown and not brown.

---

67 nor] not F   - 82 wit] ROWE; will QF   92 truth] the truth WALKER

64 **Troilus is Troilus** Tilley M243: 'A man is
a man.'
71 **Condition . . . India** Replying to Cressida
and meaning 'Troilus is himself, only if I
had gone on a pilgrimage to India –
which I haven't'.
80 **come to't** reached his maturity (or 'made
love to you'?)
82 **wit** Rowe's emendation is generally

followed, but as Hilda Hulme points out
(96), QF makes possible sense ('carnal
appetite').
82 **this year** used indefinitely, 'for many a
long day' (Deighton)
89 **brown favour** dark complexion (which
was unfashionable)
90 **for so . . . confess** (italicized in Q, perhaps
to indicate an aside, spoken to himself)

CRESSIDA To say the truth, true and not true.

PANDARUS She praised his complexion above Paris'.

CRESSIDA Why, Paris hath colour enough.

PANDARUS So he has.

CRESSIDA Then Troilus should have too much. If she praised
him above, his complexion is higher than his; he having
colour enough, and the other higher, is too flaming a
praise for a good complexion. I had as lief Helen's golden   100
tongue had commended Troilus for a copper nose.

PANDARUS I swear to you, I think Helen loves him better
than Paris.

CRESSIDA Then she's a merry Greek indeed.

PANDARUS Nay, I am sure she does. She came to him
th'other day into the compassed window and, you know,
he has not past three or four hairs on his chin –

CRESSIDA Indeed, a tapster's arithmetic may soon bring his
particulars therein to a total.

PANDARUS Why, he is very young; and yet will he within   110
three pound lift as much as his brother Hector.

CRESSIDA Is he so young a man and so old a lifter?

PANDARUS But to prove to you that Helen loves him: she
came and puts me her white hand to his cloven chin –

CRESSIDA Juno have mercy! How came it cloven?

PANDARUS Why, you know, 'tis dimpled. I think his smiling
becomes him better than any man in all Phrygia.

CRESSIDA O, he smiles valiantly.

PANDARUS Does he not?

CRESSIDA O yes, an 'twere a cloud in autumn.   120

PANDARUS Why, go to, then! But to prove to you that Helen
loves Troilus –

111 lift] F; lifte Q   112 Is he] Is he is F

97 **should** would necessarily have

101 **copper nose** red nose caused by drinking. Walker quotes Thomas Lodge, *The
Poore Mans Talentt* (c.1623; ed. 1881,
p. 11). He says that 'pimples and fierie
speckles', 'an excessive redness of the
face, either in the nose or other parts
thereof' is 'in scorne called coppernose'.
E. A. M. Colman (*The Dramatic Use of
Bawdy in Shakespeare*, 205) mentions that
Davenant wore a copper nose when he
lost his own.

104 **a merry Greek** a wanton (Tilley
M901)

106 **compassed** curved, as though drawn
with a pair of compasses

108 **tapster's arithmetic** i.e. counting on his
fingers

112 **old** experienced
lifter (a) one who lifts weights (b) sneak-
thief

120 **an** as if
in autumn i.e. that presages storms

61

CRESSIDA Troilus will stand to the proof, if you'll prove it so.

PANDARUS Troilus! Why, he esteems her no more than I
     esteem an addle egg.

CRESSIDA If you love an addle egg as well as you love an idle
     head, you would eat chickens i'th' shell.

PANDARUS I cannot choose but laugh to think how she
     tickled his chin; indeed, she has a marvellous white hand,
     I must needs confess –   130

CRESSIDA Without the rack.

PANDARUS And she takes upon her to spy a white hair on his
     chin.

CRESSIDA Alas, poor chin! Many a wart is richer.

PANDARUS But there was such laughing! Queen Hecuba
     laughed, that her eyes ran o'er.

CRESSIDA With millstones.

PANDARUS And Cassandra laughed.

CRESSIDA But there was a more temperate fire under the pot
     of her eyes. Did her eyes run o'er too?   140

PANDARUS And Hector laughed.

CRESSIDA At what was all this laughing?

PANDARUS Marry, at the white hair that Helen spied on
     Troilus' chin.

CRESSIDA An't had been a green hair, I should have laughed
 - too.

PANDARUS They laughed not so much at the hair as at his
     pretty answer.

CRESSIDA What was his answer?

PANDARUS Quoth she, 'Here's but two-and-fifty hairs on   150
     your chin, and one of them is white.'

CRESSIDA This is her question.

PANDARUS That's true; make no question of that. 'Two-

---

129 marvellous] QF (marvel's)   139 a] *not in* F   150, 154, 156 hairs] F; heires Q

123 **stand to the proof** (a) await the proof (b)
     have an erection
125 **addle** addled
126 **addle . . . idle** (a quibble in common
     use)
131 **the rack** i.e. being tortured
137 **millstones** 'To weep millstones' is usu-
     ally said of a hard-hearted person (Tilley
     M967, 'He weeps millstones') – hardly

applicable to Hecuba. Cressida is presumably registering her disbelief that
Hecuba would have laughed at so feeble
a joke.
138 **Cassandra laughed** (which she rarely
     did)
145 **An if**
148 **pretty** witty

and-fifty hairs,' quoth he, 'and one white: that white hair is my father, and all the rest are his sons.' 'Jupiter!' quoth she, 'which of these hairs is Paris my husband?' 'The forked one,' quoth he: 'pluck't out, and give it him.' But there was such laughing and Helen so blushed, and Paris so chafed, and all the rest so laughed, that it passed.

CRESSIDA So let it now; for it has been a great while going   160
by.

PANDARUS Well, cousin, I told you a thing yesterday: think on't.

CRESSIDA So I do.

PANDARUS I'll be sworn, 'tis true; he will weep you an 'twere a man born in April.

CRESSIDA And I'll spring up in his tears an 'twere a nettle against May.
    Sound a retreat

PANDARUS Hark! They are coming from the field. Shall we stand up here and see them as they pass toward Ilium?   170
Good niece, do, sweet niece Cressida.

CRESSIDA At your pleasure.

PANDARUS Here, here, here's an excellent place; here we may see most bravely. I'll tell you them all by their names as they pass by. But mark Troilus above the rest.

CRESSIDA Speak not so loud.
    Aeneas passes over the stage

PANDARUS That's Aeneas. Is not that a brave man? He's one of the flowers of Troy, I can tell you. But mark Troilus; you shall see anon.

---

160 it has] is has F   164 do] does F   168.1 *Sound a retreat*] *as here,* CAPELL; *after l.* 166 QF
170 Ilium] F; Ilion Q   176.1 *Aeneas ... stage*] ROWE; *Enter Æneas* QF (*after l. 175*)   178 tell]
not in F   179 see] see Troilus WALKER

154 **hairs** (quibbling on 'heirs')
155 **sons** Priam was reputed to have fifty sons. Walker, following A. E. Thiselton (*Notulae Criticae*, 1907), suggests that the forked hair counts as two.
157 **forked** (like horns, suggesting that Helen had cuckolded Paris)
159 **passed** outwent description
160–1 **So ... going by** Cressida, like modern audiences, finds the anecdote boring. Shakespeare, as in 3.1, was depicting the inanity of Trojan society.

167–8 **And I'll ... May** Although young nettles were an edible delicacy, Cressida seems to mean that instead of April showers leading to proverbial May flowers, she will be a stinging-nettle to Troilus.
168 **against** in anticipation of
170 **stand up here** probably not on the balcony, as this would involve an exit and an entrance (J. Q. Adams; New Variorum, 31). Possibly 'upstage', or a raised place on the stage.

Antenor passes

CRESSIDA Who's that?   180

PANDARUS That's Antenor. He has a shrewd wit, I can
tell you, and he's a man good enough; he's one o'th'
soundest judgements in Troy whosoever, and a proper
man of person. When comes Troilus? I'll show you Troilus
anon. If he see me, you shall see him nod at me.

CRESSIDA Will he give you the nod?

PANDARUS You shall see.

CRESSIDA If he do, the rich shall have more.

Hector passes

PANDARUS That's Hector, that, that, look you, that; there's
a fellow! Go thy way, Hector! There's a brave man, niece.   190
O brave Hector! Look how he looks! There's a countenance! Is't not a brave man?

CRESSIDA O, a brave man!

PANDARUS Is a not? It does a man's heart good. Look you
what hacks are on his helmet! Look you yonder, do you
see? Look you there; there's no jesting; there's laying on,
take't off who will, as they say; there be hacks!

CRESSIDA Be those with swords?

PANDARUS Swords, anything, he cares not; an the devil
come to him, it's all one. By God's lid, it does one's heart   200
good. Yonder comes Paris, yonder comes Paris.

Paris passes

Look ye yonder, niece; is't not a gallant man too, is't not?
Why, this is brave now! Who said he came home hurt
today? He's not hurt. Why, this will do Helen's heart good
now, ha! Would I could see Troilus now! You shall see
Troilus anon.

179.1 *Antenor passes*] ROWE (*subs.*); *Enter Antenor* QF (*after l. 180*)   182 a man] F; man Q
183 judgements] iudgement F   185 him] him him F   188.1 *Hector passes*] ROWE (*subs.*);
Enter Hector QF   192 a] *not in* F   194 man's] F; man Q   196 there's laying] laying F   197
will] ill F   201.1 *Paris passes*] ROWE (*subs.*); *Enter Paris* QF (*after l. 198*)   203 home hurt]
ROWE; hurt home QF   205 shall see] shall F

182 **he's one** he has one
183 **whosoever** of anyone at all
   proper man of person good-looking man
186–8 **Will he . . . more** If Troilus gives
   Pandarus a nod, making him a noddy, he
   will be richer in foolishness than he was
   before.
190 **brave** fine, as well as courageous

194 **Is a** is he
197 **take't off who will** 'and no mistake'
   (Walker); a catch-phrase, Tilley L131
200 **lid** i.e. eyelid; a common mild oath
203 **home hurt** Rowe's order seems more
   natural than that of QF.
205 **ha!** i.e. 'won't it?'

    Helenus passes

CRESSIDA Who's that?

PANDARUS That's Helenus. I marvel where Troilus is. That's
    Helenus. I think he went not forth today. That's Helenus.

CRESSIDA Can Helenus fight, uncle?   210

PANDARUS Helenus? No – yes, he'll fight indifferent well. I
    marvel where Troilus is. (*Shouts off*) Hark! Do you not
    hear the people cry 'Troilus'? Helenus is a priest.

CRESSIDA What sneaking fellow comes yonder?

    Troilus passes

PANDARUS Where? Yonder? That's Deiphobus. 'Tis Troilus!
    There's a man, niece! Hem! Brave Troilus, the prince of
    chivalry!

CRESSIDA Peace, for shame, peace!

PANDARUS Mark him; note him. O brave Troilus! Look well
    upon him, niece: look you how his sword is bloodied, and   220
    his helm more hacked than Hector's, and how he looks,
    and how he goes! O admirable youth! He ne'er saw three-
    and-twenty. Go thy way, Troilus, go thy way! Had I a
    sister were a grace, or a daughter a goddess, he should
    take his choice. O admirable man! Paris? Paris is dirt to
    him; and I warrant Helen to change would give an eye to
    boot.

    Common soldiers pass

CRESSIDA Here comes more.

PANDARUS Asses, fools, dolts! Chaff and bran, chaff and
    bran! Porridge after meat! I could live and die i'th' eyes of   230
    Troilus. Ne'er look, ne'er look; the eagles are gone; crows
    and daws, crows and daws! I had rather be such a man
    as Troilus than Agamemnon and all Greece.

206.1 *Helenus passes*] ROWE (*subs.*); *Enter Helenus* QF (*after l. 207*)   212 (*Shouts off*)] This
edition; *not in* QF   214.1 *Troilus passes*] ROWE (*subs.*); *Enter Troilus* QF   219 note] not F
222 ne'er] F; neuer Q   226 an eye] money F   227.1 *Common soldiers pass*] ROWE (*subs.*); *not
in* Q; *Enter common Souldiers* F   228 comes] come F   230 i'th'] F; in the Q

210 **Can Helenus fight** She asks either
    because he looks unwarlike, or because
    he is a priest.

211 **indifferent** fairly

214 **What sneaking fellow comes yonder**
    Cressida is teasing her uncle.

215 **Deiphobus** Pandarus, short-sighted,
    mis-identifies him, and then realizes his
    mistake.

216 **Hem!** Pandarus is either attempting to
    attract Troilus' attention, or asking
    Cressida to assent to his praise.

222 **goes** walks, marches
    ne'er The first F variant which may be
    based on the MS. See Introduction, p. 3.

226–7 **to boot** into the bargain

230 **Porridge** soup

CRESSIDA There is amongst the Greeks Achilles, a better
man than Troilus.

PANDARUS Achilles! – a drayman, a porter, a very camel.

CRESSIDA Well, well.

PANDARUS Well, well! Why, have you any discretion? Have
you any eyes? Do you know what a man is? Is not birth,
beauty, good shape, discourse, manhood, learning,   240
gentleness, virtue, youth, liberality, and such like, the
spice and salt that season a man?

CRESSIDA Ay, a minced man; and then to be baked with no
date in the pie, for then the man's date is out.

PANDARUS You are such a woman, a man knows not at
what ward you lie.

CRESSIDA Upon my back, to defend my belly; upon my wit,
to defend my wiles; upon my secrecy, to defend mine
honesty; my mask, to defend my beauty; and you, to
defend all these: and at all these wards I lie, at a thousand   250
watches.

PANDARUS Say one of your watches.

CRESSIDA Nay, I'll watch you for that; and that's one of the
chiefest of them too. If I cannot ward what I would not
have hit, I can watch you for telling how I took the blow;
unless it swell past hiding, and then it's past watching.

PANDARUS You are such another!

Enter Troilus' boy

BOY Sir, my lord would instantly speak with you.

PANDARUS Where?

---

234 amongst] among F   241 such like] so forth F   242 season] seasons F   244 date is]
dates F   245 a woman] another woman F   250 lie, at] lye at, at F   257.1 *Enter Troilus' boy*]
Q (*Enter Boy:*); *after l. 256* F (*Enter Boy.*)

236 **drayman . . . porter . . . camel** (implying that he is strong but stupid)
241 **gentleness** the characteristics of a
gentleman
243 **minced** affected, effeminate, cut up, lack-
ing in virility
243–4 **no date in the pie** (a continuation of
the previous suggestion)
244 **date is out** (a) is out of date (b) out of the
female genitalia
246 **ward** guard (in fencing)
249 **honesty** reputation
251 **watches** ways of guarding oneself. Pan-

darus takes up the word punning on the
sense 'devotional exercises'. The whole
passage plays on the common phrase
'watch and ward'.
253 **watch** keep an eye on
254 **ward** shield
255 **for** to prevent you
256 **swell past hiding** i.e. grow visibly pregnant
past watching too late to worry
257 **You are such another!** What a woman
you are! (Tilley A250)

BOY At your own house; there he unarms him.   260
PANDARUS Good boy, tell him I come.   *Exit Boy*
    I doubt he be hurt. Fare ye well, good niece.
CRESSIDA Adieu, uncle.
PANDARUS I'll be with you, niece, by and by.
CRESSIDA To bring, uncle?
PANDARUS Ay, a token from Troilus.
CRESSIDA By the same token, you are a bawd.
                        Exit Pandarus
    Words, vows, gifts, tears, and love's full sacrifice,
    He offers in another's enterprise;
    But more in Troilus thousandfold I see   270
    Than in the glass of Pandar's praise may be.
    Yet hold I off: women are angels, wooing;
    Things won are done – joy's soul lies in the doing.
    That she beloved knows nought that knows not this:
    Men prize the thing ungained more than it is.
    That she was never yet that ever knew
    Love got so sweet as when desire did sue.
    Therefore this maxim out of love I teach:
    'Achievement is command; ungained, beseech'.
    Then though my heart's content firm love doth bear,   280
    Nothing of that shall from mine eyes appear.
             Exeunt Cressida and Alexander

---

260 there . . . him] *not in* F   261 *Exit Boy*] CAPELL; *not in* QF   264 I'll be] F; I wilbe Q   267.1
Exit Pandarus] F; *not in* Q   273 lies] lives *conj.* SEYMOUR; dies *conj.* MASON   275 prize] F; price
Q   280 Then] That F   content] Contents F   281.1 *Exeunt Cressida and Alexander*] CAPELL
(*subs.*); *Exit* QF

262 **doubt** fear
265 **bring** This word, when following 'be with you' is 'a phrase of various applications but usually implying getting the upper hand in some way' (Onions).
268–81 **Words, vows . . . appear** Cressida's speech, not overheard by Alexander, explains her conduct till now: that she loves Troilus, but is afraid that his love would decline once it was satisfied. The rhymed verse and the proverbial wisdom contained in it give the impression that she is too self-possessed to be desperately in love. The fear of fruition, to be found in many Caroline poets, and later expressed by Congreve's heroines, is really a fear of disillusionment. But it should be noted that Shakespeare's heroines, from Juliet

to Miranda, are aware that their spontaneous confessions of love go against folk wisdom.
271 **glass** mirror
272 **wooing** while they are being wooed
278 **this maxim** i.e. the line that follows
279 **'Achievement . . . beseech'** The inverted commas (present in QF; and others only in Q – 272, 274) signalize a memorable saying, as frequently in books of the period. The woman who is besought before she surrenders becomes afterwards the man's slave.
    Achievement attainment
280 **content** (a) capacity (b) wish
281.1 *Exeunt . . . Alexander* But Alexander may have been forgotten by Shakespeare, or he could leave at l. 42.

1.3   *Sennet. Enter Agamemnon, Nestor, Ulysses, Diomedes,*
       Menelaus, with others

AGAMEMNON

Princes, what grief hath set the jaundice on your
      cheeks?
The ample proposition that hope makes
In all designs begun on earth below
Fails in the promised largeness. Checks and disasters
Grow in the veins of actions highest reared,
As knots, by the conflux of meeting sap,
Infects the sound pine and diverts his grain,
Tortive and errant, from his course of growth.
Nor, princes, is it matter new to us
That we come short of our suppose so far,   10
That after seven years' siege yet Troy walls stand,
Sith every action that hath gone before,
Whereof we have record, trial did draw
Bias and thwart, not answering the aim,
And that unbodied figure of the thought
That gave't surmisèd shape. Why then, you princes,
Do you with cheeks abashed behold our works,
And call them shames, which are indeed nought else
But the protractive trials of great Jove
To find persistive constancy in men?   20

1.3.0.1 *Sennet*] F; *not in* Q   1 the] F; these Q   on] F; ore Q   7 Infects] Infect F   12 every] F;
euer Q   18 call] thinke F   shames] shame F

1.3 The Greek camp, near Agamemnon's
tent. This is the first of the great debate
scenes, corresponding to the council
scene in Troy (2.2). There is, however, no
opposition to Ulysses' diagnosis; and his
proposed remedy for anarchy, suggested
by Hector's opportune challenge, is con-
veyed to Nestor alone after the departure
of the others. The vocabulary is more
Latinate than in the two previous scenes.
As Aeneas speaks of the 'long-continued
truce' (258), some editors assume that
there has been a lapse of time since the
battle described in the first two scenes.
The gap would not be noticed in performance.
0.1 *Sennet* fanfare
1–53 **Princes . . . fortune** See Introduction,
p. 26, for a comment on the style of these
speeches.

1 **jaundice** Although the word was regarded as plural, it was often treated as
singular.
2 **proposition** proposal
5 **veins** sap-vessels in plants (*OED* 3a). Obsolete by Shakespeare's day.
6 **conflux** confluence (first occurrence)
7 **his** its
8 **Tortive** twisted (first occurrence)
  errant deviating (Walker)
10 **suppose** expectation (*OED* 3)
13 **trial** testing (the subject of the sentence)
14 **Bias** awry (*OED* C2)
   thwart athwart
15 **unbodied** not having corporeal form;
   hence 'imaginary'.
17 **works** deeds
19 **protractive** long-drawn-out (first occurrence)
20 **persistive** persisting (first occurrence)

The fineness of which metal is not found
In fortune's love; for then the bold and coward,
The wise and fool, the artist and unread,
The hard and soft, seem all affined and kin.
But in the wind and tempest of her frown,
Distinction with a broad and powerful fan,
Puffing at all, winnows the light away,
And what hath mass or matter by itself
Lies rich in virtue and unminglèd.

NESTOR

With due observance of thy godlike seat,   30
Great Agamemnon, Nestor shall apply
Thy latest words. In the reproof of chance
Lies the true proof of men. The sea being smooth,
How many shallow bauble-boats dare sail
Upon her patient breast, making their way
With those of nobler bulk!
But let the ruffian Boreas once enrage
The gentle Thetis, and anon behold
The strong-ribbed bark through liquid mountains cut,
Bounding between the two moist elements   40

---

26 broad] lowd F   30 thy] F; the Q   godlike] godly F   35 patient] F; ancient Q

21 **fineness** (echoing *find* in the previous line)
  metal Carter cites Hebrews 12: 6 ('For whom the Lord loveth he chasteneth') and Job 23: 10 ('But He knoweth my way and trieth me, and I shall come forth like the gold').
23 **artist** scholar, educated in the liberal arts
24–5 **affined . . . wind** (internal rhyme, characteristic of Shakespeare's later style)
24 **affined** related
28–9 **And what . . . unminglèd** Q has a comma after *selfe*, F commas after *mass*, *itself* and *virtue*. This would make 'matter by itself' = mass. But the point is that when the chaff has been blown away, the stuff of real worth is left unmixed with chaff.
29 **unminglèd** (four syllables)
30–53 **With due . . . fortune** Nestor merely rephrases Agamemnon's argument. He is anxious, like many elder statesmen, to

parade his gifts as an orator. The theme as a whole is expressed by the proverbial 'Great courage is in greatest dangers tried' (Tilley C715).
30 **seat** Noble points out that in the Bishops' Bible, but not in the Genevan, 'seat' is used for God's throne.
32 **reproof** (a) rebuff (b) refutation (of an argument, in contrast with *proof*; OED 5)
33–44 **The sea . . . Neptune** Tilley S174: 'In a calm sea anyone can be a pilot.'
34 **bauble-boats** toy boats (first recorded use of 'bauble' thus)
35 **patient** 'ancient' (Q) may also be authorial.
37 **Boreas** the north wind
38 **Thetis** i.e. the sea. Thetis was a sea-nymph, mother of Achilles, but she was frequently confused, even in classical times, with Tethys, wife of Oceanus, and hence equated with the sea.
40 **two moist elements** sea and air

Like Perseus' horse. Where's then the saucy boat,
Whose weak untimbered sides but even now
Co-rivalled greatness? Either to harbour fled,
Or made a toast for Neptune. Even so
Doth valour's show and valour's worth divide
In storms of fortune. For in her ray and brightness
The herd hath more annoyance by the breese
Than by the tiger; but when the splitting wind
Makes flexible the knees of knotted oaks
And flies flee under shade, why then the thing of
    courage,   50
As roused with rage, with rage doth sympathize,
And with an accent tuned in selfsame key
Rechides to chiding fortune.
ULYSSES   Agamemnon,
Thou great commander, nerves and bone of Greece,
Heart of our numbers, soul and only spirit,
In whom the tempers and the minds of all
Should be shut up, hear what Ulysses speaks.
Besides th'applause and approbation
The which (*to Agamemnon*) most mighty for thy place
    and sway,
(*To Nestor*) And thou most reverend for thy stretched-out life,   60
I give to both your speeches – which were such
As, Agamemnon, all the hands of Greece
Should hold up high in brass, and such again

---

50 flee] CAPELL; fled QF   53 Rechides] STAUNTON (*conj.* LETTSOM); Retires QF; Retorts HUDSON (*conj.* DYCE)   54 nerves] Nerue F   55 spirit] F; spright Q   58 th'] the F   60 thy] F; the Q   62 all the hands] DEIGHTON (*conj.* ORGER); and the hand QF

41 **Perseus' horse** Pegasus was Bellerophon's winged horse. Shakespeare shared this mistake with the learned. See T. W. Baldwin, 'Perseus Purloins Pegasus', *Philological Quarterly*, 20 (1941), 361–70.

43 **Co-rivalled** competed with

44 **toast** toasted bread, soaked in wine; hence any tasty morsel

47 **breese** gadfly

49 **knotted** gnarled

50 **flee** Capell's emendation is an improvement, the e/d misreading being common.

53 **Rechides** This emendation seems more appropriate to Nestor's oratorical style (see 32–3, 51) than Dyce's 'retorts'

(meaning that the notes were resung twice as fast). Hulme (261) argues for 'retears' (= bluster) of which the QF reading would be a variant spelling.

57 **shut up** embodied

59–64 **The which ... Nestor** Agamemnon and Nestor are addressed alternately.

62 **all the hands** This emendation seems necessary. Ulysses is saying that Agamemnon's speech ought to be engraved on brass, and that Nestor's should be listened to by all, the 'all' repeating the word from 56. Ulysses knows that the speeches hardly deserved such praise.

As, venerable Nestor, hatched in silver,
Should with a bond of air, strong as the axle-tree
On which heaven rides, knit all the Greekish ears
To his experienced tongue – yet let it please both,
Thou great, and wise, to hear Ulysses speak.

AGAMEMNON

Speak, Prince of Ithaca; and be't of less expect
That matter needless, of importless burden,   70
Divide thy lips than we are confident,
When rank Thersites opes his mastic jaws,
We shall hear music, wit, and oracle.

ULYSSES

Troy, yet upon his bases, had been down,
And the great Hector's sword had lacked a master,
But for these instances:
The specialty of rule hath been neglected,
And look how many Grecian tents do stand
Hollow upon this plain, so many hollow factions.

66 On ... Greekish] In which the Heauens ride, knit all Greekes F   69–73 AGAMEMNON Speak
... oracle] F; *not in* Q   74 bases] basis F

64 **hatched** 'marked by parallel lines as in engraving'; but there may be an allusion to Nestor's white hair and beard which 'make him look like a figure engraved on silver' (Steevens).

65–7 **bond ... tongue** Nestor's oratory takes captive the ears of his listeners.

65 **a bond of air** In numerous pictures (e.g. Alciati, *Emblems*, 180), as Baldwin shows, there is a visible line joining the mouth of a speaker to the ear of a listener.

65–6 **strong ... rides** The heavens were thought to wheel round the earth (*axis*, 'axle of revolution of the heavens').

66 **On which ... ears** Having inserted 'the', F had to alter 'Greekish' for metrical reasons.

68 **great, and wise** Agamemnon and Nestor

69–73 AGAMEMNON **Speak ... oracle** Presumably Q's omission of this speech was accidental. It is important to call attention to Ulysses' major speech and also to forewarn the audience of Thersites' unsavoury character.

69 **expect** expectation

70 **importless** meaningless

72 **rank** Chapman uses the same epithet about Thersites (p. 531, l. 207).
   mastic gummy, mastic being used to stop

decaying teeth (Stokes, quoted in New Variorum). There may also be a reference to 'mastix' = scourge, familiar to Shakespeare's audience from *Satiromastix* and *Histriomastix*. See Introduction. p. 6.

74–136 **Troy, yet ... strength** The sources of this speech have been well discussed (New Variorum, 389 ff.). The ideas were widely diffused, but Shakespeare appears to have used at least four: Chapman's *Seven Books*, Elyot's *Book of the Governor*, Hooker's *Laws of Ecclesiastical Polity* and the *Homilies*. See K. Muir, *The Sources of Shakespeare's Plays* (1977), 151–7.

74 **yet upon his bases** i.e. still standing

76 **instances** reasons

77 **specialty** 'a special contract, obligation or bond, expressed in an instrument under seal' (*OED* 7). The specialty of rule is the obligation to obey the ruler.

78 **look how** even as

79 **Hollow ... hollow** Attempts have been made to regularize this line by the omission of one of these words; but Ulysses is playing on two meanings of the word. A tent, even if occupied, can be called hollow; and a faction, even if open, could be regarded as hollow, i.e. false, as frequently in Shakespeare.

When that the general is not like the hive,   80
To whom the foragers shall all repair,
What honey is expected? Degree being vizarded,
Th'unworthiest shows as fairly in the mask.
The heavens themselves, the planets, and this centre
Observe degree, priority, and place,
Insisture, course, proportion, season, form,
Office, and custom, in all line of order.
And therefore is the glorious planet Sol
In noble eminence enthroned and sphered
Amidst the other; whose med'cinable eye   90
Corrects the influence of evil planets,
And posts like the commandment of a king,
Sans check to good and bad. But when the planets
In evil mixture to disorder wander,
What plagues, and what portents, what mutiny,
What raging of the sea, shaking of earth,
Commotion in the winds, frights, changes, horrors,
Divert and crack, rend and deracinate
The unity and married calm of states
Quite from their fixure! O, when degree is shaked,   100
Which is the ladder of all high designs,
The enterprise is sick! How could communities,
Degrees in schools, and brotherhoods in cities,
Peaceful commerce from dividable shores,

91 influence ... planets] ill Aspects of Planets euill F   101 of] to F

80 **hive** The bee comparison, used extensive-
ly in *Henry V* (1.2), was probably derived
from Elyot's *Book of the Governor*, where
it forms part of Ulysses' attempt to cure
the anarchy in the Greek camp.

82 **vizarded** masked

84 **this centre** the earth

86 **Insisture** 'the apparent stopping when a
planet appears to become stationary at
either end of its course' (*OED*; the only
recorded use). Baldwin argues (New
Variorum, 402) that the word was
derived from Cicero's *Tusculans* ('qui er-
rantium stellarum cursus, progressiones,
institutiones [for *institiones*] notavit'),
not, Baldwin shows, from Dolman's
translation of 1561.
proportion symmetry

88 **planet Sol** According to the Ptolemaic
system, the sun was one of the planets

revolving round the earth.

89 **sphered** placed in the heavens (*OED*
sphere v. 3; first occurrence in this sense)

91 **influence of evil planets** Bacon in his
essay 'Of Envy' says that 'Astrologers call
the evil influences of the stars, *Evil Aspects*'. Both Q and F readings were
doubtless authorial.

95 **mutiny** strife

98 **deracinate** uproot. Possibly a coinage
from the French, when first used in *Henry
V* (5.2.47).

100 **fixure** fixed condition

101 **ladder of all high designs** Tilley S848:
'Step after step the ladder is ascended.'

103 **Degrees in schools** academic rank
brotherhoods guilds

104 **dividable** 'having the function of dividing' (*OED* 2; only recorded use in this
sense)

The primogeniture and due of birth,
Prerogative of age, crowns, sceptres, laurels,
But by degree stand in authentic place?
Take but degree away, untune that string,
And hark what discord follows. Each thing meets
In mere oppugnancy. The bounded waters   110
Should lift their bosoms higher than the shores,
And make a sop of all this solid globe;
Strength should be lord of imbecility,
And the rude son should strike his father dead.
Force should be right; or rather, right and wrong,
Between whose endless jar justice recides,
Should lose their names, and so should justice too.
Then everything includes itself in power,
Power into will, will into appetite;
And appetite, an universal wolf,   120
So doubly seconded with will and power,
Must make perforce an universal prey,
And last eat up himself. Great Agamemnon,
This chaos, when degree is suffocate,

---

105 primogeniture] ROWE; primogenitie Q; primogenitiue F   109 meets] F; melts Q
117 their] her F   118 includes] F; include Q

105 **primogeniture** As 'primogenitive' is not
elsewhere used as a substantive, and
'primogenitie' is not recorded elsewhere,
Q and F probably give alternative mis-
readings.
107 **authentic** of authority
108 **untune that string** Compare Hooker,
Ecclesiastical Polity, I. iii. 3.
110 **mere** total
    oppugnancy conflict (first occurrence)
113 **Strength . . . imbecility** 'brute strength
would rule and would have nothing to
rule but imbecility' (i.e. weakness)
(Dobrée)
115 **Force should be right** Tilley M922:
'Might overcomes right.'
116 **recides** All modern editors, except
Dobrée, have assumed that this is a spelling of 'resides' (as it obviously is at
3.2.138 and 1.1.99). Warburton pointed
out that it was nonsensical to represent
justice as moderating between right and
wrong; Capell retorted that justice is set
between right and wrong 'as a power to
hinder right being trampled upon by the

other'; Hanford, followed by Baldwin,
referred to the Aristotelian position of
mediocrity, 'a middle state between two
vices, one of excess and one of deficiency'
(James H. Hanford, 'A Platonic Passage in
Shakespeare's *Troilus and Cressida*',
Studies in Philology, 13 (1916), 100–9).
But right can hardly be regarded as a
vice. 'Recides' meaning 'falls down', from
Latin *recadere*, makes perfect sense, and it
is a coinage which fits in with other
words of Latin derivation.
120 **wolf** Envy is represented as feeding
upon itself, as in Alciati, *Emblems*, 71.
Baldwin suggests: 'This symbolism of
universal eating appetite induces the
figure of the wolf-pack which ate one
member at a time till only one survived.
But since here that surviving wolf is
Envy, he "last, eate up himselfe"' (New
Variorum).
123 **eat up himself** Compare e.g. *Lear*
4.2.49–50.
124 **suffocate** suffocated

Follows the choking.
And this neglection of degree it is
That by a pace goes backward with a purpose
It hath to climb. The general's disdained
By him one step below, he by the next,
That next by him beneath; so every step,   130
Exampled by the first pace that is sick
Of his superior, grows to an envious fever
Of pale and bloodless emulation.
And 'tis this fever that keeps Troy on foot,
Not her own sinews. To end a tale of length,
Troy in our weakness stands, not in her strength.

NESTOR
Most wisely hath Ulysses here discovered
The fever whereof all our power is sick.

AGAMEMNON
The nature of the sickness found, Ulysses,
What is the remedy?   140

ULYSSES
The great Achilles, whom opinion crowns
The sinew and the forehand of our host,
Having his ear full of his airy fame,
Grows dainty of his worth, and in his tent
Lies mocking our designs. With him Patroclus,
Upon a lazy bed, the livelong day
Breaks scurril jests,
And with ridiculous and awkward action,
Which, slanderer, he 'imitation' calls,
He pageants us. Sometime, great Agamemnon,   150
Thy topless deputation he puts on;
And like a strutting player, whose conceit

126 it is] is it F   127 with] in F   136 stands] liues F   148 awkward] F; sillie Q
149 'imitation'] This edition; Imitation QF

126 **neglection** neglect
127–8 **by a pace . . . climb** falls back step by
      step, because with the neglect of degree
      the wish to climb has an opposite effect
131 **first pace** i.e. the second in command
133 **emulation** jealous rivalry
141 **opinion** public opinion
142 **sinew** mainstay
      forehand foremost member
143 **airy fame** reputation

144 **dainty** fastidious
146 **lazy bed** lazily upon his bed
147 **scurril** scurrilous
148 **awkward** The Q variant 'silly' means
      'weak'.
150 **pageants** mimics, as in a play
151 **topless deputation** supreme position,
      deputed by the Greek chiefs
152 **conceit** (a) power of thought (b) vanity

Lies in his hamstring, and doth think it rich
To hear the wooden dialogue and sound
'Twixt his stretched footing and the scaffoldage,
Such to-be-pitied and o'er-wrested seeming
He acts thy greatness in; and when he speaks,
'Tis like a chime a-mending – with terms unsquared
Which, from the tongue of roaring Typhon dropped,
Would seem hyperboles. At this fusty stuff,   160
The large Achilles, on his pressed bed lolling,
From his deep chest laughs out a loud applause,
Cries 'Excellent! 'Tis Agamemnon right!
Now play me Nestor: hem, and stroke thy beard,
As he being dressed to some oration.'
That's done, as near as the extremest ends
Of parallels, as like as Vulcan and his wife.
Yet god Achilles still cries 'Excellent!
'Tis Nestor right! Now play him me, Patroclus,
Arming to answer in a night alarm.'   170
And then forsooth the faint defects of age
Must be the scene of mirth: to cough and spit,
And with a palsy, fumbling on his gorget,
Shake in and out the rivet. And at this sport
Sir Valour dies; cries 'O, enough, Patroclus,
Or give me ribs of steel! I shall split all
In pleasure of my spleen.' And in this fashion,
All our abilities, gifts, natures, shapes,

158 unsquared] F; vnsquare Q   160 seem] seemes F   163 right] iust F

154 **wooden dialogue** sound made by his steps on the planks
155 **stretched footing** long steps
     scaffoldage stage (first occurrence)
156 **o'er-wrested** wound up too high – hence 'exaggerated'
158 **chime a-mending** chime of bells being repaired (and thus making a harsh din)
     unsquared inappropriate
159 **Typhon** a monster, father of hurricanes
160 **fusty** stale, with a glance at *fustian*
165 **dressed** addressed
166–7 **extremest ends | Of parallels** parallels may be very close, though they never meet; the opposite, or extremest, ends will be as far apart as possible (Baldwin)
167 **wife** i.e. Venus
173–4 **And with a palsy ... rivet** Martin

Holmes, *Shakespeare and his Players* (1977), 160–2, has a vivid description of the difficulty of putting on a gorget: 'To imitate a doddering old man going through these contortions, half-throttling himself with the gorget-rings, getting his beard shut in between overlapping plates and finally having failure after failure with the shoulder-rivet, would be an unkind and disrespectful performance, but would be likely to make Achilles laugh, and to commend itself to the younger and still active members of a fashionable, courtly audience.'
173 **gorget** throat armour
175 **dies** i.e. laughing
177 **spleen** the seat of anger and of mirth

Severals and generals of grace exact,
Achievements, plots, orders, preventions,   180
Excitements to the field, or speech for truce,
Success or loss, what is, or is not, serves
As stuff for these two to make paradoxes.
NESTOR
And in the imitation of these twain,
Who, as Ulysses says, opinion crowns
With an imperial voice, many are infect.
Ajax is grown self-willed and bears his head
In such a rein, in full as proud a place
As broad Achilles; keeps his tent like him;
Makes factious feasts; rails on our state of war,   190
Bold as an oracle; and sets Thersites,
A slave whose gall coins slanders like a mint,
To match us in comparisons with dirt,
To weaken and discredit our exposure,
How rank soever rounded in with danger.
ULYSSES
They tax our policy and call it cowardice,
Count wisdom as no member of the war,
Forestall prescience, and esteem no act
But that of hand. The still and mental parts
That do contrive how many hands shall strike,   200
When fitness calls them on, and know by measure
Of their observant toil the enemy's weight,
Why, this hath not a finger's dignity.
They call this bed-work, mapp'ry, closet-war;
So that the ram that batters down the wall,
For the great swinge and rudeness of his poise,

---

189 keeps] and keepes F   194 and] F; our Q   201 calls] call F   206 swinge] swing F

<table>
<tr><td>179 Severals and generals individual and general (qualities)
grace exact 'consummate merit' (Walker)</td><td>194–5 discredit . . . danger discredit us, vulnerable as we are to dangers (New Variorum)</td></tr>
</table>

179 **Severals and generals** individual and
    general (qualities)
  grace exact 'consummate merit' (Walker)
183 **paradoxes** inversions of the truth
186 **infect** infected
187–8 **bears . . . rein** expresses pride, vanity
    or resentment (compare *OED* bridle, *vb.* 3)
189 **broad** hefty
190 **factious feasts** feasts of a faction
191 **Thersites** (a second warning to the
    audience about his character)
192 **gall** rancour

194–5 **discredit . . . danger** discredit us, vul-
    nerable as we are to dangers (New
    Variorum)
195 **rank** excessively
196 **tax** censure
198 **Forestall** hinder
204 **bed-work** easy work
    mapp'ry map-making (first occurrence)
206 **swinge** force; 'swing' (F) may be merely
    a spelling variant
    poise forcible impact (*OED*)

They place before his hand that made the engine
Or those that with the finesse of their souls
By reason guide his execution.

NESTOR

Let this be granted, and Achilles' horse   210
Makes many Thetis' sons.

    Tucket

AGAMEMNON   What trumpet? Look, Menelaus.

MENELAUS From Troy.

    Enter Aeneas and Trumpeter

AGAMEMNON What would you fore our tent?

AENEAS

Is this great Agamemnon's tent, I pray you?

AGAMEMNON Even this.

AENEAS

May one that is a herald and a prince
Do a fair message to his kingly ears?

AGAMEMNON

With surety stronger than Achilles' arm
Fore all the Greekish host, which with one voice
Call Agamemnon head and general.   220

AENEAS

Fair leave and large security. How may
A stranger to those most imperial looks
Know them from eyes of other mortals?

AGAMEMNON   How?

AENEAS

Ay. I ask, that I might waken reverence
And bid the cheek be ready with a blush
Modest as morning, when she coldly eyes

---

208 finesse] fineness F   211 *Tucket*] F; *not in* Q   212.1*Enter ... Trumpeter*] SISSON; *not in* Q; *Enter Æneas* F   217 ears] F; eyes Q   218 arm] arms WALKER   219 host] This edition (*conj.* KINNEAR); heads QF   225 bid] on F

208 **finesse** subtlety, cunning (a rare word; possibly merely a spelling variant of F's 'finenesse')
209 **his execution** the exercise of his powers
210–11 **Achilles' horse ... sons** Achilles' horse is worth many times more than Achilles himself.
218 **arm** Walker emends to 'arms' on the assumption that it refers to the proverbial *arma Achillea*.

219 **host** The QF reading, 'heads', anticipates 'head' in the following line.
221–3 **How may ... mortals** There is some irony in the failure to recognize Agamemnon, when he is about to be called 'that god in office'.
226 **modest as morning** The dawn, at sunrise, blushes.

The youthful Phoebus.
Which is that god in office, guiding men?
Which is the high and mighty Agamemnon?

AGAMEMNON
This Trojan scorns us, or the men of Troy   230
Are ceremonious courtiers.

AENEAS
Courtiers as free, as debonair, unarmed,
As bending angels – that's their fame in peace.
But when they would seem soldiers, they have galls,
Good arms, strong joints, true swords, and – Jove's accord –
Nothing so full of heart. But peace, Aeneas,
Peace, Trojan; lay thy finger on thy lips.
The worthiness of praise distains his worth,
If that the praised himself bring the praise forth.
But what the repining enemy commends,   240
That breath, fame blows; that praise, sole pure,
         transcends.

AGAMEMNON
Sir, you of Troy, call you yourself Aeneas?

AENEAS
Ay, Greek, that is my name.

AGAMEMNON   What's your affair, I pray you?

AENEAS
Sir, pardon: 'tis for Agamemnon's ears.

AGAMEMNON
He hears nought privately that comes from Troy.

AENEAS
Nor I from Troy come not to whisper him;
I bring a trumpet to awake his ear,
To set his sense on the attentive bent,
And then to speak.

---

235 Jove's] F; great *Ioues* Q   239 the praised] he praised F   243 affair] F; affaires Q   246
whisper] F; whisper with Q   248 sense . . . the] F; seat . . . that Q

232–6 **Courtiers as free . . . heart** One of the
   passages which arouse sympathy for the
   Trojans.
232 **free** open, generous.
233 **bending** bowing
234 **galls** spirit to resist insult (*OED* 3b)
235 **Jove's accord** Jove willing
236 **Nothing so full of heart** of unequalled
   courage

237 **lay . . . lips** Tilley F239: 'Lay thy fingers
   on thy lips.'
238–39 **The worthiness . . . forth** Noble
   compares Proverbs, 27: 2.
238 **distains** sullies
240–1 **But what . . . transcends** The praise
   of an enemy, alone disinterested, is worth
   more than any other.

AGAMEMNON   Speak frankly as the wind.
It is not Agamemnon's sleeping hour.   250
That thou shalt know, Trojan, he is awake,
He tells thee so himself.
AENEAS   Trumpet, blow loud.
Send thy brass voice through all these lazy tents,
And every Greek of mettle, let him know
What Troy means fairly shall be spoke aloud.
    Trumpet sounds
We have, great Agamemnon, here in Troy,
A prince called Hector – Priam is his father –
Who in this dull and long-continued truce
Is resty grown. He bade me take a trumpet
And to this purpose speak: 'Kings, princes, lords,   260
If there be one among the fair'st of Greece,
That holds his honour higher than his ease,
That seeks his praise more than he fears his peril,
That knows his valour and knows not his fear,
That loves his mistress more than in confession
With truant vows to her own lips he loves,
And dare avow her beauty and her worth
In other arms than hers – to him this challenge.
Hector, in view of Trojans and of Greeks,
Shall make it good, or do his best to do it,   270
He hath a lady, wiser, fairer, truer,
Than ever Greek did compass in his arms;
And will tomorrow with his trumpet call,

---

252 loud] F; alowd Q   255.1 *Trumpet sounds*] *The Trumpets sound* F; *Sound trumpet* Q
258 this] F; his Q   259 resty] rusty F   261 among] among'st F   263 That seeks] F; And
feeds Q   272 compass] F; couple Q

---

249 **frankly** freely
258 **long-continued truce** Another indication of a lapse of time after 1.2.
259 **resty** restive (more expressive than F's
'rusty')
260–79 **Kings, princes . . . much** This
chivalric challenge contrasts with the
general tone of the Greek camp, although
the challenge is accepted in similar
chivalric terms.
263 **fears** The repetition of *fear* in the next
line may suggest that this is a misprint
for *flies* (Gary Taylor, privately com-

municated) or *flees*.
266 **truant** idle (*OED* B2). The true lover to
whom the challenge is issued is one who
is more sincere than the one who swears
idle vows.
268 **other arms than hers** i.e. the arms of a
soldier
272 **compass** encompass. The Q reading,
couple, equally possible, would be an
allusion 'to the chivalric convention of a
knight's displaying some symbol of his
mistress about his armour' (Walker).

Midway between your tents and walls of Troy,
To rouse a Grecian that is true in love.
If any come, Hector shall honour him;
If none, he'll say in Troy when he retires,
The Grecian dames are sunburnt, and not worth
The splinter of a lance.' Even so much.

AGAMEMNON

This shall be told our lovers, Lord Aeneas.   280
If none of them have soul in such a kind,
We left them all at home. But we are soldiers;
And may that soldier a mere recreant prove,
That means not, hath not, or is not, in love.
If then one is, or hath, or means to be,
That one meets Hector; if none else, I am he.

NESTOR

Tell him of Nestor, one that was a man
When Hector's grandsire sucked. He is old now;
But if there be not in our Grecian host
One noble man that hath one spark of fire   290
To answer for his love, tell him from me
I'll hide my silver beard in a gold beaver,
And in my vambrace put this withered brawn,
And meeting him, will tell him that my lady
Was fairer than his grandam, and as chaste
As may be in the world. His youth in flood,
I'll prove this truth with my three drops of blood.

AENEAS

Now heavens forfend such scarcity of youth!

ULYSSES Amen.

---

285 or means] F; a meanes Q   286 I am] Ile be F   289 host] mould F   290 One ... one]
F; A ... no Q   293 this ... brawn] F; my ... braunes Q   294 will tell] F; tell Q   297 prove]
pawne F   298 forfend] forbid F   youth] F; men Q

---

278 **sunburnt** Sunburn was regarded as a
   blemish. The quibble suggested by
   Partridge (*Shakespeare's Bawdy*, 158),
   meaning 'infected with venereal disease',
   is out of keeping with the tone of the
   speech.
279 **Even so much** Probably an addition by
   Aeneas to Hector's challenge, meaning 'not even worth as much as that',
   or perhaps 'That is the sum total of

what he says'.
284 **means not, hath not** i.e. means not to
   be, and hath not been, in love
292 **beaver** face-guard of a helmet
293 **vambrace** armour to protect the arm,
   the same as *vantbrace* (F)
   brawn fleshy part of the body, especially
   the arm
296 **His youth in flood** he being in the prime
   of youth

AGAMEMNON

Fair Lord Aeneas, let me touch your hand.   300
To our pavilion shall I lead you first.
Achilles shall have word of this intent;
So shall each lord of Greece, from tent to tent.
Yourself shall feast with us before you go,
And find the welcome of a noble foe.

Exeunt all except Ulysses and Nestor

ULYSSES Nestor!

NESTOR What says Ulysses?

ULYSSES

I have a young conception in my brain;
Be you my time to bring it to some shape.

NESTOR What is't?   310

ULYSSES This 'tis.

Blunt wedges rive hard knots. The seeded pride
That hath to this maturity blown up
In rank Achilles must or now be cropped,
Or, shedding, breed a nursery of like evil
To overbulk us all.

NESTOR   Well, and how?

ULYSSES

This challenge that the gallant Hector sends,
However it is spread in general name,
Relates in purpose only to Achilles.

NESTOR

True: the purpose is perspicuous as substance,   320
Whose grossness little characters sum up;
And, in the publication, make no strain
But that Achilles, were his brain as barren

---

300 AGAMEMNON Fair] F; faire *(continuing Ulysses' speech)* Q   301 first] F; sir Q   305.1
Exeunt ... Nestor] CAPELL; *not in* Q; *Exeunt. | Manet Vlysses, and Nestor* F   311 This 'tis] F;
not in Q   320 True ... substance] The purpose is perspicuous euen as substance F

302–5 **Achilles shall . . . foe** The couplets
round off the scene, the dialogue between
Ulysses and Nestor beginning a new
phase.
306 **Nestor!** (spoken to detain him as he goes
out)
312 **Blunt wedges rive hard knots** Proverbial: Erasmus, *Adagia*, trans. Taverner
(1539, ed. 1552, 5), 'To a crabbed knot
must be sought a crabbed wedge' (New

Variorum); compare Tilley P289.
313 **blown** sprouted
314 **rank** overgrown
 or either
315 **nursery** breeding-ground; or, possibly,
 progeny or crop
320–1 **the purpose . . . up** The purpose is as
 plain as if it were expressed in numbers.
320 **substance** wealth

As banks of Libya – though, Apollo knows,
'Tis dry enough – will, with great speed of judgement,
Ay, with celerity, find Hector's purpose
Pointing on him.
ULYSSES   And wake him to the answer, think you?
NESTOR
Why, 'tis most meet. Who may you else oppose
That can from Hector bring those honours off,   330
If not Achilles? Though't be a sportful combat,
Yet in this trial much opinion dwells;
For here the Trojans taste our dear'st repute
With their fin'st palate. And trust to me, Ulysses,
Our imputation shall be oddly poised
In this wild action; for the success,
Although particular, shall give a scantling
Of good or bad unto the general;
And in such indexes, although small pricks
To their subsequent volumes, there is seen   340
The baby figure of the giant mass
Of things to come at large. It is supposed
He that meets Hector issues from our choice;
And choice, being mutual act of all our souls,
Makes merit her election, and doth boil,
As 'twere, from forth us all, a man distilled
Out of our virtues; who miscarrying,
What heart receives from hence a conquering part,
To steel a strong opinion to themselves?

---

329 Why] Yes F   330 those honours] his Honor F   332 this] F; the Q   336 wild] F; vilde
Q   348 receives ... a] from hence receyues the F

---

324 **banks of Libya** sandbanks of the Libyan
      desert
325 **dry** 'betokening a dull wit' (New
      Variorum)
335 **Our imputation shall be oddly poised**
      what is imputed to us will be unfairly
      balanced (i.e. we shall be placed at a
      disadvantage)
336 **wild** rash, irresponsible
      success result
337 **scantling** specimen
338 **general** general public

339 **indexes** preceding the volume, like
      modern tables of contents
      pricks dots, acting as checks; but as the
      word could also mean 'penis', it may
      have suggested 'baby' in l. 341.
340 **subsequent** (accent on the second syl-
      lable)
347–9 **who miscarrying ... themselves** i.e.
      if our champion is defeated, everyone's
      morale will suffer and we shall become
      defeatist
349 **steel** strengthen; with quibble on *steal*.

Which entertained, limbs are his instruments,   350
In no less working than are swords and bows
Directive by the limbs.
ULYSSES
Give pardon to my speech. Therefore 'tis meet
Achilles meet not Hector. Let us like merchants
First show foul wares, and think perchance they'll sell.
If not, the lustre of the better shall exceed
By showing the worse first. Do not consent
That ever Hector and Achilles meet,
For both our honour and our shame in this
Are dogged with two strange followers.   360
NESTOR
I see them not with my old eyes. What are they?
ULYSSES
What glory our Achilles shares from Hector,
Were he not proud, we all should share with him.
But he already is too insolent,
And we were better parch in Afric sun
Than in the pride and salt scorn of his eyes,
Should he scape Hector fair. If he were foiled,
Why then we did our main opinion crush
In taint of our best man. No, make a lott'ry,
And by device let blockish Ajax draw   370
The sort to fight with Hector; among ourselves

350–2 Which ... limbs] F; *not in* Q   350 are] F2; are in F1   353–7 Give ... first] Giue
pardon to my speech: | Therefore 'tis meet, *Achilles* meet not *Hector*: | Let vs (like Merchants)
shew our fowlest Wares, | And thinke perchance they'l sell: If not, | The luster of the better
yet to shew, | Shall shew the better. F   363 share] weare F   365 we] F; it Q   368 did] F; do Q

350–2 **Which entertained ... the limbs**
Honigmann (*Stability*, 98) believes that
the Q omission was deliberate, the lines
being unnecessary and obscure; Walker,
on the other hand, thinks the lines are
necessary to the argument. I agree. In
any case the F text, as we have argued, is
later; but it may have restored lines
deleted by Shakespeare or another.
350 **his** F2 was right to delete *in* before this
word, a false start of *instruments*.
351 **In no less** i.e. in no less a degree
354–7 **Let us ... first** Walker (*Textual
Problems*, 83) argues that Compositor B
'fouled the metre at the beginning of the

speech after dividing the first line', and
that his other alterations were an attempt
to mend matters. But, as Honigmann
points out (86), two of the four lines in F
are not regular pentameters.
360 **two strange followers** i.e. whether
Achilles wins or loses
362 **shares from** gains at the expense of
(*OED* 4d)
365 **we** The Q reading 'it' makes equally
good sense.
369 **lott'ry** Rigging the ballot (Shakespeare's
invention) is an indication that Ulysses
does not follow his own precepts.
371 **sort** lot

Give him allowance for the better man;
For that will physic the great Myrmidon,
Who broils in loud applause, and make him fall
His crest that prouder than blue Iris bends.
If the dull brainless Ajax come safe off,
We'll dress him up in voices. If he fail,
Yet go we under our opinion still
That we have better men. But, hit or miss,
Our project's life this shape of sense assumes: 380
Ajax employed plucks down Achilles' plumes.
NESTOR Ulysses,
Now I begin to relish thy advice,
And I will give a taste thereof forthwith
To Agamemnon. Go we to him straight.
Two curs shall tame each other; pride alone
Must tarre the mastiffs on, as 'twere their bone.   *Exeunt*

2.1   *Enter Ajax and Thersites*
AJAX Thersites!
THERSITES Agamemnon – how if he had boils, full, all over,
   generally?
AJAX Thersites!
THERSITES And those boils did run? Say so, did not the   5
   general run then? Were not that a botchy core?
AJAX Dog!

---

372 for] as F   better] worthier F   382–3 Ulysses, | Now] JOHNSON AND STEEVENS; Now
Vlisses QF; Ulysses now POPE (*omitting* 'begin to')   384 thereof] of it F   387 tarre] F; arre Q
their] F; a Q
    2.1.6 then] *not in* F

373 **Myrmidon** Achilles, whose soldiers
   were called Myrmidons
374 **broils** gets hot with pleasure
375 **Iris** the rainbow, which bends or bows,
   and the flower, which is blue
377 **dress him up in voices** sing his praises
   (as they do in 2.3)
379 **hit or miss** (Tilley H475)
382 **Ulysses** As Shakespeare always accents
   the second syllable of the name, the QF
   reading must be wrong. There are three
   possible remedies, although none of them
   may restore what the poet wrote: (1) omit
   'Ulysses' (2) omit 'begin to' and read
   'Ulysses, now I relish' (3) give the name

a separate line, as here, following Deighton, Walker, and others.
386 **Two curs shall tame each other** (Tilley
   C918)
387 **tarre . . . on** incite
2.1 The Greek camp. Thersites, as described
   by Ulysses in the previous scene, is
   matching the Greek chiefs in 'comparisons of dirt'.
 2 **full** i.e. of pus
 3 **generally** with a quibble on 'general'
 6 **botchy** ulcerous
   core centre of a boil (with a pos~
   quibble on *corps*, 'body')

THERSITES Then would come some matter from him; I see
    none now.

AJAX Thou bitch-wolf's son, canst thou not hear? Feel   10
    then.

    He strikes him

THERSITES The plague of Greece upon thee, thou mongrel
    beef-witted lord!

AJAX Speak then, thou vinewed'st leaven, speak! I will beat
    thee into handsomeness!

THERSITES I shall sooner rail thee into wit and holiness; but
    I think thy horse will sooner con an oration than thou
    learn a prayer without book. Thou canst strike, canst
    thou? A red murrain o'thy jade's tricks!

AJAX Toadstool, learn me the proclamation.   20

THERSITES Dost thou think I have no sense, thou strikest me
    thus?

AJAX The proclamation!

THERSITES Thou art proclaimed a fool, I think.

AJAX Do not, porpentine, do not; my fingers itch.

THERSITES I would thou didst itch from head to foot and I
    had the scratching of thee; I would make thee the loath-

---

8 would] there would F   11.1 *He strikes him*] F (*subs.*); *not in* Q   14 thou] you F   vinewed'st]
KNIGHT; vnsalted Q; whinid'st F   17 oration] F; oration without booke Q   18 a] F; *not in* Q
19 o'thy] F3; ath thy Q; o'th thy F   24 a fool] F; foole Q   26-7 foot and ... thee:] THEOBALD
(*subs.*); foote, and ... thee, QF (*subs.*)

---

8 **matter** (a) pus (b) substance
12 **plague of Greece** A plague is mentioned in
    Iliad I (Steevens) and by Lydgate, iii. 4876
    (Malone), but it is doubtful whether
    Shakespeare had either in mind. There
    may be a quibble on *grease*.
    mongrel because his mother was a
    Trojan (Malone)
13 **beef-witted** bovine (Walker). Steevens
    compared *Twelfth Night*, 1.3.80: 'I am a
    great eater of beef and I believe that does
    harm to my wit'.
14 **vinewed'st** mouldiest; the best emen-
    dation of the F reading. Shakespeare may
    also have written *unsalted*. Thersites is
    compared either to the salt that has lost
    its savour, or to the mouldy leaven which
    contaminates the whole lump. Walker
    cites 1 Corinthians 5: 8, 'The leaven of
    maliciousness and wickedness'; but com-
    pare Matthew 5: 13, 'Ye are the salt of the

earth: but if the salt have lost his savour,
wherewith shall it be salted? It is thence-
forth good for nothing, but to be cast out'
(New Variorum). Johnson pointed out
that salt was not required in leaven.
15 **handsomeness** decency, but with a
    reference to Thersites' ugliness
19 **red** 'applied to various diseases marked
    by evacuation of blood or cutaneous
    eruptions' (*OED* 16b)
20 **Toadstool** poisonous fungus; with a
    quibble on toad's stool, or excrement.
    learn me ascertain for me (Deighton)
21 **sense** feeling
25 **porpentine** an indifferent variant of 'por-
    cupine', occurring often in early texts of
    Shakespeare. 'Though the fingers of Ajax
    itch to strike the porcupine Thersites, he
    will itch from head to foot if he does'
    (Baldwin).

somest scab in Greece. When thou art forth in the
incursions, thou strikest as slow as another.

AJAX I say, the proclamation!   30

THERSITES Thou grumblest and railest every hour on
    Achilles, and thou art as full of envy at his greatness as
    Cerberus is at Proserpina's beauty, ay, that thou barkest
    at him.

AJAX Mistress Thersites!

THERSITES Thou shouldst strike him –

AJAX Cobloaf!

THERSITES He would pun thee into shivers with his fist, as
    a sailor breaks a biscuit.

AJAX You whoreson cur!   40

    He strikes him

THERSITES Do, do, Ajax, thou stool for a witch! Ay, do, do,
    thou sodden-witted lord! Thou hast no more brain than
    I have in mine elbows; an asinego may tutor thee. Thou
    scurvy-valiant ass! Thou art here but to thrash Trojans;
    and thou art bought and sold among those of any wit, like
    a barbarian slave. If thou use to beat me, I will begin at
    thy heel and tell what thou art by inches, thou thing of
    no bowels, thou!

AJAX You dog!

THERSITES You scurvy lord!   50

28–9 When ... another] *not in* F   36–42] *See Appendix 2a.*   42 brain than] QF; brain in thy
head than *conj.* CAPELL   43–4 Thou scurvy] F; you scurvy Q   44 thrash] thresh F

28–9 **When thou ... another** The F omission
    may be due to its apparent conflict with
    one's impression of Ajax's character; but
    see 5.5.18.
33 **as Cerberus ... beauty** Cerberus is the
    ugliest creature in Hades, Proserpina the
    most beautiful.
35 **Mistress** (implying that Thersites is a
    coward and a shrewish railer)
36–41 **Thou shouldst ... do** See Appendix
    2a.
36 **Thou shouldst strike him** If you were to
    strike him
37 **Cobloaf** 'a little loaf made with a round
    head' (John Minsheu, *Guide into Tongues*,
    1617). 'A crusty uneven loaf with many
    knobs and a round top ... hence, from
    appearance, a rough, loutish, misshapen

fellow' (John Foster, *A Shakespeare Word-
    Book*, 1908). One suspects that Foster
    had Thersites, rather than a loaf, in mind.
38 **pun** pound (dialectal)
41 **Do, do** go on, go on
    stool (with a quibble on Ajax/a jakes, a
    witch's jakes being particularly un-
    pleasant)
42–3 **Thou hast ... elbows** Compare Tilley
    W548, 'He has more wit in his head than
    you in both your shoulders'.
42 **brain than** Capell's addition neatly
    introduces an antithesis, but is not really
    necessary.
43 **asinego** donkey (first occurrence)
45 **bought and sold** Tilley B787: 'To be
    bought and sold.'
47–8 **of no bowels** i.e. with no compassion

AJAX You cur!
   He strikes him
THERSITES Mars his idiot! Do, rudeness; do, camel, do, do!
   Enter Achilles and Patroclus
ACHILLES
   Why, how now, Ajax! Wherefore do ye thus?
   How now, Thersites! What's the matter, man?
THERSITES You see him there, do you?
ACHILLES Ay; what's the matter?
THERSITES Nay, look upon him.
ACHILLES So I do. What's the matter?
THERSITES Nay, but regard him well.
ACHILLES 'Well'? Why, I do so.   60
THERSITES But yet you look not well upon him. For who-
   somever you take him to be, he is Ajax.
ACHILLES I know that, fool.
THERSITES Ay, but that fool knows not himself.
AJAX Therefore I beat thee.
THERSITES Lo, lo, lo, lo, what modicums of wit he utters! His
   evasions have ears thus long. I have bobbed his brain
   more than he has beat my bones. I will buy nine sparrows
   for a penny, and his pia mater is not worth the ninth part
   of a sparrow. This lord, Achilles, Ajax, who wears his   70
   wit in his belly and his guts in his head, I'll tell you what
   I say of him.
ACHILLES What?
THERSITES I say this Ajax –
   Ajax threatens him
ACHILLES Nay, good Ajax.

50.1 *He strikes him*] ROWE (*subs.*); *not in* QF   52.1 *Enter ... Patroclus*] F; *not in* Q   53 ye thus]
you this F   60 I do so] F; so I do Q   68 I] F; It Q   71 I'll tell] F; I tell Q   74.1 *Ajax threatens
him*] ROWE (*'Ajax offers to strike him'*); *not in* QF

52 **Mars his** Mars's
   camel a supposedly stupid and obstinate
   animal
61–2 **whosomever** whosoever
65 **Therefore I beat thee** He means that if he
   had not forgotten himself, he would not
   have beaten Thersites (Deighton).
66 **Lo, lo** (a sarcastic exclamation of wonder)
67 **evasions** shifts
   thus long (like an ass's)
   bobbed knocked

68–9 **nine sparrows for a penny** Compare
   Matthew 10: 29, 'Are not two sparrows
   sold for a farthing', and Luke 12: 6, 'Are
   not five sparrows bought for two far-
   things?' 'Thersites splits the difference
   and gets nine' (Baldwin).
69 **pia mater** the membrane that covers the
   brain, hence the brain itself
71 **wit in ... head** Walker cites the same
   phrase from Cornelius Agrippa as given
   in Burton's *Anatomy of Melancholy* (1621).

THERSITES Has not so much wit –

ACHILLES Nay, I must hold you.

THERSITES As will stop the eye of Helen's needle, for whom
he comes to fight.

ACHILLES Peace, fool.   80

THERSITES I would have peace and quietness, but the fool
will not – he there, that he, look you there!

AJAX O thou damned cur! I shall –

ACHILLES Will you set your wit to a fool's?

THERSITES No, I warrant you; for the fool's will shame it.

PATROCLUS Good words, Thersites.

ACHILLES What's the quarrel?

AJAX I bade the vile owl go learn me the tenor of the
proclamation, and he rails upon me.

THERSITES I serve thee not.   90

AJAX Well, go to, go to.

THERSITES I serve here voluntary.

ACHILLES Your last service was sufferance, 'twas not
voluntary. No man is beaten voluntary. Ajax was here
the voluntary, and you as under an impress.

THERSITES E'en so; a great deal of your wit too lies in your
sinews, or else there be liars. Hector shall have a great
catch an a knock out either of your brains; a were as good
crack a fusty nut with no kernel.

ACHILLES What, with me too, Thersites?   100

THERSITES There's Ulysses and old Nestor, whose wit was
mouldy ere your grandsires had nails on their toes, yoke
you like draught-oxen, and make you plough up the
wars.

ACHILLES What? What?

THERSITES Yes, good sooth. To, Achilles! To, Ajax, to! –

AJAX I shall cut out your tongue.

85 for] F; *not in* Q   the] a F   88 the vile] thee vile F   98 an] if F   a knock] KITTREDGE (*conj.*
CAMBRIDGE); he knocke F; knocke Q   out] F; at Q   102 your] THEOBALD; their QF   on their
toes] F; *not in* Q   104 wars] warre F

77 **hold** restrain
84 **Will you . . . fool's** Compare Proverbs
26: 4, 'Answer not a fool according to his
foolishness, lest thou also be like him'
(Baldwin); and Tilley W547, 'Do not set
your wit against a fool's'.
86 **Good words** *bona verba*, a phrase from
Terence's play *Andria* – '*bona verba,*

quaeso' – well known from its use in
schools; cited by Baldwin, *Small Latine*,
i. 747–8.
95 **voluntary, and you as under an impress**
volunteer and you as a conscript
106 To urging on the supposed oxen (New
Variorum)

THERSITES 'Tis no matter; I shall speak as much wit as thou afterwards.

PATROCLUS No more words, Thersites; peace!   110

THERSITES I will hold my peace when Achilles' brach bids me, shall I?

ACHILLES There's for you, Patroclus.

THERSITES I will see you hanged, like clotpolls, ere I come any more to your tents. I will keep where there is wit stirring, and leave the faction of fools.   *Exit*

PATROCLUS A good riddance.

ACHILLES (*to Ajax*)

Marry, this, sir, is proclaimed through all our host:
That Hector, by the fifth hour of the sun,
Will with a trumpet 'twixt our tents and Troy   120
Tomorrow morning call some knight to arms
That hath a stomach, and such a one that dare
Maintain – I know not what. 'Tis trash. Farewell.

AJAX Farewell. Who shall answer him?

ACHILLES

I know not. 'Tis put to lott'ry. Otherwise
He knew his man.   *Exit with Patroclus*

AJAX O, meaning you! I will go learn more of it.   *Exit*

2.2 *Enter Priam, Hector, Troilus, Paris, and Helenus*

PRIAM

After so many hours, lives, speeches spent,
Thus once again says Nestor from the Greeks:
'Deliver Helen, and all damage else –

---

108 wit] CAPELL; *not in* QF   110 peace] *not in* F   111 brach] ROWE; brooch QF   119 fifth]
F (fift); first Q   126 *Exit with Patroclus*] SELTZER (*conj.* TANNENBAUM); *not in* QF

108 **wit** As Ajax is not literally dumb, some
word is required to complete the sense.
Thersites reiterates *wit* (96, 101, 115
etc.).
111 **brach** bitch-hound, often used for 'prostitute'. A few editors retain QF 'brooch',
glossing it as 'hanger-on', but Rowe's
emendation is generally accepted.
114 **clotpolls** thickheads
119 **fifth hour** 11 o'clock, which fits the
timing of 4.5
122 **stomach** appetite
2.2 The palace in Troy. This meeting of the
Trojan leaders parallels the debate in the

Greek camp; but whereas the Greeks
discuss ways of curing anarchy and getting Achilles to fight, the Trojans, however unsatisfactorily, discuss the moral
question of whether Helen should be kept
in Troy or returned to her husband. This
debate resembles the one reported by
Caxton (ii. 515 ff.) which took place
before the war began, on whether the
Trojans should avenge the seizure of
Hesione. Hector and Helenus advise
prudence; Paris, Deiphobus and Troilus
support the expedition. It should be mentioned that grammar school pupils were

As honour, loss of time, travail, expense,
Wounds, friends, and what else dear that is consumed
In hot digestion of this cormorant war –
Shall be struck off.' Hector, what say you to't?

HECTOR

Though no man lesser fears the Greeks than I,
As far as toucheth my particular, yet, dread Priam,
There is no lady of more softer bowels,   10
More spongy to suck in the sense of fear,
More ready to cry out 'Who knows what follows?'
Than Hector is. The wound of peace is surety,
Surety secure; but modest doubt is called
The beacon of the wise, the tent that searches
To th'bottom of the worst. Let Helen go.
Since the first sword was drawn about this question,
Every tithe soul 'mongst many thousand dismes
Hath been as dear as Helen – I mean, of ours.
If we have lost so many tenths of ours   20
To guard a thing not ours, nor worth to us,
Had it our name, the value of one ten,
What merit's in that reason which denies
The yielding of her up?

TROILUS   Fie, fie, my brother!
Weigh you the worth and honour of a king,
So great as our dread father's, in a scale
Of common ounces? Will you with counters sum
The past-proportion of his infinite,
And buckle in a waist most fathomless

2.2.9 toucheth] touches F   13–14 surety. | Surety] F; surely | Surely Q   26 father's]
Father F

sometimes asked to write speeches for
and against the retention of Helen (Baldwin, *Small Latine*, i. 89). There is a
discussion on the same subject in
Greene's *Euphues his Censure to Philautus*
(1587, ed. Grosart, vi. 165) in which
Helen is referred to as a gem, a pearl and
a piece.

6 **cormorant** a voracious sea-bird; hence
 'rapacious'
7 **struck off** cancelled
9 **particular** three-syllabled: 'personal concern' (Walker)
10 **of more softer bowels** more com-
 passionate

13–14 **The wound . . . secure** Tilley W152:
 'He that is too secure is not safe.'
13 **surety** feeling of safety (*OED* 3)
15 **tent** surgeon's probe
18 **Every tithe . . . dismes** Every tenth man
 among many thousand tenths; but, as
 Deighton says, the meaning seems to be
 that every soul that has been taken as a
 tithe by war is as dear as Helen, and of
 such tithes there have been many
 thousands.
 dismes (pronounced 'dimes')
28 **past-proportion** The hyphen, inserted by
 Johnson, clarifies the meaning.

With spans and inches so diminutive   30
As fears and reasons? Fie, for godly shame!
HELENUS
No marvel though you bite so sharp at reasons,
You are so empty of them. Should not our father
Bear the great sway of his affairs with reason
Because your speech hath none that tell him so?
TROILUS
You are for dreams and slumbers, brother priest;
You fur your gloves with reason. Here are your
    reasons:
You know an enemy intends you harm;
You know a sword employed is perilous,
And reason flies the object of all harm.   40
Who marvels, then, when Helenus beholds
A Grecian and his sword, if he do set
The very wings of reason to his heels
And fly like chidden Mercury from Jove,
Or like a star disorbed? Nay, if we talk of reason,
Let's shut our gates and sleep. Manhood and honour
Should have hare hearts, would they but fat their thoughts
With this crammed reason. Reason and respect
Make livers pale and lustihood deject.
HECTOR
Brother, she is not worth what she doth cost   50
The keeping.
TROILUS   What's aught but as 'tis valued?

32 at] F; of Q   34 reason] reasons F   35 tell] tels F   44–5 And ... reason] *lines in reverse
order* F   46 Let's] F; Sets Q   47 hare] hard F   49 Make] Makes F   51 keeping] holding F

32 **reasons** quibbling on *raisins*
35 **so** i.e. not to do so
36–45 **You are ... disorbed** Troilus' speech,
    besides being an *argumentum ad hominem*,
    is also anti-rational.
37 **fur your gloves with reason** i.e. he in-
    dulges in rationalization. Walker follows
    Rowe's emendation, *reasons*; but the
    repetition of the word is awkward and the
    quibble is spoilt (*fur your gloves*, 'keep
    yourself warm and safe').
40 **the object of all harm** 'the sight of every-
    thing harmful' (Walker)
45 **like a star disorbed** 'Swift as a shooting
    star' (Baldwin)

47 **hare** i.e. timid
48 **crammed** fatted. There seems to be an
    allusion to *foie gras*.
    respect 'thinking too precisely on
    th'event' (*Hamlet*, 4.4.41)
49 **Make** Tannenbaum (74) takes 'reason
    and respect' to mean 'respective reason'
    and therefore prefers the F reading.
    livers pale Deighton cites *2 Henry IV*,
    4.3.101 ff., where a pale liver is 'the
    badge of pusillanimity and cowardice'.
51 **What's aught but as 'tis valued** Tilley
    W923: 'The worth of a thing is as it is
    valued.' Hector in his reply denies this.
    Richards (*Speculative Instruments*, 202)

HECTOR

But value dwells not in particular will:
It holds his estimate and dignity
As well wherein 'tis precious of itself
As in the prizer. 'Tis mad idolatry
To make the service greater than the god;
And the will dotes that is attributive
To what infectiously itself affects,
Without some image of th'affected merit.

TROILUS

I take today a wife, and my election   60
Is led on in the conduct of my will;
My will enkindled by mine eyes and ears,
Two traded pilots 'twixt the dangerous shores
Of will and judgement. How may I avoid,
Although my will distaste what it elected,
The wife I chose? There can be no evasion
To blench from this and to stand firm by honour.
We turn not back the silks upon the merchant
When we have soiled them; nor the remainder viands
We do not throw in unrespective sieve   70
Because we now are full. It was thought meet
Paris should do some vengeance on the Greeks;
Your breath of full consent bellied his sails;
The seas and winds, old wranglers, took a truce,

---

55 mad] made F   57 attributive] inclineable F   63 shores] F; shore Q   66 chose] F;
choose Q   69 soiled] spoyl'd F   70 sieve] same F   73 of] F; with Q

---

suggests that Hector's answer can be
read 'as a comment on Troilus' own later
struggle with this truly central problem of
all philosophy: value and fact, the ideal
and the actual, or however we care to
phrase it'.

53 **particular will** individual desire. *Will* has
a number of different meanings in
Shakespeare – desire, intention, sexual
pleasure, determination.
56 **To make ... god** As Troilus does with
Cressida, or the Trojans with Helen.
57–9 **that is ... merit** that attributes
qualities it values to a person or thing
that lacks them
57 **attributive** The F reading, *inclineable* =
prejudiced, is equally Shakespearian.

60 **wife** He is not referring to Cressida, although his situation with regard to her
doubtless suggested this example to him.
election choice
63 **traded** experienced (*OED* 2); but the word
fits in with the imagery from commerce.
pilots The choice of a wife is based partly
on sexual desire, kindled by the senses;
but it is clearly absurd to regard those
same senses as pilots, and to regard
judgement as a dangerous shore.
67 **blench** flinch
70 **unrespective sieve** a receptacle for
collecting scraps of food left over from a
meal, a 'voider' (Johnson). Unlike a
modern sieve, it is unselective.
72 **vengeance** See headnote, p. 89.
73 **bellied** swelled, as though pregnant

And did him service; he touched the ports desired;
And for an old aunt whom the Greeks held captive
He brought a Grecian queen, whose youth and freshness
Wrinkles Apollo's and makes stale the morning.
Why keep we her? The Grecians keep our aunt.
Is she worth keeping? Why, she is a pearl   80
Whose price hath launched above a thousand ships
And turned crowned kings to merchants.
If you'll avouch 'twas wisdom Paris went –
As you must needs, for you all cried 'Go, go';
If you'll confess he brought home worthy prize –
As you must needs, for you all clapped your hands
And cried 'Inestimable!'; why do you now
The issue of your proper wisdoms rate,
And do a deed that never fortune did,
Beggar the estimation which you prized   90
Richer than sea or land? O theft most base,
That we have stolen what we do fear to keep!
But thieves unworthy of a thing so stolen,
That in their country did them that disgrace
We fear to warrant in our native place!

CASSANDRA (*within*)
Cry, Trojans, cry!

PRIAM   What noise, what shriek is this?

TROILUS
'Tis our mad sister; I do know her voice.

CASSANDRA (*within*) Cry, Trojans!

---

78 stale] F; pale Q   85 he] F; be Q   worthy] Noble F   89 never fortune] Fortune neuer F
96, 98 (*within*)] THEOBALD; *not in* QF

76 **aunt** Hesione, Priam's sister
78 **stale** Pope, Johnson and others prefer Q here; but, as Theobald pointed out, *stale* is the antithesis of *freshness* in the previous line.
80 **pearl** Compare Matthew 13: 45 (Noble), 'The kingdom of heaven is like unto a merchant man, seeking goodly pearls: which when he had found one precious pearl went and sold all he had'. This may be the link with *merchants* (82).
81 **launched above a thousand ships** Echoing Faustus' address to the shade of Helen ('Is this the face that launched a thousand

ships?'); but, as Baldwin points out, both Marlowe and Shakespeare were using a well-worn statement.
88 **proper** own; with a possible quibble on the modern sense.
   rate criticize
89 **do a deed . . . did** 'Act with more inconstancy and caprice than ever did fortune' (Samuel Henley, quoted in Steevens 1793)
94–5 **That in . . . place** that we fear to justify in Troy the humiliation we gave them in Sparta

HECTOR It is Cassandra.

Enter Cassandra, raving, with her hair about her ears

CASSANDRA

Cry, Trojans, cry! Lend me ten thousand eyes,   100

And I will fill them with prophetic tears.

HECTOR Peace, sister, peace!

CASSANDRA

Virgins and boys, mid-age and wrinkled eld,

Soft infancy, that nothing canst but cry,

Add to my clamours! Let us pay betimes

A moiety of that mass of moan to come.

Cry, Trojans, cry! Practise your eyes with tears.

Troy must not be, nor goodly Ilium stand;

Our firebrand brother, Paris, burns us all.

Cry, Trojans, cry! A Helen and a woe!   110

Cry, cry! Troy burns, or else let Helen go.   *Exit*

HECTOR

Now, youthful Troilus, do not these high strains

Of divination in our sister work

Some touches of remorse, or is your blood

So madly hot that no discourse of reason,

Nor fear of bad success in a bad cause,

Can qualify the same?

TROILUS   Why, brother Hector,

We may not think the justness of each act

Such and no other than th'event doth form it,

Nor once deject the courage of our minds,   120

Because Cassandra's mad. Her brainsick raptures

Cannot distaste the goodness of a quarrel

Which hath our several honours all engaged

99.1 *Enter . . . ears*] THEOBALD; *after l. 94* QF   *raving*] *not in* F   *with . . . ears*] F; *not in* Q   103
eld] THEOBALD; elders Q; old F   104 canst] can F   105 clamours] clamour F   119 th'event]
This edition; euent QF

---

103 **eld** Theobald's emendation is a neat
    compromise. F, in correcting Q, got one
    letter wrong.
106 **moiety** share
    mass stock (*OED sb.*¹, 4b)
109 **firebrand** (alluding to Hecuba's dream,
    when pregnant with Paris, that she was
    delivered of a firebrand).
115 **discourse of reason** rational argument
    (also at *Hamlet*, 1.2.150)

119 **th'event** Shakespeare uses 'event' 26
    times, never without an epithet or an
    article. Of these half have the definite
    article, often elided. Troilus is arguing
    that we should not judge merely by
    results, and the definite article makes
    this clear.
121 **raptures** transports
122 **distaste** make distasteful

To make it gracious. For my private part,
I am no more touched than all Priam's sons;
And Jove forbid there should be done amongst us
Such things as might offend the weakest spleen
To fight for and maintain.

PARIS

Else might the world convince of levity
As well my undertakings as your counsels;   130
But I attest the gods, your full consent
Gave wings to my propension and cut off
All fears attending on so dire a project.
For what, alas, can these my single arms?
What propugnation is in one man's valour
To stand the push and enmity of those
This quarrel would excite? Yet, I protest,
Were I alone to pass the difficulties
And had as ample power as I have will,
Paris should ne'er retract what he hath done,   140
Nor faint in the pursuit.

PRIAM   Paris, you speak
Like one besotted on your sweet delights;
You have the honey still, but these the gall:
So to be valiant is no praise at all.

PARIS

Sir, I propose not merely to myself
The pleasures such a beauty brings with it,
But I would have the soil of her fair rape
Wiped off in honourable keeping her.
What treason were it to the ransacked queen,
Disgrace to your great worths, and shame to me,   150
Now to deliver her possession up
On terms of base compulsion! Can it be
That so degenerate a strain as this
Should once set footing in your generous bosoms?
There's not the meanest spirit on our party

126–8 **And Jove ... maintain** i.e. Jove for-
    bid that we should decide to do anything
    that even the most scrupulous among us
    cannot support.
129 **convince** convict (*OED* 4)

131 **attest** call to witness
132 **propension** inclination
135 **propugnation** defence, protection
138 **pass** pass through, undergo
154 **generous** noble

Without a heart to dare or sword to draw
When Helen is defended; nor none so noble
Whose life were ill bestowed or death unfamed
Where Helen is the subject. Then, I say,
Well may we fight for her whom we know well   160
The world's large spaces cannot parallel.

HECTOR

Paris and Troilus, you have both said well,
And on the cause and question now in hand
Have glozed, but superficially; not much
Unlike young men, whom Aristotle thought
Unfit to hear moral philosophy.
The reasons you allege do more conduce
To the hot passion of distempered blood
Than to make up a free determination
'Twixt right and wrong; for pleasure and revenge   170
Have ears more deaf than adders to the voice
Of any true decision. Nature craves
All dues be rendered to their owners. Now
What nearer debt in all humanity
Than wife is to the husband? If this law
Of nature be corrupted through affection,
And that great minds, of partial indulgence
To their benumbèd wills, resist the same,
There is a law in each well-ordered nation
To curb those raging appetites that are   180
Most disobedient and refractory.
If Helen then be wife to Sparta's king,

---

164 **glozed** glossed, commented

164–6 **not much . . . philosophy** Aristotle (*Nicomachean Ethics*, 1. 3) says that young men are not fitted to hear political philosophy, because they are passionate and headstrong. The substitution of *moral* for *political* is immaterial, since Aristotle was writing about 'the ethics of civil society, which are hardly distinguishable from what is commonly called "morals"' (Sidney Lee, cited in New Variorum). Erasmus, *Colloquies* (trans. Nathan Bailey, 1725, ii. 358), was probably the source of Shakespeare's information, where we are told of 'young persons, whom Aristotle accounted not to be fit Auditors of Moral Philosophy, *viz.* such as is deliver'd in serious precepts'. Mulcaster (1581) and Grimald (1556, 1600) and others make the same point (New Variorum). Shakespeare may not have realized that Aristotle lived after the date of the Trojan War.

171 **more deaf than adders** Compare Psalm 63: 4, 5 (Anders, 213); Tilley A32: 'As deaf as an adder'.

173 **All dues . . . owners** Tilley D634 'Give everyone his due' is not close in meaning.

176 **affection** emotion

177 **of** through
      partial prejudiced

As it is known she is, these moral laws
Of nature and of nations speak aloud
To have her back returned. Thus to persist
In doing wrong extenuates not wrong,
But makes it much more heavy. Hector's opinion
Is this in way of truth. Yet ne'ertheless,
My sprightly brethren, I propend to you
In resolution to keep Helen still;   190
For 'tis a cause that hath no mean dependence
Upon our joint and several dignities.

TROILUS
Why, there you touched the life of our design.
Were it not glory that we more affected
Than the performance of our heaving spleens,
I would not wish a drop of Trojan blood
Spent more in her defence. But, worthy Hector,
She is a theme of honour and renown,
A spur to valiant and magnanimous deeds,
Whose present courage may beat down our foes,   200
And fame in time to come canonize us;
For I presume brave Hector would not lose
So rich advantage of a promised glory
As smiles upon the forehead of this action
For the wide world's revenue.

HECTOR   I am yours,
You valiant offspring of great Priamus.
I have a roisting challenge sent amongst
The dull and factious nobles of the Greeks
Will strike amazement to their drowsy spirits.

---

184 nations] Nation F   209 strike] F; shrike Q

183–4 **moral laws . . . nations** O. J. Campbell (*Comicall Satyre*, 191–3) suggested
that Shakespeare was referring to Al-
berico Gentili's identification of the *jus
naturae* ('law implanted by nature in the
human mind') and *jus gentium* ('rules
common to the laws of all nations'). But
the laws of nature and of nations were
terms common in the sixteenth century
(New Variorum).
186 **extenuates** mitigates
188 **in way of truth** as an abstract question
of right (Deighton)

188 **Yet** Hector's volte-face is discussed in
the Introduction, p. 24.
189 **propend** incline (*OED* 2; first occurrence
in this sense)
195 **performance of our heaving spleens**
execution of spite and resentment (Johnson)
201 **canonize** (accent on the second syllable)
glorify
205 **revenue** (accent on the second syllable)
207 **roisting** roistering, blustering
challenge i.e. that delivered by Aeneas
in 1.3.

I was advertised their great general slept,   210
Whilst emulation in the army crept.
This, I presume, will wake him.   *Exeunt*

2.3   *Enter Thersites*

THERSITES How now, Thersites! What – lost in the labyrinth
of thy fury! Shall the elephant Ajax carry it thus? He beats
me, and I rail at him. O worthy satisfaction! Would it were
otherwise – that I could beat him, whilst he railed at me.
'Sfoot, I'll learn to conjure and raise devils but I'll see some
issue of my spiteful execrations. Then there's Achilles – a
rare engineer. If Troy be not taken till these two under-
mine it, the walls will stand till they fall of themselves.
O thou great thunder-darter of Olympus, forget that thou
art Jove, the king of gods, and, Mercury, lose all the   10
serpentine craft of thy caduceus, if ye take not that little
little, less than little wit from them that they have – which
short-armed ignorance itself knows is so abundant
scarce, it will not in circumvention deliver a fly from a
spider without drawing their massy irons and cutting the
web. After this, the vengeance on the whole camp! – or,
rather, the Neapolitan bone-ache, for that methinks is the
curse depending on those that war for a placket. I have
said my prayers, and devil Envy say 'Amen'. What ho! My
Lord Achilles!   20

PATROCLUS (*within*) Who's there? Thersites? Good Thersites,
come in and rail.

THERSITES If I could a' remembered a gilt counterfeit, thou

2.3.0.1 *Enter Thersites*] CAPELL; *Enter* Thersites *solus* QF   11 ye] thou F   15 their] the F
17 Neapolitan] *not in* F   18 depending] dependant F   21 (*within*)] WALKER (*conjectured
anonymously*, CAMBRIDGE); *Enter Patroclus* F (*after l. 20*); *not in* Q   23 a'] (a); haue F

---

210 **advertised** (accent on the second syl-
      lable)
211 **emulation** ambitious rivalry, grudge
      against the superiority of others (*OED* 2,
      3)
2.3 The Greek camp.
  2 **elephant** i.e. thick-skinned and clumsy
  5 **'Sfoot** God's foot
  7 **engineer** sapper
11 **caduceus** Mercury's staff, entwined
      with snakes. 'Mercury, the crafty thief,

would steal even the little wits possessed
by Ajax and Achilles' (Dobrée).
13 **short-armed** 'incapable of reaching far'
      (Cowden Clarke)
14 **circumvention** outwitting
15 **irons** swords
17 **Neapolitan bone-ache** syphilis
18 **placket** petticoat, hence 'woman'
19 **Envy** Thersites knows himself. Compare
      spiteful (l. 6).
23 **counterfeit** sham

wouldst not have slipped out of my contemplation; but it
is no matter – thyself upon thyself! The common curse of
mankind, folly and ignorance, be thine in great revenue!
Heaven bless thee from a tutor, and discipline come not
near thee! Let thy blood be thy direction till thy death!
Then if she that lays thee out says thou art a fair corpse,
I'll be sworn and sworn upon't she never shrouded any   30
but lazars. Amen.
> *Enter Patroclus*
Where's Achilles?

PATROCLUS
What, art thou devout? Wast thou in prayer?

THERSITES Ay; the heavens hear me.

PATROCLUS Amen.

ACHILLES (*within*) Who's there?

PATROCLUS Thersites, my lord.
> *Enter Achilles*

ACHILLES Where, where, O where? Art thou come? Why,
my cheese, my digestion, why hast thou not served thyself
in to my table so many meals? Come, what's Agamemnon?   40

THERSITES Thy commander, Achilles; then tell me,
Patroclus, what's Achilles?

PATROCLUS Thy lord, Thersites. Then tell me, I pray thee,
what's Thersites?

THERSITES Thy knower, Patroclus. Then tell me, Patroclus,
what art thou?

PATROCLUS Thou must tell, that knowest.

ACHILLES O tell, tell.

THERSITES I'll decline the whole question. Agamemnon
commands Achilles; Achilles is my lord; I am Patroclus'   50
knower, and Patroclus is a fool.

---

24 wouldst] F; couldst Q   29 art] F; art not Q   31.1 *Enter Patroclus*] WALKER (*conjectured
anonymously,* CAMBRIDGE); *not in* QF (*but see l.* 21)   33 prayer] a prayer F   35 PATROCLUS
Amen.] *not in* F   36 (*within*)] WALKER; *not in* QF   37.1 *Enter Achilles*] WALKER; *after l.* 35 QF
38 O where?] *not in* F   44 Thersites] thy selfe F   47 must] maist F

24 **slipped** quibbling on *slip*, a counterfeit
   coin
25 **thyself upon thyself!** i.e. the worst curse
   is that he should be himself
28 **Let thy blood be thy direction** be gover-
   ned by passion (rather than by reason)

31.1 Obviously Patroclus enters here, in time
   to hear the 'Amen'.
39 **cheese** supposed to be good for digestion
49 **decline** i.e. grammatically, 'as a noun is
   stated in all its cases and numbers' (Cowden Clarke)

PATROCLUS You rascal!

THERSITES Peace, fool; I have not done.

ACHILLES He is a privilegèd man. Proceed, Thersites.

THERSITES Agamemnon is a fool; Achilles is a fool; Thersites
is a fool, and, as aforesaid, Patroclus is a fool.

ACHILLES Derive this; come.

THERSITES Agamemnon is a fool to offer to command
Achilles; Achilles is a fool to be commanded of Agamem-
non; Thersites is a fool to serve such a fool; and this   60
Patroclus is a fool positive.

PATROCLUS Why am I a fool?

THERSITES Make that demand of thy Creator. It suffices me
thou art. Look you, who comes here?

ACHILLES Patroclus, I'll speak with nobody. Come in with
me, Thersites.   *Exit*

THERSITES Here is such patchery, such juggling and such
knavery! All the argument is a whore and a cuckold – a
good quarrel to draw emulous factions and bleed to death
upon! Now the dry serpigo on the subject, and war and   70
lechery confound all!   *Exit*

    Enter Agamemnon, Ulysses, Nestor, Diomedes,
    and Ajax

AGAMEMNON Where is Achilles?

PATROCLUS
Within his tent; but ill-disposed, my lord.

AGAMEMNON
Let it be known to him that we are here.
He shent our messengers, and we lay by

52–6 PATROCLUS You ... fool] F; *not in* Q   59–60 of Agamemnon] F; *not in* Q   60 this] *not
in* F   63 of] to F   thy] ROWE I 1709b; the QF   Creator] F; Prouer Q   65 Patroclus] F; Come
Patroclus Q   66 *Exit*] F; *not in* Q   68 whore and a cuckold] Cuckold and a Whore F   69
emulous$_\Lambda$] emulations, F   70–1 Now ... all] F; *not in* Q   71 *Exit*] THEOBALD; *not in* QF
71.1–2 *Enter ... Ajax*] DYCE; *after l. 64* Q; *after l. 62* F   71.2 *and Ajax*] CAPELL; *Aiax, & Calcas*
QF   75 He shent] THEOBALD; He sate Q; He sent F; We sent COLLIER (*conj.* THEOBALD)

54 **privileged** i.e. as a professional fool
57 **Derive** 'explain' (Walker)
61 **positive** absolute
63 **of thy Creator** The Q reading may be due
to the elimination of profanity: 'of' is mar-
ginally superior to 'to'; and Rowe's
emendation improves on 'the'.
67 **patchery** knavery

70 **serpigo** 'a general term for creeping skin
diseases' (*OED*)
75 **He shent** This emendation is generally
accepted, although Shakespeare
elsewhere uses *shent* only in the passive
voice. Theobald's conjecture, adopted by
Walker, *We sent*, seems weak.

Our appertainments, visiting of him.
Let him be told so, lest perchance he think
We dare not move the question of our place,
Or know not what we are.

PATROCLUS   I shall say so to him.   *Exit*

ULYSSES
We saw him at the opening of his tent –   80
He is not sick.

AJAX Yes, lion-sick, sick of proud heart. You may call it
melancholy, if you will favour the man; but, by my head,
'tis pride. But why, why? Let him show us a cause. A word,
my lord.

He takes Agamemnon aside

NESTOR What moves Ajax thus to bay at him?

ULYSSES Achilles hath inveigled his fool from him.

NESTOR Who? Thersites?

ULYSSES He.

NESTOR Then will Ajax lack matter, if he have lost his   90
argument.

ULYSSES No, you see, he is his argument that has his argument – Achilles.

NESTOR All the better – their fraction is more our wish than
their faction. But it was strong composure a fool could
disunite!

ULYSSES The amity that wisdom knits not, folly may easily
untie.

Enter Patroclus

Here comes Patroclus.

NESTOR   No Achilles with him.

---

76 appertainments] F; appertainings Q   77 so, lest] of, so F   79 say so] so say F   *Exit*] ROWE
1714; *not in* QF   83 you] *not in* F   84 'tis] it is F   a cause] the cause F   84–5 A … lord] F;
not in Q   85.1] MALONE (*subs.*); *not in* QF   95 composure] counsell that F   98.1 *Enter
Patroclus*] F; *not in* Q

---

76 **appertainments** prerogatives (Onions)
78 **move the question of our place** assert our
   authority
92–3 **he is . . . Achilles** This refers, as Z. Grey
   pointed out (*Critical . . . Notes on Shakespeare* (1754), ii. 240), to a proverb in
   Erasmus' *Adagia*: 'Denique rationem aut
   argumentum *Achilleum* vocant, quod sit
   insuperabile & insolubile' ('A reason or an

argument is called Achillean because it is
insuperable and insoluble'). One wonders
how many members of even an Inns of
Court audience saw the point of the
allusion.
94 **fraction** breaking up, quarrelling
95 **composure** combination, union
97–8 **The amity . . . untie** (aphoristic, if not
   proverbial)

ULYSSES

    The elephant hath joints, but none for courtesy.   100
    His legs are legs for necessity, not for flexure.

PATROCLUS

    Achilles bids me say he is much sorry
    If anything more than your sport and pleasure
    Did move your greatness and this noble state
    To call upon him; he hopes it is no other
    But for your health and your digestion sake,
    An after-dinner's breath.

AGAMEMNON   Hear you, Patroclus.
    We are too well acquainted with these answers;
    But his evasion, winged thus swift with scorn,
    Cannot outfly our apprehensions.   110
    Much attribute he hath, and much the reason
    Why we ascribe it to him; yet all his virtues,
    Not virtuously on his own part beheld,
    Do in our eyes begin to lose their gloss,
    Yea, like fair fruit in an unwholesome dish,
    Are like to rot untasted. Go and tell him
    We come to speak with him; and you shall not sin
    If you do say we think him over-proud
    And under-honest, in self-assumption greater
    Than in the note of judgement; and worthier than himself   120
    Here tend the savage strangeness he puts on,
    Disguise the holy strength of their command,
    And underwrite in an observing kind

---

101 legs are] legge are F   flexure] flight F   113 on] of F   115 Yea,] Yea, and F   117 come]
came F   121 tend] tends F

100–1 **The elephant . . . flexure** Referring to
    the vulgar error that elephants have no
    knees. Erasmus, *Adagia*, has a proverb
    (from Carollus Bovillus) about the
    haughty man, *Homo genibus elephantinis*
    (Baldwin, cited in New Variorum).
104 **state** official representatives
106 **digestion** i.e. digestion's, the 's often
    being omitted before a word beginning in
    's'.
107 **breath** breath of fresh air, a stroll
110 **Cannot outfly . . . apprehensions** can-
    not escape capture by flight, with a
    quibble on *apprehensions*

111 **attribute** reputation, honour
113 **Not virtuously . . . beheld** not regarded
    as a virtuous man should
119–20 **self-assumption . . . judgement**
    overestimating oneself, rather than
    giving a judicious assessment
121 **tend** attend
    savage strangeness barbarous unfriendli-
    ness
122 **holy** Agamemnon, too, is guilty of self-
    assumption.
123 **underwrite in an observing kind** sub-
    scribe in a compliant way

His humorous predominance; yea, watch
His pettish lunes, his ebbs and flows, as if
The passage and whole carriage of this action
Rode on his tide. Go tell him this, and add
That if he overhold his price so much
We'll none of him; but let him, like an engine
Not portable, lie under this report: 130
'Bring action hither; this cannot go to war.
A stirring dwarf we do allowance give
Before a sleeping giant.' Tell him so.

PATROCLUS
I shall; and bring his answer presently.   *Exit*

AGAMEMNON
In second voice we'll not be satisfied.
We come to speak with him. Ulysses, enter you.
                                               Exit Ulysses

AJAX What is he more than another?

AGAMEMNON No more than what he thinks he is.

AJAX Is he so much? Do you not think he thinks himself a
better man than I am?   140

AGAMEMNON No question.

AJAX Will you subscribe his thought and say he is?

AGAMEMNON No, noble Ajax. You are as strong, as valiant,
as wise, no less noble, much more gentle, and altogether
more tractabie.

AJAX Why should a man be proud? How doth pride grow?
I know not what pride is.

AGAMEMNON Your mind is the clearer, Ajax, and your virtues the fairer. He that is proud eats up himself. Pride is
his own glass, his own trumpet, his own chronicle; and   150
whatever praises itself but in the deed, devours the deed
in the praise.

---

125 pettish lunes] HANMER; course, and time Q; pettish lines F   and flows] his flowes F   as if]
F; and if Q   126 carriage of this action] F; streame of his commencement Q   134 *Exit*] ROWE;
not in QF   136 enter you] F; entertaine Q   136.1 *Exit Ulysses*] F; *not in* Q   147 pride is] it is F
148 Ajax] F; *not in* Q

---

124 **humorous predominance** the pre-
     dominance of his particular humours; or
     his strange assumption of superiority
124–7 **yea, watch . . . tide** See Appendix 2*b*.

125 **pettish** ill-humoured (Walker)
128 **overhold** overestimate
135 **In second voice** by a substitute, i.e. by
     Patroclus

Enter Ulysses

AJAX I do hate a proud man as I hate the engendering of
toads.

NESTOR (*aside*)
And yet he loves himself. Is't not strange?

ULYSSES
Achilles will not to the field tomorrow.

AGAMEMNON
What's his excuse?

ULYSSES   He doth rely on none,
But carries on the stream of his dispose
Without observance or respect of any,
In will peculiar and in self-admission.   160

AGAMEMNON
Why will he not, upon our fair request,
Untent his person and share the air with us?

ULYSSES
Things small as nothing, for request's sake only,
He makes important; possessed he is with greatness,
And speaks not to himself but with a pride
That quarrels at self-breath. Imagined worth
Holds in his blood such swollen and hot discourse
That 'twixt his mental and his active parts
Kingdomed Achilles in commotion rages
And batters down himself. What should I say?   170
He is so plaguey proud that the death-tokens of it
Cry 'No recovery'.

AGAMEMNON   Let Ajax go to him.
Dear lord, go you and greet him in his tent.
'Tis said he holds you well and will be led,
At your request, a little from himself.

ULYSSES
O Agamemnon, let it not be so!

153 I hate] F; I do hate Q   155 And yet] Yet F   162 the air] F;   th'ayre Q   166 worth]
wroth F   170 down himself] gainst it selfe F   174 led] F; lead Q

158 **dispose** disposition   too proud to speak
160 **In will peculiar and in self-admission**   168–70 **That 'twixt . . . himself** Compare
     self-willed and self-satisfied (Walker)   *Caesar* 2.1.67–9: 'The state of man | Like
163 **for request's sake only** 'merely because   to a little kingdom, suffers then | The
     they are requested' (Seymour, quoted in   nature of an insurrection'.
     New Variorum)   171 **death-tokens** fatal symptoms
166 **That quarrels at self-breath** almost

We'll consecrate the steps that Ajax makes
When they go from Achilles. Shall the proud lord
That bastes his arrogance with his own seam
And never suffers matter of the world   180
Enter his thoughts, save such as doth revolve
And ruminate himself, shall he be worshipped
Of that we hold an idol more than he?
No, this thrice-worthy and right valiant lord
Must not so stale his palm, nobly acquired,
Nor, by my will, assubjugate his merit,
As amply titled as Achilles is,
By going to Achilles –
That were to enlard his fat-already pride,
And add more coals to Cancer when he burns   190
With entertaining great Hyperion.
This lord go to him? Jupiter forbid,
And say in thunder 'Achilles go to him'.
NESTOR (*aside*)
O, this is well; he rubs the vein of him.
DIOMEDES (*aside*)
And how his silence drinks up this applause!
AJAX
If I go to him, with my armèd fist
I'll pash him o'er the face.
AGAMEMNON   O, no, you shall not go.
AJAX
An a be proud with me, I'll feeze his pride.
Let me go to him.
ULYSSES
Not for the worth that hangs upon our quarrel.   200
AJAX A paltry, insolent fellow!
NESTOR (*aside*) How he describes himself!
AJAX Can he not be sociable?

---

181 doth] doe F   185 Must] F; Shall Q   187 titled] F; liked Q   195 this] F; his Q   197
pash] F; push Q   198 a] F; he Q

179 **seam** fat, grease   enters Cancer on 21 June, when it is al-
181 **revolve** consider   ready very hot.
186 **assubjugate** reduce to subjection (first   197 **pash** strike violently, smash
    occurrence)   198 **a** he
190–1 **And add . . . Hyperion** The sun   **feeze** 'settle the business of' (*OED*)

ULYSSES (*aside*) The raven chides blackness.

AJAX I'll let his humour's blood.

AGAMEMNON (*aside*) He will be the physician that should be
the patient.

AJAX An all men were o'my mind –

ULYSSES (*aside*) Wit would be out of fashion.

AJAX A should not bear it so; a should eat swords first. Shall   210
pride carry it?

NESTOR (*aside*) An 'twould, you'd carry half.

⌈ULYSSES⌉ (*aside*) A would have ten shares. I will knead him,
I'll make him supple. He's not yet through warm.

NESTOR (*aside*) Force him with praises. Pour in, pour in; his
ambition is dry.

ULYSSES (*to Agamemnon*)
My lord, you feed too much on this dislike.

NESTOR
Our noble general, do not do so.

DIOMEDES
You must prepare to fight without Achilles.

ULYSSES
Why, 'tis this naming of him does him harm.   220
Here is a man – but 'tis before his face.
I will be silent.

NESTOR   Wherefore should you so?
He is not emulous, as Achilles is.

ULYSSES
Know the whole world, he is as valiant –

AJAX
A whoreson dog, that shall palter with us thus!
Would he were a Trojan!

NESTOR
What a vice were it in Ajax now –

ULYSSES
If he were proud –

205 let] F; tell Q   humour's] F; humorous Q   208 o'] F (a); of Q   213 ULYSSES] F; *Aiax* Q
I will] *Aia⟨x⟩*. I will F   215 praises] F; praiers Q   in; his] F; his Q   220 does] doth F   224
valiant –] Q; valiant. F   225 with us thus] thus with vs F

210 **eat swords** be stabbed, with a quibble on
     'eat's words'
213–16 **A would . . . dry** See Appendix 2c.
213 **ten shares** i.e. the whole, all pride; pos-

sibly alluding to the ten shares into which
the Globe property was divided.
214 **through warm** warm all through
215 **Force** stuff

106

DIOMEDES   Or covetous of praise –
ULYSSES
  Ay, or surly borne –
DIOMEDES   Or strange, or self-affected!
ULYSSES
  Thank the heavens. lord, thou art of sweet composure;   230
  Praise him that got thee, she that gave thee suck;
  Famed be thy tutor, and thy parts of nature
  Thrice famed beyond, beyond all erudition.
  But he that disciplined thine arms to fight,
  Let Mars divide eternity in twain,
  And give him half; and, for thy vigour,
  Bull-bearing Milo his addition yield
  To sinewy Ajax. I will not praise thy wisdom,
  Which, like a bourn, a pale, a shore, confines
  Thy spacious and dilated parts. Here's Nestor,   240
  Instructed by the antiquary times;
  He must, he is, he cannot but be wise;
  But pardon, father Nestor, were your days
  As green as Ajax', and your brain so tempered,
  You should not have the eminence of him,
  But be as Ajax.
AJAX   Shall I call you father?
NESTOR
  Ay, my good son.
DIOMEDES   Be ruled by him, Lord Ajax.
ULYSSES
  There is no tarrying here. The hart Achilles

231 got] F; gat Q   232 Famed] Fame F   233 beyond, beyond all] F; beyond all thy Q   234
thine] thy F   239 bourn] F; boord Q   240 Thy] F; This Q   244 Ajax'] HANMER; *Aiax* QF
247 NESTOR] *Ulis⟨ses⟩*. F

229 **self-affected** egotistical
230 **composure** temperament
231 **Praise him . . . suck** Warburton suggested that the corresponding passage in
Shrew – 'Happy the parents of so fair a
child; | Happier the man whom favour-
able stars | Allots thee for his lovely bed-
fellow' (4.5.38–40) – was derived from
Golding's Ovid, but for the present
passage he noted a parallel with Luke
11: 27 ('Blessed is the womb that bare
thee and the paps which gave thee suck').
Baldwin claimed that Shakespeare was
echoing the original of the Ovid passage

(iv. 322–6) 'qui te genuere beati . . . quae
dedit ubera' (New Variorum).
237 **Milo** an athlete of the sixth century BC,
who carried a four-year-old bull on his
shoulders
addition title
238 **wisdom** Actors often pause after this
word, so that Ajax can register
annoyance.
239 **pale** boundary
240 **dilated** extended
241 **antiquary** ancient
245 **eminence of** superiority to

Keeps thicket. Please it our great general
To call together all his state of war.   250
Fresh kings are come to Troy; tomorrow
We must with all our main of power stand fast;
And here's a lord, come knights from east to west,
And cull their flower, Ajax shall cope the best.

AGAMEMNON
Go we to council. Let Achilles sleep.
Light boats sail swift, though greater hulks draw deep.

Exeunt

3.1   *Enter Pandarus and a Servant. Music sounds within*

PANDARUS Friend, you, pray you, a word. Do you not follow
   the young Lord Paris?

SERVANT Ay sir, when he goes before me.

PANDARUS You depend upon him, I mean.

SERVANT Sir, I do depend upon the Lord.

PANDARUS You depend upon a notable gentleman: I must
   needs praise him.

SERVANT The Lord be praised!

PANDARUS You know me, do you not?

SERVANT Faith, sir, superficially.   10

PANDARUS Friend, know me better. I am the Lord Pandarus.

SERVANT I hope I shall know your honour better.

PANDARUS I do desire it.

SERVANT You are in the state of grace?

PANDARUS Grace? Not so, friend: 'honour' and 'lordship' are
   my titles. What music is this?

SERVANT I do but partly know, sir. It is music in parts.

PANDARUS Know you the musicians?

---

249 great] *not in* F   254 cull] F; call Q   256 sail] may saile F   hulks] bulkes F   256.1
Exeunt] Exeunt. Musicke sounds within. F
    3.1.0.1 *and a Servant]* F; *not in* Q   *Music sounds within]* F (*after 'Exeunt'*, 2.3.256.1); *not in*
Q; *at l.* 15 CAPELL   1 you not] not you F   6 notable] noble F   16 titles] title F

---

250 **state** council

251 **Fresh kings** i.e. to fight on the Trojan
   side

256 **Light boats . . . deep** (possibly proverbial)

3.1 A room in the Palace.

  5 **Lord** (a) Paris (b) God. The Servant has a
   number of remarks which can be taken in

a religious sense. Pandarus always as-
suming a secular meaning. Compare ll. 8,
14, 15.

14 **You are in the state of grace** If Pandarus
   desires to be better, as opposed to being
   better acquainted, he is perhaps in a state
   of grace.

SERVANT Wholly, sir.

PANDARUS Who play they to?   20

SERVANT To the hearers, sir.

PANDARUS At whose pleasure, friend?

SERVANT At mine, sir, and theirs that love music.

PANDARUS Command, I mean.

SERVANT Who shall I command, sir?

PANDARUS Friend, we understand not one another. I am too
courtly, and thou too cunning. At whose request do these
men play?

SERVANT That's to't, indeed, sir. Marry, sir, at the request of
Paris my lord, who is there in person; with him, the   30
mortal Venus, the heart-blood of beauty, love's invisible
soul –

PANDARUS Who? My cousin Cressida?

SERVANT No, sir, Helen. Could you not find out that by her
attributes?

PANDARUS It should seem, fellow, that thou hast not seen
the Lady Cressida. I come to speak with Paris from the
Prince Troilus. I will make a complimental assault upon
him, for my business seethes.

SERVANT Sodden business! There's a stewed phrase indeed.   40

Enter Paris and Helen, attended

PANDARUS Fair be to you, my lord, and to all this fair company! Fair desires, in all fair measure, fairly guide them!
Especially to you, fair Queen, fair thoughts be your fair
pillow!

HELEN Dear lord, you are full of fair words.

---

24 mean] Q (meane:); meane friend F   27 thou too] thou art too F   30 who is] who's F
31 invisible] indivisible WALKER (*conj.* DANIEL); invincible *conj.* TANNENBAUM   32 soul –] Q
(soule:); soule. F   34 you not] F; not you Q   36 that thou] F; thou Q   37 Cressida] F;
Cressid Q   40.1 *attended*] THEOBALD; *not in* QF

31–2 **love's invisible soul** the quintessential
spirit of love. Walker, however, argues for
Daniel's conjecture 'indivisible', meaning
that Helen is the embodiment of love and
beauty. Tannenbaum (76) suggests 'invincible', on the grounds that in *1 Henry
IV*, 3.2.304, 'invisible' is misprinted as
'invincible'.

38 **complimental assault** In anticipation of
the compliments in the scene which
follows (Walker).

39 **seethes** is urgent

40 **Sodden** boiled, stewed – whether by being
overworked in the brothel, or treated for
venereal disease in the sweating tub (Colman). Walker thinks the remark is an
aside.

41 ff. In the ensuing dialogue the word 'fair' is
used eleven times, 'sweet' fifteen times,
thereby helping to create the sentimental
and enervating atmosphere of the court.

PANDARUS You speak your fair pleasure, sweet Queen. Fair
    prince, here is good broken music.
PARIS You have broke it, cousin; and, by my life, you shall
    make it whole again. You shall piece it out with a piece
    of your performance. Nell, he is full of harmony.   50
PANDARUS Truly, lady, no.
HELEN O, sir!
PANDARUS Rude, in sooth; in good sooth, very rude.
PARIS Well said, my lord! Well, you say so in fits.
PANDARUS I have business to my lord, dear Queen. My lord,
    will you vouchsafe me a word?
HELEN Nay, this shall not hedge us out. We'll hear you sing,
    certainly.
PANDARUS Well, sweet Queen, you are pleasant with me. –
    But, marry, thus, my lord. My dear lord, and most es-   60
    teemed friend, your brother Troilus –
HELEN My Lord Pandarus, honey-sweet lord –
PANDARUS Go to, sweet Queen, go to – commends himself
    most affectionately to you –
HELEN You shall not bob us out of our melody. If you do, our
    melancholy upon your head!
PANDARUS Sweet Queen, sweet Queen; that's a sweet
    Queen, i'faith –
HELEN And to make a sweet lady sad is a sour offence.
PANDARUS Nay, that shall not serve your turn, that shall it   70
    not, in truth, la. Nay, I care not for such words; no, no. –
    And, my lord, he desires you, that if the King call for him
    at supper you will make his excuse.
HELEN My Lord Pandarus –

---

50 Nell, he] Q (*Nel.* he); HELEN He ALEXANDER   60 my lord.] THEOBALD; my Lord$_A$ Q; my
Lord, F

47 **broken music** music 'employing different
    families of instruments' (Walker)
48 **broke it** i.e. by interrupting it
    cousin There was another Pandarus,
    grandson of Priam by his former wife; but
    it is unlikely that Shakespeare fused this
    character with Chaucer's. The word was
    often used about people who were not
    related.
50 **Nell** Alexander argues plausibly that this
    is a speech-prefix, the next five words
    being given to Helen. But Paris does later

refer to her as Nell; she is not given this
form of prefix anywhere else in the scene;
and even though the words are spoken by
Paris, it is natural in the circumstances
for Pandarus to address Helen.
54 **in fits** at times; with a quibble, a 'fit' being
part of a song or poem
57 **hedge us out** shut us out. Walker suggests 'fob us off'.
59 **pleasant** engaging in pleasantries and
jokes
65 **bob** cheat

PANDARUS What says my sweet Queen, my very very sweet
Queen?

PARIS What exploit's in hand? Where sups he tonight?

HELEN Nay, but, my lord –

PANDARUS What says my sweet Queen? My cousin will fall
out with you.   80

HELEN *(to Paris)* You must not know where he sups.

PARIS I'll lay my life, with my disposer Cressida.

PANDARUS No, no, no such matter. You are wide. Come,
your disposer is sick.

PARIS Well, I'll make 's excuse.

PANDARUS Ay, good my lord. Why should you say Cressida?
No, your poor disposer's sick.

PARIS I spy.

PANDARUS You spy! What do you spy? Come, give me an
instrument. Now, sweet Queen.   90

HELEN Why, this is kindly done.

PANDARUS My niece is horribly in love with a thing you
have, sweet Queen.

HELEN She shall have it, my lord, if it be not my Lord Paris.

PANDARUS He? No, she'll none of him; they two are twain.

HELEN Falling in, after falling out, may make them three.

81 You ... sups] *continuing previous speech* CAPELL   82 I'll ... life] *not in* F   85 make 's] Q
(makes); make F   87 poor] F; *not in* Q   92 horribly] horrible F

79–80 **My cousin will fall out with you** Paris
will be annoyed with you, if you flirt with
me like this (compare Tannenbaum,
p. 76, cited by Baldwin). Although Paris
has previously called Pandarus cousin,
Walker thinks the word here refers to
Cressida, thus letting the cat out of the
bag. Pandarus is flustered by the difficulty
of giving Troilus' message to Paris, with
Helen continually interrupting. But,
presumably, Helen knows as well as Paris
that Troilus has an assignation with
Cressida.

82 **disposer** The word normally means 'one
who arranges or commands'. It may here
be used, ironically, in the sense of
'mistress'; but no one, as the long note in
the New Variorum makes apparent, has
given a convincing explanation of the
word in the context, or a comparable use
in Elizabethan literature. Perhaps 'my' is
used vaguely.

85 **make 's** make his

89–90 **Come, give me an instrument**
addressed to an attendant (or to one of the
musicians who had entered with Paris
and Helen)

91 **kindly done** (because he has agreed to
sing)

92–3 **a thing you have** Walker assumes that
this remark is to distract attention from
the question of Troilus' assignation.
Theobald (letter to Warburton, cited in
New Variorum) asked if Pandarus was
hinting that Cressida wanted a man like
Paris as her bedfellow. It is more likely to
refer to some unspecified material
possession. See next note.

94 **Paris** This might be Paris', i.e. his sexual
organ, the 'thing' he has.

96 **Falling in ... three** 'The reconciliation
and wanton dalliance of two lovers after a
quarrel may produce a child' (Tollet, cited
in New Variorum); Tilley F40: 'The falling
out of lovers is the renewing of love'.

PANDARUS Come, come, I'll hear no more of this. I'll sing
   you a song now.
HELEN Ay, ay, prithee now. By my troth, sweet lord, thou
   hast a fine forehead.   100
PANDARUS Ay, you may, you may.
HELEN Let thy song be love. 'This love will undo us all.' O
   Cupid, Cupid, Cupid!
PANDARUS Love? Ay, that it shall, i'faith.
PARIS Ay, good now, 'Love, love, nothing but love'.
PANDARUS In good troth, it begins so.
   (*Sings*) Love, love, nothing but love, still love, still more!
           For, O, love's bow
           Shoots buck and doe;
           The shaft confounds   110
           Not that it wounds,
       But tickles still the sore.
       These lovers cry 'O, O, they die!'
         Yet that which seems the wound to kill
       Doth turn O! O! to ha! ha! he!
         So dying love lives still.
         'O! O!' a while, but 'ha! ha! ha!'
         'O! O!' groans out for 'ha! ha! ha!'
   Heigh-ho!
HELEN In love, i'faith, to the very tip of the nose.   120
PARIS He eats nothing but doves, love, and that breeds hot
   blood, and hot blood begets hot thoughts, and hot
   thoughts beget hot deeds, and hot deeds is love.

---

99 lord] F; lad Q   106 In … so] F (*continuing Paris' speech*, F *uncorr.*; *attrib. to* 'Pan.' F *corr.*);
not in Q   107 still love] *not in* F   110 shaft confounds] F; shaftes confound Q   119 Heigh-
ho] JOHNSON AND STEEVENS 1785 (*conj.* RITSON); hey ho QF (*as part of the song*)

101 **you may** Helen is caressing him.
102 **'This love will undo us all'** A catch-
   phrase, to be found in Nathan Field's *A
   Woman is a Weathercock* (*c.*1609), 3.3
   (Verity, cited in New Variorum).
105 **'Love, love, nothing but love'** Paris is
   giving the first line of the song, possibly
   because he recognizes it from the opening
   bars of the tune.
109 **buck and doe** male and female
110–1 **confounds | Not that it wounds** Am-
   biguous: 'that' may mean 'that which' (S.
   Musgrave, quoted in Johnson and
   Steevens 1778) and this interpretation

would be supported by printing in one
line (as in QF), as Walker suggests. An
alternative interpretation is that the shaft
confounds (overwhelms) the recipient not
so much by the *wound* (the penetration by
the male organ) as by the subsequent
tickling (erotic stimulation).
110 **shaft** (a) arrow (b) penis
112 **sore** quibble on *sore* = buck of the
   fourth year, as in *LLL* 4.2.54 ff.
113 **die** referring to sexual orgasm
114 **wound to kill** 'killing wound' (Mason,
   Comments)
119 **Heigh-ho!** (a sigh, not part of the song)

PANDARUS Is this the generation of love? Hot blood, hot
thoughts, and hot deeds? Why, they are vipers. Is love a
generation of vipers? Sweet lord, who's afield today?

PARIS Hector, Deiphobus, Helenus, Antenor, and all the
gallantry of Troy. I would fain have armed today, but my
Nell would not have it so. How chance my brother Troilus
went not?   130

HELEN He hangs the lip at something. You know all, Lord
Pandarus.

PANDARUS Not I, honey-sweet Queen. I long to hear how
they sped today. You'll remember your brother's excuse?

PARIS To a hair.

PANDARUS Farewell, sweet Queen.

HELEN Commend me to your niece.

PANDARUS I will, sweet Queen.   *Exit*
          Sound a retreat

PARIS
They're come from the field. Let us to Priam's hall
To greet the warriors. Sweet Helen, I must woo you   140
To help unarm our Hector. His stubborn buckles
With these your white enchanting fingers touched,
Shall more obey than to the edge of steel
Or force of Greekish sinews. You shall do more
Than all the island kings – disarm great Hector.

HELEN
'Twill make us proud to be his servant, Paris;
Yea, what he shall receive of us in duty
Gives us more palm in beauty than we have,
Yea, overshines ourself.

PARIS Sweet, above thought I love thee.   *Exeunt*   150

3.2   *Enter Pandarus and Troilus' Man, meeting*

PANDARUS How now! Where's thy master? At my cousin
Cressida's?

---

138 *Exit*] ROWE; *not in* QF   139 They're] F; Their Q   the field] fielde F   142 these] F;
this Q   150 PARIS] *not in* F   thee.] F; her? Q
   3.2.0.1 *Enter ... man*] F; *Enter. Pandarus Troylus, man* Q   *meeting*] CAPELL; *not in* QF

124 **generation** genealogy
126 **generation of vipers** Pandarus uses the
    Biblical phrase (Matthew 3: 7, where it
    means 'offspring' or 'race' of vipers).

135 **To a hair** to the last detail (Tilley H26)
143 **edge of steel** sword-blade
3.2 The garden of Cressida's house. It ap-
    pears from 1.2.260 that Pandarus and

MAN No, sir; he stays for you to conduct him thither.

    Enter Troilus

PANDARUS O, here he comes. How now, how now!

TROILUS Sirrah, walk off.   *Exit Man*

PANDARUS Have you seen my cousin?

TROILUS

  No, Pandarus; I stalk about her door,
  Like a strange soul upon the Stygian banks
  Staying for waftage. O, be thou my Charon,
  And give me swift transportance to those fields   10
  Where I may wallow in the lily beds
  Proposed for the deserver! O gentle Pandarus,
  From Cupid's shoulder pluck his painted wings,
  And fly with me to Cressid!

PANDARUS Walk here i'th' orchard; I'll bring her straight.

                                         Exit

---

3 he] F; *not in* Q   3.1 *Enter Troilus*] F; *not in* Q   5 *Exit Man*] KITTREDGE; *not in* QF; *Exit Servant* CAPELL   8 Like] F; Like to Q   10 those] F; these Q   12 Pandarus] F; Pandar Q   15.1 *Exit*] F (*subs.*); *not in* Q

Cressida are not living in the same house, but from 4.1 that the lovers meet at Calchas' house. At 4.3.5 it is referred to as 'her house'. Walker argues that the references are puzzling unless we assume that Pandarus' house adjoined Calchas', where Cressida is living. It may be mentioned that Chaucer's hero consummates his love in Pandarus' house. The audience would not be aware of any discrepancies.

Robert Boyle (*Englische Studien*, 30 (1902), 21–59) drew attention to several parallels with the corresponding scene in *Merchant* (3.2). Baldwin, in the New Variorum edition, added others, arguing that 'the rhetorical relationships tend to indicate that the passage in *Troilus and Cressida* represents the earlier stage'. Whatever we may think of Baldwin's dating, the parallels are striking. Compare l. 16 with *Merchant* 3.2.144 ('Giddy in spirit, still gazing in a doubt'); ll. 22–5 with *Merchant* ll. 111–14 ('O love, be moderate, allay thy ecstasy, | In measure rain thy joy, scant this excess! | I feel too much thy blessing. Make it less, | for fear I surfeit') and 177–84 ('Only my blood speaks to you in my veins; | And there is such confusion in my powers | As, after some oration fairly spoke | By a beloved

prince, there doth appear | Among the buzzing pleased multitude, | Where every something, being blent together, | Turns to a wild of nothing, save of joy | Express'd and not express'd'); and l. 51 with *Merchant* l. 176 ('Madam, you have bereft me of all words').

  9 **waftage** passage
 10 **transportance** conveyance (first occurrence)
 11 **wallow** 'befouling his Elysium with porcine lust' (Baldwin); and other critics have made similar remarks. But in Shakespeare's only other use of *wallow* (*Richard II*, 1.3.298), Bolingbroke speaks of wallowing in December snow, not exactly associated with lust.
   lily beds Baldwin suggests that these were derived from the Song of Solomon, Chaps. 2, 4, 6, 7, and that the general idea of the underworld and Elysium came from *Aeneid* VI, especially ll. 637–9.
 12 **Proposed for** promised to
 13 **Cupid's shoulder . . . wings** The idea of Pandarus wearing Cupid's wings is not, of course, wholly serious.
   painted as in a painting
 15 **orchard** garden (not necessarily with fruit trees)

TROILUS

    I am giddy. Expectation whirls me round.
    Th'imaginary relish is so sweet
    That it enchants my sense. What will it be
    When that the wat'ry palate tastes indeed
    Love's thrice repurèd nectar? – death, I fear me,   20
    Swooning destruction, or some joy too fine,
    Too subtle-potent, tuned too sharp in sweetness,
    For the capacity of my ruder powers.
    I fear it much, and I do fear besides
    That I shall lose distinction in my joys,
    As doth a battle, when they charge on heaps
    The enemy flying.

        Enter Pandarus

PANDARUS She's making her ready; she'll come straight.
    You must be witty now – she does so blush, and fetches her
    wind so short as if she were frayed with a sprite. I'll fetch   30
    her. It is the prettiest villain; she fetches her breath as
    short as a new-ta'en sparrow.   *Exit*

TROILUS

    Even such a passion doth embrace my bosom;
    My heart beats thicker than a feverous pulse;
    And all my powers do their bestowing lose,
    Like vassalage at unawares encountering
    The eye of majesty.

        Enter Pandarus, and Cressida, veiled

PANDARUS Come, come, what need you blush? Shame's a
    baby. (*To Troilus*) Here she is now. Swear the oaths now to
    her that you have sworn to me. (*To Cressida*) What, are   40
    you gone again? You must be watched ere you be made

19 palate tastes] HANMER; pallats taste QF   20 repurèd] reputed F   22 subtle-potent] THEO-
BALD; subtill, potent QF   tuned] and F   27.1 *Enter Pandarus*] F; *not in* Q   30 sprite] F; spirite
Q   31–2 as short] so short F   32 *Exit*] F (*Exit Pand⟨arus⟩.*); *not in* Q   36 unawares] F
(*corr.*); vnwares Q, F (*uncorr.*)   37.1 *veiled*] BEVINGTON; *not in* QF

16–27 **I am giddy . . . flying** See Introduction, p. 31.
19 **palate tastes** Most modern editors retain
the QF reading, but the plural seems awkward.
25 **distinction** capacity to discriminate, or
separate one joy from another
26 **battle** army
29 **be witty** keep your wits about you
30 **frayed with** frightened (from *affrayed*) by

31 **villain** Used playfully, as a term of endear-
ment, as 'rogue' often is in Restoration
comedy.
34 **thicker** faster
35 **bestowing** use
36 **vassalage** vassals, humble people.
Theseus makes the same point. *Dream*
5.1.93–9.
41 **watched** as hawks were tamed by
preventing them from sleeping

tame, must you? Come your ways, come your ways; an
you draw backward, we'll put you i'th' thills. (*To Troilus*)
Why do you not speak to her? Come, draw this curtain,
and let's see your picture. Alas the day, how loath you are
to offend daylight! An 'twere dark, you'd close sooner. So,
so; rub on, and kiss the mistress. How now! A kiss in fee-
farm! – Build there, carpenter; the air is sweet. Nay, you
shall fight your hearts out ere I part you – the falcon as the
tercel, for all the ducks i'th' river. Go to, go to.   50

TROILUS You have bereft me of all words, lady.

PANDARUS Words pay no debts, give her deeds; but she'll
bereave you o'th' deeds too, if she call your activity in
question. What, billing again? Here's 'In witness whereof
the parties interchangeably'. – Come in, come in; I'll go get
a fire.   *Exit*

CRESSIDA Will you walk in, my lord?

TROILUS

O Cressid, how often have I wished me thus!

CRESSIDA

Wished, my lord? The gods grant – O, my lord!

TROILUS What should they grant? What makes this pretty   60
abruption? What too curious dreg espies my sweet lady in
the fountain of our love?

CRESSIDA

More dregs than water, if my fears have eyes.

---

43 thills] This edition; filles QF   49 fight] sigh *conj.* KELLNER   56 *Exit*] F2 (*subs.*); *not in* Q, F1
58 Cressid] Cressida F   63 fears] ROWE 1709b; teares QF

---

43 **thills** shafts (QF *filles* is an obsolete
  variant.)
44 **curtain** Cressida's veil
45 **picture** alluding to the custom of hanging
  curtains before paintings
47 **rub** a term in bowls
  mistress a small ball in a game of bowls;
  balls are said to kiss when they touch
  gently (Nares, cited in New Variorum) (a
47–8 **A kiss in fee-farm** a prolonged kiss (a
  fee-farm being a grant of land in perpetu-
  ity)
48 **Build there, carpenter** Deighton cites
  Macbeth 1.6.1 ff. for the idea of building
  where the air is sweet, the martlet approv-
  ing. Pandarus means, perhaps, that the
  lovers will build a permanent relationship.

49 **fight your hearts out** 'love's wars' (Baldwin)
49–50 **falcon . . . river** 'Pandarus will bet all
  the ducks in the river that the falcon
  (female) is as eager as the tercel (male).'
  (Dobrée)
52 **Words pay . . . deeds** Tilley W820: 'Not
  words but deeds.'
53 **activity** virility
54–5 **In witness whereof the parties interchangeably** Pandarus is giving a garbled
  version of a betrothal ceremony.
56 **fire** to warm their bedroom, perhaps implying that the lovers need warming up
61 **abruption** breaking off (first occurrence)
  curious finicky, minute

TROILUS Fears make devils of cherubins; they never see truly.

CRESSIDA Blind fear, that seeing reason leads, finds safer footing than blind reason stumbling without fear. To fear the worst oft cures the worse.

TROILUS O, let my lady apprehend no fear; in all Cupid's pageant there is presented no monster.   70

CRESSIDA Nor nothing monstrous neither?

TROILUS Nothing but our undertakings, when we vow to weep seas, live in fire, eat rocks, tame tigers; thinking it harder for our mistress to devise imposition enough than for us to undergo any difficulty imposed. This is the monstruosity in love, lady – that the will is infinite and the execution confined; that the desire is boundless and the act a slave to limit.

CRESSIDA They say all lovers swear more performance than they are able, and yet reserve an ability that they never   80 perform; vowing more than the perfection of ten, and discharging less than the tenth part of one. They that have the voice of lions and the act of hares, are they not monsters?

TROILUS Are there such? Such are not we. Praise us as we are tasted, allow us as we prove. Our head shall go bare till merit crown it; no perfection in reversion shall have a praise in present. We will not name desert before his birth; and, being born, his addition shall be humble. Few words to fair faith – Troilus shall be such to Cressid as what envy   90

66 safer] safe F   71 Nor] Not F   75 This is] F: This Q   87 crown...perfection] F: louer part no affection Q

66–7 **To fear...worse** Tilley W912: 'It is good to fear the worst.'
70 **no monster** Spenser, however, describes many monstrous shapes in the masque of Cupid in *The Faerie Queene* III. xii.
72–5 **Nothing...imposed** (paraphrased by Cressida in her next speech)
75–6 **monstruosity** variant of monstrosity, but derived not from Latin but from the French *monstruosité*
78 **act** the sexual act, but with wider implications about human endeavour
79–80 **They say...able** Tilley L570: 'Lovers' vows are not to be trusted.'
81 **perfection** accomplishment (Onions)
83 **lions...hares** Proverbial contrast, as in

Erasmus, *Adagia*, under *Inconstantia* (Walker).
85–6 **Praise...prove** Tilley P83: 'Praise at parting.'
87 **perfection in reversion** accomplishment at some future date, as an estate may revert to a grantor (Clarkson and Warren, p. 72, cited in New Variorum)
89 **addition** title
89–90 **Few words to fair faith** Tilley W828: 'Where many words are the truth goes by.'
90–1 **as what envy...truth** 'even malice ...shall not be able to impeach his truth, or attack him in any other way except by ridiculing him for his constancy' (Malone)

can say worst shall be a mock for his truth; and what
truth can speak truest, not truer than Troilus.

CRESSIDA Will you walk in, my lord?

    Enter Pandarus

PANDARUS What, blushing still? Have you not done talking
yet?

CRESSIDA Well, uncle, what folly I commit, I dedicate to you.

PANDARUS I thank you for that. If my lord get a boy of you,
you'll give him me. Be true to my lord. If he flinch, chide
me for it.

TROILUS You know now your hostages – your uncle's word   100
and my firm faith.

PANDARUS Nay, I'll give my word for her too. Our kindred,
though they be long ere they are wooed, they are constant being won. They are burrs, I can tell you; they'll
stick where they are thrown.

CRESSIDA
Boldness comes to me now and brings me heart:
Prince Troilus, I have loved you night and day
For many weary months.

TROILUS
Why was my Cressid then so hard to win?

CRESSIDA
Hard to seem won; but I was won, my lord,   110
With the first glance that ever – pardon me;
If I confess much, you will play the tyrant.
I love you now; but not, till now, so much
But I might master it. In faith, I lie!
My thoughts were like unbridled children, grown
Too headstrong for their mother. See, we fools!
Why have I blabbed? Who shall be true to us,
When we are so unsecret to ourselves?
But, though I loved you well, I wooed you not;
And yet, good faith, I wished myself a man,   120
Or that we women had men's privilege

93.1 *Enter Pandarus*] F; *not in* Q   103 are wooed] F; bee wooed Q   111 glance that ever –
pardon] F2 (*subs.*); glance; that ever pardon Q, F1   113 not, till now] F; till now not Q   115
grown] grow F

98 **flinch** i.e. sexually
115 **unbridled** unrestrained
120 **I wished myself a man** Baldwin

compares *Othello*, 1.3.163 ('Yet she
wish'd | That heaven had made her such
a man.')

Of speaking first. Sweet, bid me hold my tongue;
For in this rapture I shall surely speak
The thing I shall repent. See, see, your silence,
Cunning in dumbness, from my weakness draws
My very soul of counsel! Stop my mouth.

TROILUS

And shall, albeit sweet music issues thence.

He kisses her

PANDARUS Pretty, i'faith.

CRESSIDA

My lord, I do beseech you, pardon me.
'Twas not my purpose thus to beg a kiss.   130
I am ashamed. O heavens! What have I done?
For this time will I take my leave, my lord.

TROILUS Your leave, sweet Cressid?

PANDARUS

Leave! An you take leave till tomorrow morning –

CRESSIDA

Pray you, content you.

TROILUS   What offends you, lady?

CRESSIDA

Sir, mine own company.

TROILUS   You cannot shun yourself.

CRESSIDA Let me go and try.
I have a kind of self resides with you,
But an unkind self that itself will leave
To be another's fool. I would be gone.   140
Where is my wit? I know not what I speak.

TROILUS

Well know they what they speak that speak so wisely.

---

125 Cunning] POPE; Comming QF   126 very ... counsell] soule of counsell from me F   127.1
He kisses her] ROWE (*subs.*); *not in* QF   134 morning –] F2 (*subs.*); morning. Q, F1   140–1
I ... speak.] Where is my wit? | I would be gone: I speake I know not what. F   142 that speak]
that speakes F

---

125 **Cunning** The emendation is generally
accepted. The word could easily be misread, and not corrected in F by oversight.
Greg, however (*Principles of Emendation*,
12), argued for the retention of *coming*,
on the grounds that Q and F agreed. He
wrote before the relationship between the

two texts had been clearly demonstrated.
139 **unkind** unnatural, quibbling on 'kind
of'
140 **fool** In reacting against her love for
Troilus, Cressida reverts to her feeling
that a woman who confesses her love
loses her dominance.

CRESSIDA

    Perchance, my lord, I show more craft than love,
    And fell so roundly to a large confession
    To angle for your thoughts; but you are wise,
    Or else you love not. For to be wise and love
    Exceeds man's might; that dwells with gods above.

TROILUS

    O that I thought it could be in a woman –
    As, if it can, I will presume in you –
    To feed for aye her lamp and flame of love;   150
    To keep her constancy in plight and youth,
    Outliving beauties outward, with a mind
    That doth renew swifter than blood decays!
    Or that persuasion could but thus convince me
    That my integrity and truth to you
    Might be affronted with the match and weight
    Of such a winnowed purity in love,
    How were I then uplifted! But, alas,
    I am as true as truth's simplicity,
    And simpler than the infancy of truth!   160

CRESSIDA

    In that I'll war with you.

TROILUS   O virtuous fight,
    When right with right wars who shall be most right!

---

150 aye] F; age Q   flame] WALKER (*conj.* TANNENBAUM); flames QF

144 **roundly** openly
    large whole-hearted
146 **Or else** These words seem to contradict
    the rest of the speech, unless we take
    them to mean 'in other words'. Cressida
    has fished for Troilus' thoughts, without
    success; and she concludes that he is too
    wise, or too cunning, to be caught, or else
    that he does not love her. This reminds
    her of the proverb, 'and she whimsically
    rounds off her sentence with, "for you
    know, you cannot both love *and* be wise."
    It is an admirable *non sequitur*' (Verity,
    quoted in New Variorum). Baldwin adds
    that 'The answering speech of Troilus is
    built on that paradox'.
147–8 **For to . . . above** Malone pointed out
    that the origin of this was *Amare et sapere
    vix deo conceditur* (included by Publilius
    Syrus, a writer of the age of Julius Caesar,

in his *Sententiae*; Tilley L558). Shakespeare could have taken it from Spenser's
Shepheards Calendar, March, 119–20.
150 **flame** As Walker points out, the sin-
    gular is more appropriate to the idea of
    constancy.
151 **To keep . . . youth** 'to preserve in all its
    freshness the constancy she has plighted'
    (Deighton)
152 **beauties outward** outward beauties; or
    perhaps we should read 'beauty's out-
    ward'
153 **blood** passion
156 **affronted** confronted, matched
159–60 **I am . . . truth** 'I am as true as Truth
    in its pristine state, and sincerer even
    than Truth in its infancy (before it
    became tarnished)'. Tilley T565: 'It is as
    true as truth itself.'
161 **war** compete

True swains in love shall in the world to come
Approve their truth by Troilus. When their rhymes,
Full of protest, of oath, and big compare,
Want similes, truth tired with iteration –
'As true as steel, as plantage to the moon,
As sun to day, as turtle to her mate,
As iron to adamant, as earth to th'centre' –
Yet, after all comparisons of truth,   170
As truth's authentic author to be cited,
'As true as Troilus' shall crown up the verse
And sanctify the numbers.

CRESSIDA   Prophet may you be!
If I be false, or swerve a hair from truth,
When time is old and hath forgot itself,
When waterdrops have worn the stones of Troy,
And blind oblivion swallowed cities up,
And mighty states characterless are grated
To dusty nothing, yet let memory,
From false to false, among false maids in love,   180
Upbraid my falsehood! When they've said, 'as false
As air, as water, wind or sandy earth,
As fox to lamb, as wolf to heifer's calf,
Pard to the hind, or stepdame to her son',
Yea, let them say, to stick the heart of falsehood,
'As false as Cressid'.

---

164 truth] truths F   166 Want] F2; Wants Q, F1   170 Yet] F: *not in* Q   175 and] F: or Q
182 wind or] as Winde, as F   183 as wolf] F: or Wolfe Q

163–96 **True swains . . . amen** The characters assume for a moment the roles they
afterwards became in legend. This 'ap-
pealed to what everybody knew was
going to be the story' (William Empson,
Seven Types of Ambiguity (1930), 265–6).
165 **compare** comparison
167 **As true as steel** proverbial (Tilley S840)
plantage vegetation. Farmer (in Johnson
and Steevens 1778, cited in New
Variorum) quoted R. Scot, *Discoverie of
Witchcraft* (1584), 169: 'the increase of
the moone maketh plants . . . frutefull: so
as in the full moone they are in best
strength, decaieng in the wane, and in

the conjunction doo utterlie wither and
vade'.
168 **turtle** turtle-dove (Tilley T624: 'As true
as turtle to her mate.')
169 **adamant** lode-stone
centre the point to which all things are
attracted
178 **characterless** leaving no mark behind
(Onions) (accent on the second syllable)
181–2 **false . . . as water** Tilley W86: 'As
false as ever water wet.'
184 **pard** leopard
185 **stick the heart** hit the centre of the tar-
get

PANDARUS Go to, a bargain made. Seal it, seal it. I'll be the
witness. Here I hold your hand; here my cousin's. If ever
you prove false one to another, since I have taken such
pains to bring you together, let all pitiful goers-between be   190
called to the world's end after my name – call them all
Pandars. Let all constant men be Troiluses, all false
women Cressids, and all brokers-between Pandars! Say
'Amen'.

TROILUS Amen.

CRESSIDA Amen.

PANDARUS Amen. Whereupon I will show you a chamber
with a bed: which bed, because it shall not speak of your
pretty encounters, press it to death. Away.

                         Exeunt Troilus and Cressida
And Cupid grant all tongue-tied maidens here   200
Bed, chamber, pander, to provide this gear!   *Exit*

3.3   *Flourish. Enter Agamemnon, Ulysses, Nestor, Diomedes,*
          Ajax, Menelaus, and Calchas

CALCHAS
    Now, princes, for the service I have done,
    Th'advantage of the time prompts me aloud
    To call for recompense. Appear it to your mind
    That, through the sight I bear in things to come,

190 pains] F; paine Q   198 with a bed: which bed] HANMER; which bed QF   199.1 *Exeunt*
... *Cressida*] CAPELL; *Exeunt* Q; *not in* F   201 pander] and Pander F   *Exit] Exeunt* F
    3.3.0.1 *Flourish*] F (*after 'Chalcas.'*); *not in* Q (*which reads 'Enter Vlisses, Diomed, Nestor,*
Agamem, Chalcas')   *Diomedes*] F; *Diomed* Q   0.2 *Ajax*] THEOBALD; *not in* QF   *Menelaus*]
F; *not in* Q   1 done] done you F   3 your] F; *not in* Q   mind] minds WALKER   4 come] F4;
loue QF

187–8 **I'll be . . . cousin's** Taking hands
    before a witness was a normal betrothal
    ceremony, and could be a valid marriage,
    though not, apparently, here.
188–92 **If ever . . . Pandars** Pandarus is
    referring only to his own name (Pandar).
198 **with a bed** Sisson, supporting Hanmer,
    suggested that the eye could jump from
    with to *which*, especially if both words
    were abbreviated. The eye, moreover,
    could easily jump from one bed to the
    other.
199 **press it to death** the punishment – *peine*
    forte et dure – legally imposed on those
    'who stood mute and would not plead'
    (*OED*)

200–1 **And Cupid . . . gear** Addressed di-
    rectly to the audience, and so undercut-
    ting the solemnity of the previous vow.
201 **gear** i.e. the room and bed
3.3.0.1 Theobald's order, adopted here, puts
    the General first.
2 **advantage . . . time** suitable opportunity
3 **mind** Walker's emendation, *minds*, is
    unnecessary. Calchas can turn to
    Agamemnon, or address the collective
    mind of the Greek leaders.
4 **come** This emendation 'fits the occasion
    as detailed in the sources' (New
    Variorum), and, as Tannenbaum (76)
    says, could easily be misread as *loue*.

I have abandoned Troy, left my possessions,
Incurred a traitor's name, exposed myself
From certain and possessed conveniences,
To doubtful fortunes; sequest'ring from me all
That time, acquaintance, custom and condition
Made tame and most familiar to my nature;   10
And here, to do you service, am become
As new into the world, strange, unacquainted.
I do beseech you, as in way of taste,
To give me now a little benefit
Out of those many registered in promise,
Which, you say, live to come in my behalf.

AGAMEMNON
What wouldst thou of us, Trojan? Make demand.

CALCHAS
You have a Trojan prisoner called Antenor,
Yesterday took. Troy holds him very dear.
Oft have you – often have you thanks therefore –   20
Desired my Cressid in right great exchange,
Whom Troy hath still denied; but this Antenor
I know is such a wrest in their affairs,
That their negotiations all must slack,
Wanting his manage; and they will almost
Give us a prince of blood, a son of Priam,
In change of him. Let him be sent, great princes,
And he shall buy my daughter; and her presence
Shall quite strike off all service I have done
In most accepted pain.

AGAMEMNON   Let Diomedes bear him,   30
And bring us Cressid hither; Calchas shall have
What he requests of us. Good Diomed,
Furnish you fairly for this interchange;

---

5 possessions] CAPELL; possession QF

5 **possessions** As F is not a check on Q in this passage, the emendation is a permissible improvement.
9 **condition** position
13 **as in way of taste** as a foretaste
16 **live to come** wait to be fulfilled
23 **wrest** tuning-key; 'that upon which the harmonious ordering of their affairs

depends' (Deighton, citing Cowden Clarke)
25 **manage** management
27 **change of** exchange for
30 **most accepted pain** trouble willingly endured (or, less probably, cordially accepted by the Greeks)

Withal bear word that Hector will tomorrow
Be answered in his challenge. Ajax is ready.

DIOMEDES

This shall I undertake, and 'tis a burden
Which I am proud to bear.   *Exeunt Diomedes and Calchas*
          Enter Achilles and Patroclus, in the entrance of
          their tent

ULYSSES

Achilles stands i'th' entrance of his tent.
Please it our general pass strangely by him,
As if he were forgot; and, princes all,   40
Lay negligent and loose regard upon him.
I will come last. 'Tis like he'll question me
Why such unplausive eyes are bent, why turned on him.
If so, I have derision medicinable
To use between your strangeness and his pride,
Which his own will shall have desire to drink.
It may do good. Pride hath no other glass
To show itself but pride; for supple knees
Feed arrogance and are the proud man's fees.

AGAMEMNON

We'll execute your purpose and put on   50
A form of strangeness as we pass along;

---

34 bear word that] This edition; bring word If QF   37 *Exeunt ... Calchas*] CAPELL; *Exit* QF
37.1–2 *Enter ... tent*] This edition; Achilles *and* Patro. *stand in their tent* Q; *Enter* Achilles *and*
Patroclus *in their Tent* F   39 pass] to passe F

34 **bear word that** Although editors have
not commented on the QF reading at this
point, it would appear to be one of the
places where the absence of a separate F
reading has allowed a Q error to stand.
Diomedes cannot discover in Troy if Hector will be answered in his challenge; and
it would seem that *that* (y^t) was misread
as *yf* and that *bring* was copied inadvertently from 31.

37.1 **in the entrance of their tent** Probably
Achilles and Patroclus stand at the
entrance to the tiring-house, under the
balcony, or in a tent erected on the stage.

39 **strangely** as if we were strangers

41 **loose** casual

43 **unplausive** unapproving (first occurrence)
     bent It seems possible that the words
bent and *turn'd* were alternatives, one or

other intended as a replacement. Greg,
however (*Principles of Emendation*, 36),
argued against the extrusion of 'why
turned'.

44 **derision medicinable** As Deighton points
out, 'nothing is less like derision in its
ordinary sense than the line which
Ulysses takes'. Although Baldwin argues
that the 'strangeness of the Princes is the
derision', surely the words 'if so' imply
that Ulysses' derision is to follow, not
precede, Achilles' question.

45 **use between** act as a go-between
     strangeness Compare *strangely*, l. 39.

47–9 **Pride hath . . . fees** Our proud
behaviour will teach Achilles that he is
proud, whereas our meekness would
make him worse.

49 **fees** reward

So do each lord, and either greet him not
Or else disdainfully, which shall shake him more
Than if not looked on. I will lead the way.

ACHILLES (*to Patroclus*)

What, comes the general to speak with me?
You know my mind – I'll fight no more 'gainst Troy.

AGAMEMNON (*to Nestor*)

What says Achilles? Would he aught with us?

NESTOR Would you, my lord, aught with the general?

ACHILLES No.

NESTOR Nothing, my lord.   60

AGAMEMNON The better.   *Exeunt Agamemnon and Nestor*

ACHILLES (*to Menelaus*) Good day, good day.

MENELAUS How do you? How do you?   *Exit*

ACHILLES What! Does the cuckold scorn me?

AJAX How now, Patroclus!

ACHILLES Good morrow, Ajax.

AJAX Ha!

ACHILLES Good morrow.

AJAX Ay, and good next day too.   *Exit*

ACHILLES

What mean these fellows? Know they not Achilles?   70

PATROCLUS

They pass by strangely. They were used to bend,
To send their smiles before them to Achilles,
To come as humbly as they used to creep
To holy altars.

ACHILLES   What, am I poor of late?
'Tis certain, greatness, once fall'n out with fortune,
Must fall out with men too. What the declined is
He shall as soon read in the eyes of others
As feel in his own fall; for men, like butterflies,
Show not their mealy wings but to the summer,
And not a man, for being simply man,   80

---

61 *Exeunt . . . Nestor*] CAPELL; *not in* QF   63 *Exit*] CAPELL; *not in* QF   69 *Exit*] CAPELL; *Exeunt* QF

59–67 No . . . **Ha!** (possibly verse, divided 59–62, 63–4, 65–7)

69 *Exit* Either here or during the next two speeches Ulysses starts reading a book.

73 **used** W. S. Walker's conjecture *use*, adopted by Dyce 1864 and Hudson 1881, is attractive, but not strictly necessary.

74–6 **What, am I . . . too** Carter cites Ecclesiasticus 13: 22: 'If a rich man fall, his friends set him up again, but when the poor falleth, his friends drive him away'.

79 **mealy** powdery

Hath any honour but honour for those honours
That are without him – as place, riches, and favour,
Prizes of accident as oft as merit;
Which, when they fall, as being slippery standers,
The love that leaned on them, as slippery too,
Doth one pluck down another, and together
Die in the fall. But 'tis not so with me:
Fortune and I are friends; I do enjoy
At ample point all that I did possess,
Save these men's looks; who do, methinks, find out   90
Something not worth in me such rich beholding
As they have often given. Here is Ulysses.
I'll interrupt his reading.
How now, Ulysses!
ULYSSES   Now, great Thetis' son!
ACHILLES
What are you reading?
ULYSSES   A strange fellow here
Writes me that man, how dearly ever parted,
How much in having, or without or in,
Cannot make boast to have that which he hath,
Nor feels not what he owes, but by reflection;
As when his virtues, shining upon others,   100

---

81 but honour] but honour'd F   100 shining] F; ayming Q

82 **place, riches, and favour** Seneca, *Letters
   to Lucilius*, trans. E. P. Barker (2 vols,
   Oxford, 1932, i. 280), cited in New
   Variorum, makes the same triple division,
   as Baldwin points out: 'Money will come
   unsought, official distinction will be set in
   your way, rank and popularity will perhaps be thrust on you: virtue will never
   fall into your lap'.
83 **of accident** come by chance
86 **Doth one** i.e. one doth
89 **At ample point** to the full (Onions)
95 **A strange fellow** The identity of this
   author has been much debated – as much
   as the satirical rogue quoted by Hamlet
   (2.2.195 ff.). R.G. White (*Studies in Shakespeare* (1886), 298) followed by J. Chur-
   ton Collins (*Studies in Shakespeare* (1904),
   33–5) argued on the strength of a parallel
   with the *First Alcibiades* (Section 133)
   that the strange fellow was Plato. J. M.
   Robertson (*Montaigne and Shakespeare*
   (1909), 97 ff.) retorted that the parallel

was not with Ulysses' speech, but with
that of Achilles. He argued that the idea
that the eye could not see itself except by
reflection was a commonplace, to be
found in, e.g., Davies' *Nosce Teipsum*,
Cicero's *Tusculans* (trans. Dolman), and
Montaigne. Steevens had earlier cited a
parallel with Marston's *The Fawn* (ed.
David A. Blostein, Manchester, 1978:
'The eye sees all things but his proper
self', 4.4.565). As Shakespeare is known
to have read Davies' poem and Dolman's
translation (entitled *Those Fyve Questions*)
one of these may be the immediate
source, but it is unlikely that Shakespeare
had any particular author in mind. Dolman (sig. E6ᵛ) reads: 'the soule is not able
in this bodye to see him selfe. No more is
the eye whyche although he seeth all
other thinges, (that whiche is one of the
leaste) can not discerne his owne shape'.
96 **parted** endowed with parts or qualities
99 **owes** owns

Heat them and they retort that heat again
To the first giver.
ACHILLES   This is not strange, Ulysses.
The beauty that is borne here in the face
The bearer knows not, but commends itself
To others' eyes; nor doth the eye itself,
That most pure spirit of sense, behold itself,
Not going from itself; but eye to eye opposed
Salutes each other with each other's form;
For speculation turns not to itself
Till it hath travelled and is mirrored there   110
Where it may see itself. This is not strange at all.
ULYSSES
I do not strain at the position –
It is familiar – but at the author's drift;
Who in his circumstance expressly proves
That no man is the lord of anything,
Though in and of him there be much consisting,
Till he communicate his parts to others;
Nor doth he of himself know them for aught
Till he behold them formèd in th'applause
Where they're extended; who, like an arch, reverb'rate   120
The voice again; or, like a gate of steel
Fronting the sun, receives and renders back
His figure and his heat. I was much rapt in this,
And apprehended here immediately
The unknown Ajax. Heavens! What a man is there!

---

102 giver] F; giuers Q   105–6 To ... itself] *not in* F   110 mirrored] SINGER (*see Commentary note*);   married QF   112 at] it at F   115 man] may F   116 be] is F   119 th'applause] F; the applause Q   120 they're] Q (th'are); they are F   125 The] F; Th' Q

105–7 **nor doth the eye ... behold itself** proverbial (Tilley E231a)
106 **That most ... sense** See 1.1.57 n.
110 **mirrored** This emendation, made anonymously by hand in a copy of F2, is generally accepted. The word 'mirroring' was used by Nashe, *Christ's Tears over Jerusalem* (1593), ed. McKerrow, ii. 76.15.
112 **strain at** object to
114 **circumstance** discourse, context
115–23 **That no man ... heat** Walker cites Erasmus, *Adagia*, 'occultae musices nullus respectus', with his commentary:

'however much you are endowed with extraordinary talents, if you don't display them it is just as though you did not have them'. Compare *Measure*, 1.1.35–6.
119 **applause** Ulysses is concerned merely with popularity, not with desert.
120 **extended** displayed
who Used, as frequently, for *which*.
reverb'rate The applause is thought of as plural because it is given by many people.
121 **gate of steel** a door plated with polished steel (New Variorum)
125–7 **The unknown ... are** Tannenbaum (*Critique*, 133), noting the short line and

A very horse, that has he knows not what.
Nature, what things there are
Most abject in regard and dear in use!
What things again most dear in the esteem
And poor in worth! Now shall we see tomorrow –   130
An act that very chance doth throw upon him –
Ajax renowned. O heavens, what some men do,
While some men leave to do!
How some men creep in skittish Fortune's hall,
Whiles others play the idiots in her eyes!
How one man eats into another's pride,
While pride is fasting in his wantonness!
To see these Grecian lords! Why, even already
They clap the lubber Ajax on the shoulder,
As if his foot were on brave Hector's breast   140
And great Troy shrieking.

ACHILLES

I do believe it; for they passed by me
As misers do by beggars, neither gave to me
Good word nor look. What, are my deeds forgot?

ULYSSES

Time hath, my lord, a wallet at his back,
Wherein he puts alms for oblivion,

---

128 abject] F; obiect Q   137 fasting] feasting F   140 on] F; one Q   141 shrieking] Q
(shriking); shrinking F

alexandrine in F, suggested that these
lines were the result of a marginal substitution. The Q arrangement, here
followed, is more satisfactory; and Tannenbaum's complaint that 125 is
unmetrical is unjustified – 'Heavens' is
monosyllabic.

126 **that has he knows not what** who is ignorant of himself
131 **chance** But since the ballot was rigged,
Ajax was not chosen by chance.
134 **creep** i.e. without drawing attention to
themselves
135 **Whiles others . . . eyes** While others
attract the attention of Fortune, even by
behaving absurdly. Walker, however,
believes that 134 refers to Ajax, 135 to
Achilles.
137 **fasting** 'One man eats, while another
fasts. Achilles . . . capriciously abstains

from those active exertions which would
furnish new food for his pride' (Malone,
quoted in New Variorum). Ajax is eating
into Achilles' pride.
137 **wantonness** perversity
141 **shrieking** Those who support this reading (Q) compare 5.3.84–5, where roars,
cries and dolours shrilled forth accom-
pany the fall of Troy. Those who support
the F reading say that Hector and Troy
'would shrink under the blow of Ajax;
they would not shriek' (Baldwin).
145–80 **Time hath . . . object** See Introduction, p. 27.
145 **Time hath . . . a wallet at his back** A
commonplace, derived ultimately from
Phaedrus, but found in Erasmus' *Adagia*,
Spenser's *Faerie Queene* (VI. viii. 23–4),
and elsewhere.
wallet satchel

A great-sized monster of ingratitude.
Those scraps are good deeds past, which are devoured
As fast as they are made, forgot as soon
As done. Perseverance, dear my lord,   150
Keeps honour bright; to have done is to hang
Quite out of fashion, like a rusty mail
In monumental mock'ry. Take the instant way;
For honour travels in a strait so narrow
Where one but goes abreast. Keep then the path;
For emulation hath a thousand sons
That one by one pursue. If you give way,
Or hedge aside from the direct forthright,
Like to an entered tide they all rush by
And leave you hindmost;   160
Or, like a gallant horse fall'n in first rank,
Lie there for pavement to the abject rear,
O'errun and trampled on. Then what they do in present,
Though less than yours in past, must o'ertop yours;
For Time is like a fashionable host
That slightly shakes his parting guest by th'hand
And, with his arms outstretched as he would fly,
Grasps in the comer. Welcome ever smiles,

147 ingratitude] HANMER; ingratitudes QF   155 one] F; on Q   158 hedge] F; turne Q   160
hindmost] F; him, most Q   161–3 Or . . . on] F; *not in* Q   162 abject rear] HANMER; abiect,
neere F   164 past] F; passe Q   168 Welcome] POPE; the welcome QF

147 **monster** i.e. Time (not oblivion)
ingratitude Although Foxe, *Acts*, ed.
1570, ii. 2042, writes of an archbishop
'casting into the satchell behinde hym all
those Syr *Iohn* Gostewickes ingratitudes'
(cited in New Variorum) the singular was
more usual. Jonson, in *Every Man in his
Humour* (revised version, 3.3.57), has
'monster of ingratitude' (Walker); and
Lear compares ingratitude to a sea monster (1.4.261).
148–50 **Those scraps . . . lord** The mislin-
eation in QF may indicate that there were
marginal alterations; 'soon | As done' is
an awkward enjambement and 150 is a
short line. Perhaps some words have
dropped out, e.g. '(As) they are (done)', as
Dyce suggested.
153 **monumental mock'ry** Walker takes this
to mean 'mocking commemoration'.
Riverside explains 'a suit of armour
grown rusty from disuse set up as a mocking trophy of past action'. Possibly there

was a link between this and the monu-
ments of dead soldiers in churches. The
armour of the Black Prince still hangs in
Canterbury Cathedral.
153 **instant** quickest
154 **strait** narrow path. Noble cites Matthew
7: 14 'Because strait is the gate, and narrow is the way which leadeth unto life',
and he argues for the spelling *straight* (i.e.
'a straight path so narrow').
158 **hedge** go aside from the straight way
(*OED v.* 9)
forthright strait path (not previously
recorded in this sense)
161–3 **Or, like . . . on** These lines may have
been intended for cancellation (Walker).
The rest of 163 joins smoothly with 160.
166 **slightly** casually, slightingly
168 **Welcome** As Walker rightly says, 'The
restoration of the article by recent editors
spoils the personification'. Malone suggested that 'the' was inadvertently
repeated by the compositor.

And Farewell goes out sighing. O, let not virtue seek
Remuneration for the thing it was;   170
For beauty, wit,
High birth, vigour of bone, desert in service,
Love, friendship, charity, are subjects all
To envious and calumniating Time.
One touch of nature makes the whole world kin –
That all with one consent praise new-born gauds,
Though they are made and moulded of things past,
And give to dust that is a little gilt
More laud than gilt o'er-dusted.
The present eye praises the present object: 180
Then marvel not, thou great and complete man,
That all the Greeks begin to worship Ajax;
Since things in motion sooner catch the eye
Than what not stirs. The cry went once on thee,
And still it might, and yet it may again,
If thou wouldst not entomb thyself alive
And case thy reputation in thy tent,
Whose glorious deeds but in these fields of late
Made emulous missions 'mongst the gods themselves,
And drave great Mars to faction.

ACHILLES   Of this my privacy   190
    I have strong reasons.

ULYSSES   But 'gainst your privacy
    The reasons are more potent and heroical.
    'Tis known, Achilles, that you are in love
    With one of Priam's daughters.

ACHILLES   Ha! Known?

ULYSSES   Is that a wonder?
    The providence that's in a watchful state

---

169 Farewell] farewels F   O] F; *not in* Q   173 subjects] subject WALKER   178 give] THEOBALD
(*conj.* THIRLBY); goe QF   183 sooner] begin to F   184 Than ... stirs] F; That what stirs not Q
once] out F

---

176 **gauds** toys, trifles
181 **complete** (accent on the first syllable)
189–90 **Made emulous ... faction** 'the des-
    cent of deities to combat on either side'
    (Steevens). Although the incident to
    which he refers was not included in the
    books translated by Chapman at this
    time, the knowledge would be widely

disseminated.
194 **one of Priam's daughters** Polyxena.
    Shakespeare here departs from Caxton's
    account (ii. 620 ff.) which tells how
    Achilles first met Polyxena on the anni-
    versary of Hector's death.
195 **providence** foresight; but see 202 n.

Knows almost every grain of Pluto's gold,
Finds bottom in th'uncomprehensive deeps,
Keeps place with thought and almost like the gods
Does thoughts unveil in their dumb cradles.
There is a mystery, with whom relation   200
Durst never meddle, in the soul of state,
Which hath an operation more divine
Than breath or pen can give expressure to.
All the commerce that you have had with Troy
As perfectly is ours as yours, my lord;
And better would it fit Achilles much
To throw down Hector than Polyxena.
But it must grieve young Pyrrhus now at home,
When fame shall in our islands sound her trump,
And all the Greekish girls shall tripping sing: 210
'Great Hector's sister did Achilles win,
But our great Ajax bravely beat down him.'
Farewell, my lord. I as your lover speak.
The fool slides o'er the ice that you should break.   *Exit*

PATROCLUS

To this effect, Achilles, have I moved you.
A woman impudent and mannish grown
Is not more loathed than an effeminate man
In time of action. I stand condemned for this:
They think my little stomach to the war
And your great love to me restrains you thus.   220
Sweet, rouse yourself, and the weak wanton Cupid
Shall from your neck unloose his amorous fold

---

196 every ... gold] F; euery thing Q   197 th'] F; the Q   deeps] F; depth Q   199 Does] F2;
Do Q, F1   209 our islands] her Iland F   214 *Exit*] POPE; *not in* QF

196 **Pluto's** Pluto, the god of the underworld,
    and Plutus, the god of wealth, were
    frequently confused or identified, even in
    classical times.
197 **uncomprehensive** illimitable (Onions)
    (first occurrence)
199 **in their dumb cradles** before they are
    spoken. Various halting attempts have
    been made to mend the metre.
200 **relation** report
202 **divine** This epithet fits the confusion
    of theology and political theory apparent

in Ulysses' earlier oration in 1.3.
203 **expressure** expression; used by Shake-
    speare in *Merry Wives* (5.5.73) and
    Twelfth Night (2.3.147).
208 **Pyrrhus** Achilles' son, who came to
    Troy later
213 **lover** friend
214 **The fool ... break** Walker cites Eras-
    mus, *Adagia, 'scindere glaciem'*, 'break the
    ice'.
    fool i.e. Ajax
216 **impudent** shameless (possibly Lesbian)

And, like a dew-drop from the lion's mane,
Be shook to air.
ACHILLES   Shall Ajax fight with Hector?
PATROCLUS
Ay, and perhaps receive much honour by him.
ACHILLES
I see my reputation is at stake;
My fame is shrewdly gored.
PATROCLUS   O, then, beware;
Those wounds heal ill that men do give themselves.
Omission to do what is necessary
Seals a commission to a blank of danger;   230
And danger, like an ague, subtly taints
Even then when we sit idly in the sun.
ACHILLES
Go call Thersites hither, sweet Patroclus;
I'll send the fool to Ajax and desire him
T'invite the Trojan lords after the combat
To see us here unarmed. I have a woman's longing,
An appetite that I am sick withal,
To see great Hector in his weeds of peace,
To talk with him, and to behold his visage,
Even to my full of view.
            Enter Thersites
                         A labour saved!   240
THERSITES A wonder!
ACHILLES What?
THERSITES Ajax goes up and down the field, asking for
    himself.
ACHILLES How so?

223 a] F; *not in* Q   224 air] *ayrie ayre* F   232 we] F; they Q   240 *Enter Thersites*] WHITE
1883; *after* 'saved' Q; *after l. 238* F

224 **air** Although 'ayrie ayre' has had some
     defenders, it seems likely that *ayre* was
     meant to replace a word misread as *ayrie*.
228 **Those wounds . . . themselves** Aphor-
     istic, but not recorded as a proverb.
230 **Seals . . . danger** i.e. gives danger a
     blank cheque
231–2 **danger . . . sun** Two ideas seem to be
     combined here – of suffering from an
     ague, and of meat going bad if left in the
     sun. The combination was helped by the

belief that agues could be caused by sitting in the sun in March. Compare *1*
Henry IV, 4.1.111–12.
234 **the fool** Thersites is, among other
     things, a professional fool.
236 **a woman's longing** i.e. like the fanciful
     cravings of pregnant women
239 **behold his visage** (which he could not do
     when Hector was wearing armour)
243–4 **for himself** i.e. for a jakes (privy)

THERSITES He must fight singly tomorrow with Hector, and
is so prophetically proud of an heroical cudgelling that he
raves in saying nothing.

ACHILLES How can that be?

THERSITES Why, a stalks up and down like a peacock – a   250
stride and a stand; ruminates like an hostess that hath no
arithmetic but her brain to set down her reckoning; bites
his lip with a politic regard, as who should say 'There were
wit in this head, an 'twould out' – and so there is; but it lies
as coldly in him as fire in a flint, which will not show
without knocking. The man's undone for ever, for if Hector
break not his neck i'th' combat he'll break't himself in vain-
glory. He knows not me. I said 'Good morrow, Ajax,' and
he replies 'Thanks, Agamemnon.' What think you of this
man, that takes me for the general? He's grown a very   260
land-fish, languageless, a monster. A plague of opinion! A
man may wear it on both sides, like a leather jerkin.

ACHILLES Thou must be my ambassador to him, Thersites.

THERSITES Who, I? Why, he'll answer nobody. He professes
not answering. Speaking is for beggars; he wears his
tongue in's arms. I will put on his presence. Let Patroclus
make demands to me, you shall see the pageant of
Ajax.

ACHILLES To him, Patroclus. Tell him I humbly desire the
valiant Ajax to invite the most valorous Hector to come   270
unarmed to my tent, and to procure safe-conduct for his
person of the magnanimous and most illustrious six-or-
seven-times-honoured captain-general of the Grecian
army, Agamemnon, et cetera. Do this.

PATROCLUS Jove bless great Ajax!

THERSITES 'Hum!'

PATROCLUS I come from the worthy Achilles –

250 a stalks] he stalkes F   254 this] his F   263 to him] F; *not in* Q   267 demands] his
demands F   270 most] F; *not in* Q   273 Grecian] F; *not in* Q   274 et cetera] F; *not in* Q

252 **arithmetic** a book or calculator
255 **fire in a flint** Tilley F371: 'In the coldest
flint there is hot fire.'
261 **land-fish** 'a fish that lives on land; hence
an unnatural creature' (*OED*)
of on
262 **A man . . . jerkin** Referring to the low

opinion people had of Ajax before he was
chosen to fight with Hector, contrasted
with their present adulation.
264–5 **professes not** does not regard as his
job
266 **put on** perform

THERSITES 'Ha!'

PATROCLUS Who most humbly desires you to invite Hector
to his tent –   280

THERSITES 'Hum!'

PATROCLUS And to procure safe-conduct from Agamemnon.

THERSITES 'Agamemnon?'

PATROCLUS Ay, my lord.

THERSITES 'Ha!'

PATROCLUS What say you to't?

THERSITES 'God buy you, with all my heart.'

PATROCLUS Your answer, sir?

THERSITES 'If tomorrow be a fair day, by eleven o'clock it will
go one way or other. Howsoever, he shall pay for me ere   290
he has me.'

PATROCLUS Your answer, sir?

THERSITES 'Fare you well, with all my heart.'

ACHILLES
Why, but he is not in this tune, is he?

THERSITES No, but out o'tune thus. What music will be in
him when Hector has knocked out his brains, I know not;
but, I am sure, none, unless the fiddler Apollo get his
sinews to make catlings on.

ACHILLES
Come, thou shalt bear a letter to him straight.

THERSITES Let me carry another to his horse; for that's the   300
more capable creature.

ACHILLES
My mind is troubled like a fountain stirred,
And I myself see not the bottom of it.

> *Exeunt Achilles and Patroclus*

THERSITES Would the fountain of your mind were clear
again, that I might water an ass at it! I had rather be a tick
in a sheep than such a valiant ignorance.   *Exit*

---

289 o'clock] F (a clocke); of the clock Q   293 you] F; yee Q   295 out] he's out F   o'] F (a); of
Q   300 carry] F; beare Q   303.1 *Exeunt ... Patroclus*] CAPELL; *not in* QF   306 *Exit*] CAPELL;
not in QF; *Exeunt* ROWE

---

287 **buy** A corruption of 'be with', confused
with *buy*, meaning 'redeem' (Cercignani,
365).

298 **catlings** strings for musical instruments,
made of catgut

4.1 *Enter, at one door, Aeneas and a torchbearer; at another,*
Paris, Deiphobus, Antenor, Diomedes, and others, with
torches

PARIS See, ho! Who is that there?

DEIPHOBUS It is the Lord Aeneas.

AENEAS Is the Prince there in person?
　　Had I so good occasion to lie long
　　As you, Prince Paris, nothing but heavenly business
　　Should rob my bed-mate of my company.

DIOMEDES
　　That's my mind too. Good morrow, Lord Aeneas.

PARIS
　　A valiant Greek, Aeneas – take his hand –
　　Witness the process of your speech, wherein
　　You told how Diomed, a whole week by days,　　　　　10
　　Did haunt you in the field.

AENEAS　　　　　　　　　　Health to you, valiant sir,
　　During all question of the gentle truce;
　　But when I meet you armed, as black defiance
　　As heart can think or courage execute.

DIOMEDES
　　The one and other Diomed embraces.
　　Our bloods are now in calm; and so long, health!
　　But when contention and occasion meet,
　　By Jove, I'll play the hunter for thy life
　　With all my force, pursuit, and policy.

AENEAS
　　And thou shalt hunt a lion, that will fly　　　　　20
　　With his face backward. In humane gentleness,
　　Welcome to Troy! Now, by Anchises' life,
　　Welcome indeed! By Venus' hand I swear

4.1.0.1 *and a torchbearer*] This edition; *not in* Q; *with a Torch* F 0.2 *Diomedes, and others*]
CAPELL (*subs.*); *Diomed the Grecian* QF 5 you] F; your Q 9 wherein] within F 10 a] in a F
17 But] F; Lul'd Q meet] meetes F

4.1 A street in Troy.
0.3 *torches* (to indicate it is before dawn)
9 **process** gist
10 **a whole week by days** every day for a
　　week
17 **But** Q's *Lul'd* suggests that a line, begin-
　　ning with this word, has dropped out.

17 **when contention and occasion meet**
　　when it is time for fighting
21 **humane** This word and 'human' were
　　spelt the same.
22–3 **Anchises . . . Venus** the parents of
　　Aeneas

No man alive can love in such a sort
The thing he means to kill more excellently.

DIOMEDES

We sympathize. Jove, let Aeneas live,
If to my sword his fate be not the glory,
A thousand complete courses of the sun!
But, in mine emulous honour, let him die
With every joint a wound, and that tomorrow.   30

AENEAS We know each other well.

DIOMEDES

We do; and long to know each other worse.

PARIS

This is the most despiteful-gentle greeting,
The noblest-hateful love that e'er I heard of.
What business, lord, so early?

AENEAS

I was sent for to the King; but why, I know not.

PARIS

His purpose meets you. 'Twas to bring this Greek
To Calchas' house, and there to render him,
For the enfreed Antenor, the fair Cressid.
Let's have your company or, if you please,   40
Haste there before us. (*Aside to Aeneas*) I constantly do
        think –
Or rather, call my thought a certain knowledge –
My brother Troilus lodges there tonight.
Rouse him and give him note of our approach,
With the whole quality wherefore. I fear
We shall be much unwelcome.

AENEAS (*aside to Paris*)   That I assure you;
Troilus had rather Troy were borne to Greece
Than Cressid borne from Troy.

PARIS (*aside to Aeneas*)   There is no help;
The bitter disposition of the time
Will have it so. – On, lord, we'll follow you.   50

AENEAS Good morrow all.   *Exit, with torchbearer*

---

30 tomorrow.] F; to morrow – Q   33 despiteful] despightful'st F   37 'Twas] it was F
38 Calchas'] F (*Calcha's*); *Calcho's* Q   41 do think] F; beleeue Q   45 wherefore] whereof F
51 *Exit, with torchbearer*] DYCE (*subs.*); *not in* Q; *Exit.* F

26 **sympathize** agree   51 As Aeneas came in with a torchbearer, he
45 **quality** cause (Onions)   should go out with him.

PARIS

And tell me, noble Diomed, faith tell me true,
Even in the soul of sound good-fellowship,
Who, in your thoughts, deserves fair Helen best,
Myself or Menelaus?

DIOMEDES   Both alike.

He merits well to have her that doth seek her,
Not making any scruple of her soil,
With such a hell of pain and world of charge;
And you as well to keep her that defend her,
Not palating the taste of her dishonour,   60
With such a costly loss of wealth and friends.
He, like a puling cuckold, would drink up
The lees and dregs of a flat tamed piece;
You, like a lecher, out of whorish loins
Are pleased to breed out your inheritors.
Both merits poised, each weighs nor less nor more;
But he as he, the heavier for a whore.

PARIS

You are too bitter to your countrywoman.

DIOMEDES

She's bitter to her country. Hear me, Paris;
For every false drop in her bawdy veins   70
A Grecian's life hath sunk; for every scruple
Of her contaminated carrion weight
A Trojan hath been slain; since she could speak,
She hath not given so many good words breath
As for her Greeks and Trojans suffered death.

PARIS

Fair Diomed, you do as chapmen do,

53 the] F: *not in* Q   54 deserves . . . best] merits . . . most F   57 soil] soylure F   66 nor less]
no lesse F   67 the] which F: each *conj.* HEATH

54 **deserves . . . best** Both readings may be
authorial, but *merits* may be an anticipation of 56. See Walker, *Textual
Problems*, 80. She prefers F.
57 **soil** Although 'soylure' fits the diction of
the play, Shakespeare may have changed
it to avoid the 'unfortunate tripping effect' (Honigmann, *Stability*, 92) of a
sequence of words with a stress on the
first syllable.
58 **charge** expense
63 **flat** stale (of drink)

63 **tamed** pierced, broached (*OED* tame *v.*²;
aphetic form of *attame*, used especially of
casks and bottles)
piece cask of wine (*OED sb.* 5); probably
playing on 'piece of flesh', contemptuous-
ly.
67 **the** Heath's conjecture, as Walker says, is
'very tempting', and it could be misread as
which; but as 'each' is used in 66, the
meaning is perfectly clear without the
repetition.
77 **chapmen** traders, shopkeepers

Dispraise the thing that you desire to buy;
But we in silence hold this virtue well,
We'll not commend what we intend to sell.
Here lies our way.   *Exeunt*   80

4.2   *Enter Troilus and Cressida*

TROILUS

Dear, trouble not yourself; the morn is cold.

CRESSIDA

Then, sweet my lord, I'll call mine uncle down;
He shall unbolt the gates.

TROILUS   Trouble him not.
To bed, to bed! Sleep kill those pretty eyes,
And give as soft attachment to thy senses
As infants' empty of all thought!

CRESSIDA   Good morrow, then.

TROILUS

I prithee now, to bed!

CRESSIDA   Are you aweary of me?

TROILUS

O Cressida! But that the busy day,
Waked by the lark, hath roused the ribald crows,
And dreaming night will hide our joys no longer,   10
I would not from thee.

CRESSIDA   Night hath been too brief.

TROILUS

Beshrew the witch! With venomous wights she stays

---

77 you] F; they Q   79 not] but WHITE (*conj.* JACKSON)

   4.2.4 kill] seal ROWE 1714; lull HUDSON 1881 (*conj.* LETTSOM); still *conj.* JACKSON   10 joys]
eyes F

79 **We'll not ... sell** Compare *Sonnets* 21.14
   ('I will not praise that purpose not to sell'),
   and *LLL* 4.3.238 ('To things of sale a
   seller's praise belongs'). It is clear that
   Paris means, as Johnson explains,
   'Though you practise the buyer's art, we
   will not practise the seller's'. Paris implies
   that Helen is not for sale. The suggestion
   by Brinsley Nicholson (*N. & Q.*, 1866,
   p. 164) that the line refers to Cressida has
   had no supporters.
4.2 The courtyard of Cressida's house. See
   headnote to 3.2.
  4 **kill** overpower (Deighton). Walker argues
   that Lettsom's conjecture ('lull') is 'wan-

ted as a link with the simile of sleeping
infants'; but Shakespeare often dispenses
with such links.
  5 **attachment** imprisonment
  9 **ribald** J. Bab, *Shakespeare* (1925), 290,
   speaks of 'the crows of an obscene reality';
   but too much has been made of the
   contrast between this scene and the dawn
   scene in *Romeo and Juliet*. This is not the
   dialogue of two sated sensualists as O. J.
   Campbell supposed (*Comicall Satyre*,
   213).
 12 **venomous wights** Not 'witches' (Warburton), nor *venefici*, 'those who practise noc-
   turnal sorcery' (Steevens), nor 'one who

138

As tediously as hell, but flies the grasps of love
With wings more momentary-swift than thought.
You will catch cold, and curse me.
CRESSIDA   Prithee, tarry.
You men will never tarry.
O foolish Cressid! I might have still held off,
And then you would have tarried. Hark! There's one up.
PANDARUS (*within*) What's all the doors open here?
TROILUS It is your uncle.   20
CRESSIDA A pestilence on him! Now will he be mocking; I
shall have such a life.
        Enter Pandarus
PANDARUS How now, how now! How go maidenheads?
Here, you maid! Where's my cousin Cressid?
CRESSIDA
Go hang yourself, you naughty mocking uncle!
You bring me to do – and then you flout me too.
PANDARUS To do what? To do what? Let her say what! What
have I brought you to do?
CRESSIDA
Come, come, beshrew your heart! You'll ne'er be good,
Nor suffer others.   30
PANDARUS Ha, ha! Alas, poor wretch! A poor *capocchia*! Has't
not slept tonight? Would he not, a naughty man, let it
sleep? A bugbear take him!
CRESSIDA
Did not I tell you? Would he were knocked i'th' head!

---

13 tediously] hideously F   19 (*within*)] F; *not in* Q   22.1 *Enter Pandarus*] CAPELL;
after l. 20 F; *not in* Q   31 Has't] WALKER (*conj.* TANNENBAUM); hast QF

is in distasteful company' (Walker), but
people who lie awake, hating.

14 **With wings . . . thought** Tilley T240: 'as
swift as thought.'
16 **You men will never tarry** This does not
mean that Cressida has had previous
lovers (see 23 n.); it is one of her frequent
scraps of worldly wisdom.
19 **What's** why are
24 **Here . . . Cressid?** Pandarus implies that
he cannot recognize her because she is no
longer a virgin.
    cousin The word was used loosely in
Shakespeare's day (see 3.1.79).

29 **You'll ne'er be good** By 'good' Cressida
probably means 'decent in speech',
though she may refer to his acting as a
pander.
31 *capocchia* simpleton (Theobald); but, as
Malone pointed out, Florio, *Worlde of
Wordes* (1598), defines the word as 'the
foreskin or prepuce of a mans privie member'. Theobald was clearly correct in his
interpretation of his own modernization;
but Pandarus, and perhaps Cressida,
would relish the alternative meaning.
32 **it** Often used in talking to or of children,
e.g. *Romeo* 1.4.30 ff.
34 **knocked i'th' head** killed (*OED v.* 3a)

Knocking within

Who's that at door? Good uncle, go and see.

My lord, come you again into my chamber.

You smile and mock me, as if I meant naughtily.

TROILUS Ha, ha!

CRESSIDA

Come, you are deceived; I think of no such thing.

Knocking within

How earnestly they knock! Pray you, come in;   40

I would not for half Troy have you seen here.

Exeunt Troilus and Cressida

PANDARUS Who's there? What's the matter? Will you beat

down the door? How now! What's the matter?

Enter Aeneas

AENEAS Good morrow, lord, good morrow.

PANDARUS

Who's there? My Lord Aeneas! By my troth

I knew you not. What news with you so early?

AENEAS

Is not Prince Troilus here?

PANDARUS   Here! What should he do here?

AENEAS

Come, he is here, my lord. Do not deny him.

It doth import him much to speak with me.

PANDARUS Is he here, say you? 'Tis more than I know, I'll   50

be sworn. For my own part, I came in late. What should

he do here?

AENEAS Whoa! Nay, then. Come, come, you'll do him wrong

ere you are ware: you'll be so true to him, to be false to

him. Do not you know of him, but yet go fetch him hither;

go.

Enter Troilus

TROILUS How now! What's the matter?

34.1 *Knocking within*] DYCE 1864; *One knocks* QF (*after l.* 35 Q, *after l.* 33 F)   39.1 *Knocking within*] DYCE 1864; *Knock* QF (*after l.* 40)   41.1 *Exeunt ... Cressida*] CAPELL; *Exeunt* QF   43.1 *Enter Aeneas*] ROWE; *not in* QF   50 'Tis] F; *its* Q   53 Whoa!] QF (*Who*); Ho! WALKER (*conj.* TANNENBAUM)   56.1 *Enter Troilus*] F; *not in* Q

37 **naughtily** What Cressida thinks of love-
making?
49 **doth import him much** is of great impor-
tance to him.

53 **Whoa!** 'Stop! esp. as a call to a horse'
(*OED*)
54 **true** loyal
to be as to be

AENEAS

My lord, I scarce have leisure to salute you,
My matter is so rash. There is at hand
Paris your brother and Deiphobus,   60
The Grecian Diomed, and our Antenor
Delivered to us; and for him forthwith,
Ere the first sacrifice, within this hour,
We must give up to Diomedes' hand
The Lady Cressida.

TROILUS   Is it so concluded?

AENEAS

By Priam and the general state of Troy.
They are at hand and ready to effect it.

TROILUS How my achievements mock me!
I will go meet them; and, my Lord Aeneas,
We met by chance: you did not find me here.   70

AENEAS

Good, good, my lord, the secrets of nature
Have not more gift in taciturnity.

Exeunt Troilus and Aeneas

PANDARUS

Is't possible? No sooner got but lost?
The devil take Antenor! The young prince will go mad.
A plague upon Antenor! I would they had broke 's neck.

Enter Cressida

CRESSIDA

How now! What's the matter? Who was here?

PANDARUS Ah, ah!

CRESSIDA

Why sigh you so profoundly? Where's my lord?
Gone? Tell me, sweet uncle, what's the matter?

---

62 us; and for him] F; him, and Q   64 Diomedes'] *Diomeds* F   66 so concluded?] concluded
so? F   71 nature] F; neighbor Pandar Q   72.1 *Exeunt Troilus and Aeneas*] CAPELL; *Exeunt* QF
75.1 *Enter Cressida*] Q (*in place of speech prefix*); *Enter Pandarus and Cressid* F (*after l. 72*)
77 Ah, ah!] Ah, ha! F

59 **rash** urgent
67 **state** council, government
71 **secrets of nature** The Q reading was accepted by Pope, Johnson, and Walker; the
latter thinks it alludes to Pandarus' denial
of Troilus' presence and to the fact that he
and Cressida live in adjacent houses. But,

as Pandarus is hardly taciturn, and in-
effectively secretive (as is apparent from
3.1), the Q reading would not be reassur-
ing to Troilus. Nature's secrets are said
to be taciturn because they are not
revealed. Sisson compares *Antony* 1.2.9–
10 (*New Readings*, ii. 115).

PANDARUS Would I were as deep under the earth as I am   80
   above!

CRESSIDA O the gods! What's the matter?

PANDARUS Pray thee, get thee in. Would thou hadst ne'er
   been born! I knew thou wouldst be his death. O, poor
   gentleman! A plague upon Antenor!

CRESSIDA Good uncle, I beseech you, on my knees I beseech
   you, what's the matter?

PANDARUS Thou must be gone, wench, thou must be gone;
   thou art changed for Antenor; thou must to thy father,
   and be gone from Troilus. 'Twill be his death; 'twill be   90
   his bane; he cannot bear it.

CRESSIDA

   O you immortal gods! I will not go.

PANDARUS Thou must.

CRESSIDA

   I will not, uncle. I have forgot my father;
   I know no touch of consanguinity;
   No kin, no love, no blood, no soul so near me
   As the sweet Troilus. O you gods divine!
   Make Cressid's name the very crown of falsehood,
   If ever she leave Troilus! Time, force, and death,
   Do to this body what extremes you can,   100
   But the strong base and building of my love
   Is as the very centre of the earth,
   Drawing all things to it. I'll go in and weep –

PANDARUS Do, do.

CRESSIDA

   Tear my bright hair and scratch my praisèd cheeks,
   Crack my clear voice with sobs, and break my heart
   With sounding 'Troilus'. I will not go from Troy.

                                                      Exeunt

83 Pray thee] Prythee F   86–7 knees I beseech you, what's] F: Knees, whats Q   100 ex-
tremes] extremitie F   103 I'll] I will F   107 *Exeunt*] F; *not in* Q

95 I know . . . consanguinity Noble   neither father nor mother').
   cites Matthew 19: 5 ('For this cause   106 clear voice The same expression is used
   shall a man leave father and mother,   by Henryson, *Testament of Cresseid*,
   and cleave unto his wife'), and   l. 443.
   Baldwin 1 Esdras 4:21 ('remembreth

4.3   *Enter Paris, Troilus, Aeneas, Deiphobus, Antenor, and
        Diomedes*

PARIS
It is great morning, and the hour prefixed
For her delivery to this valiant Greek
Comes fast upon. Good my brother Troilus,
Tell you the lady what she is to do
And haste her to the purpose.

TROILUS   Walk into her house.
I'll bring her to the Grecian presently:
And to his hand when I deliver her,
Think it an altar, and thy brother Troilus
A priest, there off'ring to it his own heart.   ⌈*Exit*⌉

PARIS (*aside*) I know what 'tis to love,   10
And would, as I shall pity, I could help. –
Please you walk in, my lords.   *Exeunt*

4.4   *Enter Pandarus and Cressida*

PANDARUS Be moderate, be moderate.

CRESSIDA
Why tell you me of moderation?
The grief is fine, full perfect, that I taste
And violenteth in a sense as strong
As that which causeth it. How can I moderate it?   5
If I could temporize with my affection,
Or brew it to a weak and colder palate,
The like allayment could I give my grief.

4.3.0.1 *and*] F: *not in* Q   2 For] Of F   3 upon] upon us POPE   5 her house] th'house WALKER
9 own] *not in* F   Exit] STEEVENS: *not in* QF
    4.4.0.1 Cressida] Cressid F   3 full perfect] F: full, perfect Q   4 violenteth] no lesse F
6 affection] F: affections Q

4.3 Near Cressida's house.
  1 **great morning** broad daylight
  3 **upon** Pope's insertion mends the metre
     and Walker declares that there is no
     parallel in Shakespeare for the QF read-
     ing. But compare 'draws on apace',
     'comes on apace'.
  5 **her house** Walker's conjecture is linked
     with her attempt to straighten out the
     references to location. She also argues
     that the stress falls very awkwardly on
     walk, but the main stress is surely on
     house.
  9 *Exit* Some editors follow QF and let

Troilus remain on stage to the end of the
scene. Capell was the first to have Troilus
exit at this point. In any case Paris's next
two lines would be spoken aside, either to
Troilus or to himself.
4.4 Within the house.
  3 **full perfect** quite perfect. Q's comma is
     unnecessary (Craig).
  4 **violenteth** rages with violence (not other-
     wise recorded as an intransitive verb)
  7 **brew** mix with water, dilute
  8 **allayment** dilution, mitigation (first oc-
     currence)

My love admits no qualifying dross;
No more my grief, in such a precious loss.   10
    Enter Troilus
PANDARUS Here, here he comes. Ah sweet ducks!
CRESSIDA O Troilus! Troilus!
    She embraces him
PANDARUS What a pair of spectacles is here! Let me embrace
too. 'O heart', as the goodly saying is,
    O heart, O heavy heart,
      Why sigh'st thou without breaking?
where he answers again,
    Because thou canst not ease thy smart
      By friendship nor by speaking.
There was never a truer rhyme. Let us cast away nothing,   20
for we may live to have need of such a verse. We see it, we
see it. How now, lambs!
TROILUS
    Cressid, I love thee in so strained a purity,
    That the blest gods, as angry with my fancy,
    More bright in zeal than the devotion which
    Cold lips blow to their deities, take thee from me.
CRESSIDA Have the gods envy?
PANDARUS Ay, ay, ay, ay; 'tis too plain a case.
CRESSIDA
    And is it true that I must go from Troy?
TROILUS
    A hateful truth.
CRESSIDA   What, and from Troilus too?   30
TROILUS
    From Troy and Troilus.
CRESSIDA   Is't possible?

---

9 dross] crosse F   10.1 *Enter Troilus*] *after l.* 9 F   11 Ah] QF (a)   ducks] ducke F   12.1 *She
... him*] CAPELL (*subs.*); *not in* QF   15 O heavy] POPE; heauy QF   16 sigh'st] sighest F   23
strain'd] strange F   31 Is't] Is it ROWE

---

13 **spectacles** (a) sights (b) glasses
19 **friendship** Hudson thought that Pan-
    darus meant that 'relief must come from
    another sort of love than that of friend-
    ship', i.e. sexual. He means rather that his
    own friendship for the lovers, although
    genuine, is powerless to help.

20 **There . . . rhyme** The source, if any, has
    not been discovered.
23 **strained** with all its impurities strained off
31 **Troy and Troilus** A quibble, even though
    'Troilus' is once apparently pronounced
    with three syllables (5.2.161).
    Is't Rowe's emendation is often accepted

TROILUS

And suddenly; where injury of chance
Puts back leave-taking, jostles roughly by
All time of pause, rudely beguiles our lips
Of all rejoindure, forcibly prevents
Our locked embrasures, strangles our dear vows
Even in the birth of our own labouring breath.
We two, that with so many thousand sighs
Did buy each other, must poorly sell ourselves
With the rude brevity and discharge of one.   40
Injurious Time now with a robber's haste
Crams his rich thiev'ry up, he knows not how.
As many farewells as be stars in heaven,
With distinct breath and consigned kisses to them,
He fumbles up into a loose adieu,
And scants us with a single famished kiss,
Distasted with the salt of broken tears.

AENEAS (*within*) My lord, is the lady ready?

TROILUS

Hark! You are called. Some say the genius so
Cries 'Come!' to him that instantly must die.   50
(*To Aeneas*) Bid them have patience; she shall come anon.

PANDARUS

Where are my tears? Rain, to lay this wind,
Or my heart will be blown up by the root!   *Exit*

---

36 embrasures] embraces POPE   40 one] our F   42 thiev'ry] theeuerie F   47 Distasted]
Distasting F   tears] teares. *Enter Æneas* F   49–50 the genius so | Cries 'Come!'] F;   the *Genius*
cries so Q   53 the root] F;   my throate Q   *Exit*] THEOBALD (*subs.*);   *not in* QF

for metrical reasons, but some roughness
is frequent when a line is split between
two speakers. Cressida could pause a moment before speaking; and see previous
note.

33 **Puts back** prevents
35 **rejoindure** rejoining (first occurrence)
36 **embrasures** Walker accepted Pope's
   emendation on the grounds that the
   original audience would understand *embrasures* to mean 'windows'. Cotgrave,
   however, gives 'embraces' as the primary
   meaning of the word.
42 **thiev'ry** stolen property
44 **consigned** delivered, given in trust
46–7 **scants ... tears** Walter Whiter cites
   this passage (*Specimen of a Commentary on*

Shakespeare, ed. Alan Over and Mary Bell,
1967, 121) and says that broken meats
were 'suggested by the *culinary* language,
and the ideas annexed to it, into which he
has fallen; – Scants-famished-distasted-
Salt.' This is one of the passages cited by
Spurgeon in discussing the cooking
imagery. See Introduction, p. 29.

47 **broken** interrupted with sobs (Onions)
49 **genius** guardian spirit
52 **Rain, to lay this wind** i.e. tears to stop my
   sighs. Tilley R16: 'Small rain lays great
   winds.'
53 *Exit* As Pandarus has nothing more to
   say during the rest of the scene, Shakespeare doubtless intended him to leave at
   this point.

CRESSIDA

I must then to the Grecians?

TROILUS   No remedy.

CRESSIDA

A woeful Cressid 'mongst the merry Greeks!

When shall we see again?

TROILUS

Hear me, my love: be thou but true of heart –

CRESSIDA

I true! How now! What wicked deem is this?

TROILUS

Nay, we must use expostulation kindly,

For it is parting from us.   60

I speak not 'be thou true' as fearing thee,

For I will throw my glove to Death himself

That there's no maculation in thy heart;

But 'be thou true' say I, to fashion in

My sequent protestation – be thou true,

And I will see thee.

CRESSIDA

O, you shall be exposed, my lord, to dangers

As infinite as imminent! But I'll be true.

TROILUS

And I'll grow friend with danger. Wear this sleeve.

CRESSIDA

And you this glove. When shall I see you?   70

TROILUS

I will corrupt the Grecian sentinels

To give thee nightly visitation.

But yet, be true.

CRESSIDA   O heavens! 'Be true' again!

TROILUS Hear why I speak it, love.

---

57 my] F; *not in* Q   63 there's] F; there is Q

55 **merry Greeks** See 1.2.104 n.
56 **see** i.e. see each other
58 **deem** surmise (first occurrence)
59 **expostulation** (referring to Cressida's in-
      dignant protest)
60 **it is parting from us** the opportunity is
      leaving us

63 **maculation** stain of impurity (Onions) or
      of infidelity
64 **to fashion in** as a way of introducing
69 **sleeve** Sleeves were detachable.
      Chaucer's Criseyde (v. 1043) gives
      Diomed 'a pencel of hir sleve', as a love-
      token.

The Grecian youths are full of quality;
Their loving well composed with gifts of nature,
And flowing o'er with arts and exercise.
How novelty may move and parts with person –
Alas, a kind of godly jealousy,
Which, I beseech you, call a virtuous sin –   80
Makes me afeard.

CRESSIDA   O heavens! You love me not.

TROILUS Die I a villain then!
In this I do not call your faith in question
So mainly as my merit. I cannot sing,
Nor heel the high lavolt, nor sweeten talk,
Nor play at subtle games – fair virtues all,
To which the Grecians are most prompt and pregnant;
But I can tell that in each grace of these
There lurks a still and dumb-discoursive devil
That tempts most cunningly. But be not tempted.   90

CRESSIDA Do you think I will?

TROILUS
No; but something may be done that we will not,
And sometimes we are devils to ourselves,
When we will tempt the frailty of our powers,
Presuming on their changeful potency.

AENEAS (*within*)
Nay, good my lord!

TROILUS   Come, kiss, and let us part.

PARIS (*within*)
Brother Troilus!

TROILUS   Good brother, come you hither;

76 Their ... nature] F; *not in* Q   gifts] THEOBALD; guift F   77 And flowing] STAUNTON; And
swelling Q; Flawing and swelling F   78 novelty] nouelties F   person] F; portion Q   81
afeard] affraid F

77 **And flowing** In the manuscript used for F, *Flowing* was added to, instead of being substituted for, *swelling*; this was then misprinted as *Flawing*.
arts and exercise the exercise of arts
78 **parts with person** accomplishments with handsomeness
79 **godly jealousy** Biblical; Theobald compared 2 Corinthians 11: 2.
84 **mainly** much
85 **heel** perform
lavolt a lively dance with 'high and active

bounds' (Nares); an anglicized form of *lavolta* (*OED*).
87 **pregnant** resourceful
89 **dumb-discoursive** silently persuasive
92 No (followed, perhaps, by a pause)
but something ... not Compare Romans 7: 18–20.
95 **changeful potency** power of change; or, more probably, as Dyce suggested, 'their potency which is subject to variation, and therefore imperfect and not to be rashly relied on'

And bring Aeneas and the Grecian with you.

CRESSIDA My lord, will you be true?

TROILUS

Who, I? Alas, it is my vice, my fault!   100
Whiles others fish with craft for great opinion,
I with great truth catch mere simplicity;
Whilst some with cunning gild their copper crowns,
With truth and plainness I do wear mine bare.
Fear not my truth: the moral of my wit
Is plain and true; there's all the reach of it.

 Enter Aeneas, Paris, Antenor, Deiphobus, and
 Diomedes

Welcome, Sir Diomed: here is the lady
Which for Antenor we deliver you.
At the port, lord, I'll give her to thy hand,
And by the way possess thee what she is.   110
Entreat her fair; and, by my soul, fair Greek,
If e'er thou stand at mercy of my sword,
Name Cressid, and thy life shall be as safe
As Priam is in Ilium.

DIOMEDES   Fair Lady Cressid,
So please you, save the thanks this prince expects.
The lustre in your eye, heaven in your cheek,
Pleads your fair usage; and to Diomed
You shall be mistress, and command him wholly.

TROILUS

Grecian, thou dost not use me courteously,
To shame the zeal of my petition to thee   120
In praising her. I tell thee, lord of Greece,
She is as far high-soaring o'er thy praises
As thou unworthy to be called her servant.
I charge thee use her well, even for my charge;
For, by the dreadful Pluto, if thou dost not,

---

99 true?] true? *Exit.* F 106.1 *Enter ... Diomedes*] MALONE; *not in* Q; *Enter the Greekes* F (*after*
l. 104); *Enter Æneas, Paris and Diomedes* ROWE (*after l. 106*) 117 usage] visage F 120 zeal]
WARBURTON (*conj.* THEOBALD); scale QF to thee] towards F; towards thee ROWE 121 In] I F

---

102 **I with ... simplicity** my sincerity merely
 earns me a reputation for naivety
109 **port** gate
111 **Entreat** treat

120 **zeal** with a quibble on *seal*, which fits
 petition
124 **for my charge** because I request it

Though the great bulk Achilles be thy guard,
I'll cut thy throat.

DIOMEDES   O, be not moved, Prince Troilus.
Let me be privileged by my place and message
To be a speaker free. When I am hence,
I'll answer to my lust; and know you, lord,   130
I'll nothing do on charge. To her own worth
She shall be prized; but that you say 'Be't so',
I'll speak it in my spirit and honour 'No!'

TROILUS
Come, to the port. I'll tell thee, Diomed,
This brave shall oft make thee to hide thy head.
Lady, give me your hand; and, as we walk,
To our own selves bend we our needful talk.

                    Exeunt Troilus, Cressida, and Diomedes
          Trumpet sounds

PARIS
Hark! Hector's trumpet.

AENEAS   How have we spent this morning!
The Prince must think me tardy and remiss,
That swore to ride before him to the field.   140

PARIS
'Tis Troilus' fault. Come, come, to field with him.

DEIPHOBUS Let us make ready straight.

AENEAS
Yea, with a bridegroom's fresh alacrity
Let us address to tend on Hector's heels.
The glory of our Troy doth this day lie
On his fair worth and single chivalry.   *Exeunt*

---

130 you] my F   133 I'll] F; I Q   137.1 *Exeunt . . . Diomedes*] RANN (*conj.* RITSON); *not in* QF
137.2 *Trumpet sounds*] F (*Sound Trumpet*); *not in* Q   140 to the] in the F   142–6 Let . . .
chivalry] F; *not in* Q   142 DEIPHOBUS] MALONE (*conj.* RITSON); *Dio.* F; *Par⟨is⟩.* RANN (*conj.* RIT-
SON, MASON)   146 *Exeunt*] ROWE; *after l.* 142 QF

---

130 **I'll answer . . . lust** Ambiguous: (a) I'll do
what I please (b) I'll do what my lust suggests (c) I'll treat Cressida well because I
wish to do so (not because of your instruc-
tions) (d) I'll answer you as I wish, in
battle.
131 **charge** command
132 **but that** i.e. he would refuse Troilus' request, were it not for Cressida's own worth
135 **brave** bravado, boast
137 *Exeunt . . . Diomedes* Troilus, Cressida

and Diomedes must leave here: they
should not overhear the remarks of
Aeneas and Paris.
142–6 **Let us . . . chivalry** These lines were
apparently added to the original text,
since the direction *Exeunt* precedes them.
This may be due to the use of printed
copy, with a cramped insertion. As
Diomedes must leave with Troilus and
Cressida, l. 142 is universally ascribed to
Deiphobus, instead of to *Dio.*

4.5   *Enter Ajax, armed, Agamemnon, Achilles, Patroclus,*
          Ulysses, Menelaus, Nestor, and others

AGAMEMNON

Here art thou in appointment fresh and fair,
Anticipating time with starting courage.
Give with thy trumpet a loud note to Troy,
Thou dreadful Ajax, that the appallèd air
May pierce the head of the great combatant
And hale him hither.

AJAX   Thou trumpet, there's my purse.
Now crack thy lungs, and split thy brazen pipe;
Blow, villain, till thy spherèd bias cheek
Outswell the colic of puffed Aquilon.
Come, stretch thy chest, and let thy eyes spout blood;   10
Thou blow'st for Hector.

          Trumpet sounds

ULYSSES

No trumpet answers.

ACHILLES   'Tis but early days.

AGAMEMNON

Is not yond Diomed, with Calchas' daughter?

ULYSSES

'Tis he; I ken the manner of his gait:
He rises on the toe; that spirit of his
In aspiration lifts him from the earth.

          Enter Diomedes, with Cressida

AGAMEMNON

Is this the Lady Cressid?

DIOMEDES   Even she.

4.5.0.1–2] QF *include* Calchas (*om.* THEOBALD); *names reordered*   2 time with ... courage.]
THEOBALD; time. With ... courage. QF   9 colic] choller WALKER   11 blow'st] POPE; blowest
QF   11.1 *Trumpet sounds*] HANMER; *not in* QF   13 yond] yong F   16.1 *Enter ... Cressida*]
THEOBALD; *not in* QF

4.5 Near the Greek camp. Lists set out. All
     editors have placed this scene in the
     Greek camp, but see 1.3.274–5.
1 **appointment** accoutrement
   fresh and fair spick and span
2 **starting courage** 'courage in coming into
   the field before the challenger' (Theobald); or 'with courage to get things
   started' (New Variorum)

6 **trumpet** trumpeter
8 **bias** 'On old maps the winds were represented as heads, puffing from the
   appropriate direction; in profile or three-
   quarter face this gave them a "bias"
   cheek' (Walker).
9 **colic** Swollen, as though with colic, like
   the pictures of winds on old maps.
   Aquilon the north (or north-east) wind

AGAMEMNON

Most dearly welcome to the Greeks, sweet lady.
He kisses her

NESTOR

Our general doth salute you with a kiss.

ULYSSES

Yet is the kindness but particular;   20
'Twere better she were kissed in general.

NESTOR

And very courtly counsel. I'll begin.
He kisses her
So much for Nestor.

ACHILLES

I'll take that winter from your lips, fair lady.
Achilles bids you welcome.
He kisses her

MENELAUS

I had good argument for kissing once.

PATROCLUS

But that's no argument for kissing now;
For thus popped Paris in his hardiment,
And parted thus you and your argument.
He kisses her

ULYSSES

O deadly gall, and theme of all our scorns!   30
For which we lose our heads to gild his horns.

PATROCLUS

The first was Menelaus' kiss; this, mine.
Patroclus kisses you.
He kisses her again

MENELAUS   O, this is trim!

PATROCLUS

Paris and I kiss evermore for him.

MENELAUS

I'll have my kiss, sir. Lady, by your leave.

18.1 *He kisses her*] DYCE 1864 (*subs.*); *not in* QF   22.1 *He kisses her*] DYCE 1864 (*subs.*); *not in* QF   25.1 *He kisses her*] KITTREDGE (*subs.*); *not in* QF   29 And ... argument] *not in* F   29.1 *He kisses her*] DYCE 1864 (*subs.*); *not in* QF   33 *He ... again*] DYCE 1864; *not in* QF

21 **in general** (quibbling on the two meanings of 'general')
28 **hardiment** boldness

34 **Paris ... him** As Paris kisses Helen, so I kiss you.

151

CRESSIDA

In kissing, do you render or receive?

MENELAUS

Both take and give.

CRESSIDA   I'll make my match to live,

The kiss you take is better than you give;

Therefore no kiss.

MENELAUS

I'll give you boot, I'll give you three for one.   40

CRESSIDA

You're an odd man; give even, or give none.

MENELAUS

An odd man, lady? Every man is odd.

CRESSIDA

No, Paris is not; for you know 'tis true

That you are odd, and he is even with you.

MENELAUS

You fillip me o'th' head.

CRESSIDA   No, I'll be sworn.

ULYSSES

It were no match, your nail against his horn.

May I, sweet lady, beg a kiss of you?

CRESSIDA

You may.

ULYSSES   I do desire it.

CRESSIDA   Why, beg too.

ULYSSES

Why then, for Venus' sake, give me a kiss

When Helen is a maid again and his.   50

CRESSIDA

I am your debtor; claim it when 'tis due.

ULYSSES

Never's my day, and then a kiss of you.

---

37 MENELAUS] WHITE (*conj.* TYRWHITT); *Patr⟨oclus⟩.* QF   41 You're] CAPELL; You are QF   48
too] WALKER (*conj.* RITSON); then Q; then? F; then, too *conj.* KINNEAR   50 his.] CAPELL; his – QF

37 **I'll . . . live** I'll wager my life
40 **boot** advantage, odds
41, 42, 44 **odd** Shakespeare plays on various meanings of the word – single, singular, uneven number, on terms of enmity.

46 **nail** i.e. Cressida's
48 **too** As Cressida's banter with the Greeks is in rhymed verse, this emendation is an obvious improvement.
50 **his** Menelaus'

DIOMEDES

Lady, a word; I'll bring you to your father.

Exeunt Diomedes and Cressida

NESTOR

A woman of quick sense.

ULYSSES   Fie, fie upon her!

There's language in her eye, her cheek, her lip,

Nay, her foot speaks; her wanton spirits look out

At every joint and motive of her body.

O, these encounterers, so glib of tongue,

That give accosting welcome ere it comes,

And wide unclasp the tables of their thoughts   60

To every tickling reader! Set them down

For sluttish spoils of opportunity

And daughters of the game.

Trumpet within

ALL

The Trojans' trumpet.

AGAMEMNON   Yonder comes the troop.

*Flourish. Enter Hector, armed, Aeneas, Troilus, and
other Trojans with Attendants*

AENEAS

Hail, all the state of Greece! What shall be done

To him that victory commands? Or do you purpose

A victor shall be known? Will you the knights

Shall to the edge of all extremity

53.1 *Exeunt...Cressida*] POPE 1728 (*subs.*); *not in* QF   55 language] a language F   59 accost-
ing] HUDSON (*conj.* THEOBALD); a coasting QF   61 tickling] F; ticklish Q   63.1 *Trumpet within*]
THEOBALD; *Flowrish enter all of Troy* Q; *Exeunt* F   64.1-2 *Flourish ... Attendants*] MALONE
(*subs.*); Q *includes entry in previous direction* (*l.* 63.1); *Enter all of Troy, Hector, Paris, Æneas,
Helenus and Attendants. Florish.* F   65 the] you F

57 **motive** a moving limb

59 **accosting** As Shakespeare does not
elsewhere use *coasting* in the sense
required, and as he does use *accost* to
mean 'woo' (*Twelfth Night*, 1.3.52),
Theobald's conjecture is probably right;
but many editors-prefer to retain the
reading of QF, paraphrasing 'give a welcome in advance to a tentative approach
of a suitor'.

60 **tables** writing-tablet

61 **tickling** Shakespeare may have altered
ticklish (Q) to avoid the repetition of
sound in *sluttish* (62). Both words make
good sense: the admirers can be described

as making lustful advances, or as being
sexually aroused by daughters of the
game. Greene (*Euphues his Censure*, 195)
speaks of 'the tickling desire of a new
chaunge'. Walker suggests that since *accost* was derived from Latin *costa*, 'rib',
this would explain Shakespeare's use of
tickling.

64 **Trojans' trumpet** A. P. Rossiter (*Angel
with Horns* (1961), 133) pointed out that
these words would be heard as 'Trojans'
strumpet'. It may be doubted whether
Shakespeare intended an allusion to
Cressida.

65 **state** important people

Pursue each other, or shall they be divided
By any voice or order of the field?   70
Hector bade ask.
AGAMEMNON   Which way would Hector have it?
AENEAS
He cares not; he'll obey conditions.
AGAMEMNON
'Tis done like Hector.
ACHILLES   But securely done,
A little proudly, and great deal misprizing
The knight opposed.
AENEAS   If not Achilles, sir,
What is your name?
ACHILLES   If not Achilles, nothing.
AENEAS
Therefore Achilles. But whate'er, know this:
In the extremity of great and little,
Valour and pride excel themselves in Hector;
The one almost as infinite as all,   80
The other blank as nothing. Weigh him well,
And that which looks like pride is courtesy.
This Ajax is half made of Hector's blood;
In love whereof half Hector stays at home;
Half heart, half hand, half Hector comes to seek
This blended knight, half Trojan and half Greek.
ACHILLES
A maiden battle then? O, I perceive you.
          Enter Diomedes
AGAMEMNON
Here is Sir Diomed. Go, gentle knight,
Stand by our Ajax. As you and Lord Aeneas
Consent upon the order of their fight,   90

69 they] *not in* F   73 ACHILLES] WALKER (*conj.* THEOBALD); *not in* QF   74 misprizing] disprizing
F   87.1 *Enter Diomedes*] POPE 1728 (*subs.*); *not in* QF

69–70 **shall they ... field?** shall the combatants be made to desist by a referee or by
set rules?
73–5 **AGAMEMNON... opposed** QF gives the
whole speech to Agamemnon. In view of
Aeneas' defence of Hector's modesty,
Theobald gave the whole speech to
Achilles. I follow Walker in giving only
the first four words to Agamemnon. The

speech prefix for the remainder of the
speech could easily have been overlooked.
73 **securely** over-confidently
83 **Ajax ... blood** Ajax was thought to be
the son of Priam's sister, Hesione (see
1.2.13, 2.2.76). Caxton, Lydgate, and
Cooper agree on this.
87 **maiden battle** bloodless combat

So be it; either to the uttermost,
Or else a breath. The combatants being kin
Half stints their strife before their strokes begin.
        Ajax and Hector enter the lists
ULYSSES They are opposed already.
AGAMEMNON
What Trojan is that same that looks so heavy?
ULYSSES
The youngest son of Priam, a true knight;
Not yet mature, yet matchless-firm of word;
Speaking in deeds and deedless in his tongue;
Not soon provoked nor, being provoked, soon calmed;
His heart and hand both open and both free;   100
For what he has he gives, what thinks he shows;
Yet gives he not till judgement guide his bounty,
Nor dignifies an impair thought with breath;
Manly as Hector, but more dangerous;
For Hector in his blaze of wrath subscribes
To tender objects, but he in heat of action
Is more vindicative than jealous love;
They call him Troilus, and on him erect
A second hope, as fairly built as Hector.
Thus says Aeneas, one that knows the youth   110
Even to his inches, and with private soul
Did in great Ilium thus translate to me.
        Alarum. Hector and Ajax fight
AGAMEMNON They are in action.
NESTOR Now, Ajax, hold thine own!

---

92 breath] breach F   93.1 *Ajax . . . lists*] MALONE; *not in* QF   94 ULYSSES They . . . already] F; *not in* Q   95 AGAMEMNON What] F; *Vlisses: what* Q   96 The . . . knight] *The yongest Sonne of Priam;* | *A true Knight; they call him Troylus* F   98 Speaking in] F; *Speaking* Q   112.1 *Hector and Ajax fight*] ROWE; *not in* QF

92 **breath** gentle exercise
95 **heavy** sad, depressed
96–112 **The youngest . . . me** Ulysses is given a character-sketch of Troilus to balance his previous description of Cressida; we must accept both, or neither; both prepare the way for the development of the two characters before the end of the play as slut and Trojan leader.
98 **Speaking . . . tongue** Tilley W797: 'Few words and many deeds.'
100 **free** open, generous

103 **impair** There are three explanations: (1) unworthy, from Latin *impar*; (2) unconsidered, from Latin *imparatus*; (3) injurious, from the noun 'impair', meaning injury. As it is a nonce-word various emendations have been proposed, all unnecessary.
105 **subscribes** yields
107 **vindicative** vindictive (first occurrence). The line ironically foreshadows Troilus' jealousy.
111 **to his inches** from top to toe (Deighton)

TROILUS Hector, thou sleep'st. Awake thee!
AGAMEMNON His blows are well disposed. There, Ajax!
    Trumpets cease
DIOMEDES
    You must no more.
AENEAS   Princes, enough, so please you.
AJAX
    I am not warm yet; let us fight again.
DIOMEDES
    As Hector pleases.
HECTOR   Why, then will I no more.
    Thou art, great lord, my father's sister's son,   120
    A cousin-german to great Priam's seed;
    The obligation of our blood forbids
    A gory emulation 'twixt us twain.
    Were thy commixtion Greek and Trojan so,
    That thou couldst say 'This hand is Grecian all,
    And this is Trojan; the sinews of this leg
    All Greek, and this all Troy; my mother's blood
    Runs on the dexter cheek, and this sinister
    Bounds in my father's', by Jove multipotent,
    Thou shouldst not bear from me a Greekish member   130
    Wherein my sword had not impressure made
    Of our rank feud; but the just gods gainsay
    That any drop thou borrow'dst from thy mother,
    My sacred aunt, should by my mortal sword
    Be drained! Let me embrace thee, Ajax.
    By him that thunders, thou hast lusty arms;
    Hector would have them fall upon him thus.
    Cousin, all honour to thee!
AJAX   I thank thee, Hector.
    Thou art too gentle and too free a man.
    I came to kill thee, cousin, and bear hence   140
    A great addition earnèd in thy death.

---

132 Of ... feud] F; *not in* Q   133 drop] F; day Q

121 **cousin-german** i.e. first cousin   131 **impressure** impression
124 **commixtion** commixture   141 **addition** something added to a coat of
129 **multipotent** most mighty (first occur-   arms
    rence)

HECTOR

Not Neoptolemus so mirable,
On whose bright crest Fame with her loud'st oyez
Cries 'This is he', could promise to himself
A thought of added honour torn from Hector.

AENEAS

There is expectance here from both the sides
What further you will do.

HECTOR   We'll answer it.

The issue is embracement. (*They embrace*) Ajax, farewell.

AJAX

If I might in entreaties find success,
As seld I have the chance, I would desire   150
My famous cousin to our Grecian tents.

DIOMEDES

'Tis Agamemnon's wish; and great Achilles
Doth long to see unarmed the valiant Hector.

HECTOR

Aeneas, call my brother Troilus to me,
And signify this loving interview
To the expecters of our Trojan part;
Desire them home. Give me thy hand, my cousin;
I will go eat with thee, and see your knights.

Agamemnon and the rest of the Greeks approach

AJAX

Great Agamemnon comes to meet us here.

HECTOR

The worthiest of them tell me name by name;   160
But for Achilles, my own searching eyes
Shall find him by his large and portly size.

---

143 oyez] DYCE (*subs.*); (O yes) QF   144 could] could'st F   148 (*They embrace*)] This edition:
not in QF   158.1 *Agamemnon ... approach*] ROWE (*subs.*); *not in* Q; *Enter Agamemnon and the
rest.* F   161·my] mine F

142 **Neoptolemus** Johnson suggested that as
Achilles' son was Pyrrhus Neoptolemus,
Shakespeare supposed that the latter was
a family name. Baldwin, however,
believes that Shakespeare was referring
to the prophecy that Troy would be cap-
tured by Neoptolemus – of which Hector

may have heard, though Pyrrhus had not
yet arrived in Troy. See 3.3.208.
142 **mirable** wonderful
143 **oyez** Call of the town-crier, pronounced
to rhyme with 'joys'.
150 **seld** seldom

AGAMEMNON

Worthy of arms! – as welcome as to one
That would be rid of such an enemy.
But that's no welcome; understand more clear,
What's past and what's to come is strewed with husks
And formless ruin of oblivion;
But in this extant moment, faith and troth,
Strained purely from all hollow bias-drawing,
Bids thee, with most divine integrity,   170
From heart of very heart, great Hector, welcome.

HECTOR

I thank thee, most imperious Agamemnon.

AGAMEMNON (*to Troilus*)

My well-famed lord of Troy, no less to you.

MENELAUS

Let me confirm my princely brother's greeting;
You brace of warlike brothers, welcome hither.

HECTOR

Who must we answer?

AENEAS   The noble Menelaus.

HECTOR

O, you, my lord! By Mars his gauntlet, thanks!
Mock not that I affect th'untraded oath;
Your quondam wife swears still by Venus' glove.
She's well, but bade me not commend her to you.   180

MENELAUS

Name her not now, sir; she's a deadly theme.

HECTOR O! pardon; I offend.

NESTOR

I have, thou gallant Trojan, seen thee oft,
Labouring for destiny, make cruel way
Through ranks of Greekish youth; and I have seen thee,
As hot as Perseus, spur thy Phrygian steed,

---

163 Worthy of arms] F; Worthy all armes Q   165–70 But . . . integrity] F; *not in* Q   178 that
. . . oath] F; thy affect, the vntraded earth Q   179 quondam] F; *quandom* Q

---

169 **bias-drawing** turning away from the
   truth (Onions), insincerity
172 **imperious** imperial
178 **untraded** unhackneyed (yet the

oath does not appear unusual)
184 **Labouring for destiny** i.e. doing the
   work of the Fates by killing men
186 **Perseus** See note on 1.3.41.

Despising many forfeits and subduements,
When thou hast hung thy advancèd sword i'th' air,
Not letting it decline on the declined,
That I have said to some my standers-by   190
'Lo, Jupiter is yonder, dealing life!'
And I have seen thee pause and take thy breath,
When that a ring of Greeks have hemmed thee in,
Like an Olympian wrestling. This have I seen,
But this thy countenance, still locked in steel,
I never saw till now. I knew thy grandsire,
And once fought with him. He was a soldier good;
But, by great Mars, the captain of us all,
Never like thee. O, let an old man embrace thee;
And, worthy warrior, welcome to our tents.   200

AENEAS 'Tis the old Nestor.

HECTOR

Let me embrace thee, good old chronicle,
That hast so long walked hand in hand with Time;
Most reverend Nestor, I am glad to clasp thee.

NESTOR

I would my arms could match thee in contention,
As they contend with thee in courtesy.

HECTOR   I would they could.

NESTOR

Ha! By this white beard, I'd fight with thee tomorrow.
Well, welcome, welcome! I have seen the time.

ULYSSES

I wonder now how yonder city stands   210
When we have here her base and pillar by us.

HECTOR

I know your favour, Lord Ulysses, well.
Ah, sir, there's many a Greek and Trojan dead,

---

187 Despising many] And seene thee scorning F   188 thy] F; th' Q   190 to some] vnto F
193 hemmed] F; shrupd Q; shraped SISSON   199 O, let] Let F   206 As...courtesy] F; *not in* Q

187 **subduements** conquests (first occurrence)
193 **hemmed** Walker rightly supposes that
shrupd (Q) conceals the true reading; but
no emendations have been convincing,
the best being *shraped* (Sisson, *New Readings*, ii. 118) = caught or trapped (dia-

lectal). But Shakespeare may himself
have altered an unfamiliar word.
194 **Olympian wrestling** Olympic wrestling-
match
195 **still** up till now
212 **favour** appearance

Since first I saw yourself and Diomed
In Ilium, on your Greekish embassy.

ULYSSES

Sir, I foretold you then what would ensue.
My prophecy is but half his journey yet;
For yonder walls, that pertly front your town,
Yon towers, whose wanton tops do buss the clouds,
Must kiss their own feet.

HECTOR   I must not believe you.   220
There they stand yet; and modestly I think
The fall of every Phrygian stone will cost
A drop of Grecian blood. The end crowns all;
And that old common arbitrator, Time,
Will one day end it.

ULYSSES   So to him we leave it.
Most gentle and most valiant Hector, welcome.
After the general, I beseech you next
To feast with me and see me at my tent.

ACHILLES

I shall forestall thee, Lord Ulysses, thou!
Now Hector, I have fed mine eyes on thee;   230
I have with exact view perused thee, Hector,
And quoted joint by joint.

HECTOR   Is this Achilles?

ACHILLES I am Achilles.

HECTOR

Stand fair, I pray thee; let me look on thee.

ACHILLES

Behold thy fill.

HECTOR   Nay, I have done already.

ACHILLES

Thou art too brief. I will the second time,
As I would buy thee, view thee limb by limb.

---

234 pray thee] prythee F

215 **In Ilium . . . embassy** When they cap-
tured Tenedos at the start of their expedition, the Greeks sent Ulysses and
Diomedes to Troy with an offer of peace,
on condition that Helen was restored to
Menelaus (Caxton, ii. 559 ff.).

219 **buss** kiss
223–4 **The end . . . Time** Tilley E116 ('The
end crowns all'); T336 ('Time tries all
things').
231 **exact** (accent on the first syllable)
232 **quoted** scrutinized

HECTOR

O, like a book of sport thou'lt read me o'er;
But there's more in me than thou understand'st.
Why dost thou so oppress me with thine eye?   240

ACHILLES

Tell me, you heavens, in which part of his body
Shall I destroy him? – whether there, or there, or there? –
That I may give the local wound a name,
And make distinct the very breach whereout
Hector's great spirit flew. Answer me, heavens!

HECTOR

It would discredit the blest gods, proud man,
To answer such a question. Stand again:
Think'st thou to catch my life so pleasantly
As to prenominate in nice conjecture
Where thou wilt hit me dead?

ACHILLES   I tell thee yea.   250

HECTOR

Wert thou an oracle to tell me so,
I'd not believe thee. Henceforth guard thee well;
For I'll not kill thee there, nor there, nor there;
But, by the forge that stithied Mars his helm,
I'll kill thee everywhere, yea o'er and o'er.
You wisest Grecians, pardon me this brag.
His insolence draws folly from my lips;
But I'll endeavour deeds to match these words,
Or may I never –

AJAX   Do not chafe thee, cousin;
And you, Achilles, let these threats alone   260
Till accident or purpose bring you to't.
You may have every day enough of Hector,
If you have stomach. The general state, I fear,
Can scarce entreat you to be odd with him.

HECTOR

I pray you, let us see you in the field;

---

251 an] the F   254 stithied] F; stichied Q   262 have] *not in* F

238 **of sport** about hunting
247 **Stand again** Achilles is still kneeling, his previous speech being addressed to the gods.
249 **prenominate** mention in advance

249 **nice** accurate, precise
254 **stithied** forged
    Mars his Mars's
264 **odd** at odds. Ajax implies that Achilles is a coward.

We have had pelting wars since you refused
The Grecians' cause.

ACHILLES   Dost thou entreat me, Hector?
Tomorrow do I meet thee, fell as death;
Tonight all friends.

HECTOR   Thy hand upon that match.

AGAMEMNON
First, all you peers of Greece, go to my tent;   270
There in the full convive we. Afterwards,
As Hector's leisure and your bounties shall
Concur together, severally entreat him.
Beat loud the taborins, let the trumpets blow,
That this great soldier may his welcome know.

                    Flourish. Exeunt all except Troilus and Ulysses

TROILUS
My Lord Ulysses, tell me, I beseech you,
In what place of the field doth Calchas keep?

ULYSSES
At Menelaus' tent, most princely Troilus.
There Diomed doth feast with him tonight;
Who neither looks upon the heaven nor earth,   280
But gives all gaze and bent of amorous view
On the fair Cressid.

TROILUS
Shall I, sweet lord, be bound to you so much,
After we part from Agamemnon's tent,
To bring me thither?

ULYSSES   You shall command me, sir.
As gentle tell me, of what honour was
This Cressida in Troy? Had she no lover there
That wails her absence?

271 we] you F   274 Beat ... taborins] F: To taste your bounties Q   275.1 *Flourish*] CAPELL;
not in QF   *all except Troilus and Ulysses*] ROWE: *not in* QF   280 upon ... nor] on heauen, nor
on F   283 you] thee F   286 As] F; But Q

266 **pelting** petty
271 **convive** feast together (the only recorded use)
274 **Beat loud the taborins** The Q reading
seems an awkward repetition of 'your
bounties' (273) and may therefore have
been altered by Shakespeare.
taborins small drums, each beaten with
one stick

279–82 **There Diomed ... Cressid** Ulysses
has not left the stage during the whole
scene and could not have obtained this
information; but no audience would
notice this telescoping, which was a con-
venient way of getting Ulysses to act as
Troilus' guide, and of preparing the
audience for Cressida's seduction.
286 **gentle** courteously

TROILUS

O, sir, to such as boasting show their scars,
A mock is due. Will you walk on, my lord?   290
She was beloved, she loved; she is, and doth;
But still sweet love is food for fortune's tooth.   *Exeunt*

5.1   *Enter Achilles and Patroclus*

ACHILLES

I'll heat his blood with Greekish wine tonight,
Which with my scimitar I'll cool tomorrow.
Patroclus, let us feast him to the height.

PATROCLUS

Here comes Thersites.
        Enter Thersites

ACHILLES   How now, thou core of envy!
Thou crusty botch of nature, what's the news?

THERSITES Why, thou picture of what thou seemest, and idol
of idiot-worshippers, here's a letter for thee.

ACHILLES From whence, fragment?

THERSITES Why, thou full dish of fool, from Troy.
        Achilles reads the letter

PATROCLUS Who keeps the tent now?   10

THERSITES The surgeon's box, or the patient's wound.

PATROCLUS Well said, adversity! And what need these
tricks?

THERSITES Prithee, be silent, boy; I profit not by thy talk.
Thou art said to be Achilles' male varlet.

PATROCLUS Male varlet, you rogue! What's that?

---

291 she loved] F; my Lord Q
    5.1.4 core] F; curre Q   5 botch] THEOBALD;   batch QF   9.1 *Achilles ... letter*] CAPELL
(*subs.*); *not in* QF   12 need these] F; needs this Q   14 boy] F; box Q   15 said] thought F

5.1 The Greek camp.

3 **to the height** to the utmost degree
5 **botch** Theobald's emendation, meaning
  'ulcer' or 'boil', fits in with the disease
  imagery; and with *core* in the previous
  line, the word recalls Thersites' own
  phrase 'botchy core' (2.1.6). On the other
  hand, the QF reading, *batch*, suits the food
  imagery. Thersites has been called a *cobloaf* (2.1.37), and *crusty* is appropriate to
  loaves.

8 **fragment** a scrap of left-over food
10 **keeps the tent** (because Achilles now
  seems determined to fight Hector)
11 **the surgeon's box** Thersites deliberately
  supposes him to have used *tent* in the
  sense '(surgeon's) probe' or 'lint used to
  clean and probe a wound'.
12 **adversity** contrariety – because Thersites
  deliberately misunderstands
15 **male varlet** man-servant, with an innu-
  endo explained in l. 17

THERSITES Why, his masculine whore. Now the rotten
diseases of the south, the guts-griping, ruptures, catarrhs,
loads o'gravel i'th' back, lethargies, cold palsies, raw eyes,
dirt-rotten livers, wheezing lungs, bladders full of impos-   20
tume, sciaticas, lime-kilns i'th' palm, incurable bone-
ache, and the rivelled fee-simple of the tetter, take and
take again such preposterous discoveries!

PATROCLUS Why, thou damnable box of envy, thou; what
mean'st thou to curse thus?

THERSITES Do I curse thee?

PATROCLUS Why, no, you ruinous butt; you whoreson indis-
tinguishable cur, no.

THERSITES No? Why art thou then exasperate, thou idle
immaterial skein of sleave-silk, thou green sarcenet flap   30
for a sore eye, thou tassel of a prodigal's purse, thou? Ah,
how the poor world is pestered with such waterflies,
diminutives of nature!

PATROCLUS Out, gall!

THERSITES Finch-egg!

18 the guts-griping] guts-griping F   guts-griping, ruptures] F4: guts griping ruptures Q
catarrhs] F; *not in* Q   19 i'th'] F; in the Q   19–22 raw . . . tetter] and the like F   25 mean'st]
F; meanes Q   28 cur, no] Curre F   30 sleave-silk] Sleyd silke F   sarcenet] F; sacenet Q   31
tassel] F; toslell Q

17 **masculine whore** The nature of the
relationship between Achilles and
Patroclus (i.e. friendship or sexual love)
was much discussed in classical times,
and later. See New Variorum, 255.
18 **diseases of the south** 'Shakespeare often
speaks of the south as unhealthy' (Deighton), but may here be referring to the
south wind.
18–22 **guts-griping . . . tetter** A. H. G.
Doran, in *Shakespeare's England* (1916),
i. 437–8, says that the names may be
translated into modern terms as 'syphilis,
colic, hernias, catarrhs, pain in the loins
ascribed . . . to gravel or stone in the kid-
neys, apoplectic stroke with unconscious-
ness, permanent paralysis of the limbs,
chronic inflammation of the lids with inverted lashes, obscure diseases ascribed to
the liver, asthma, chronic cystitis, lum-
bago or sciatica (possibly a euphemism),
psoriasis of the palm, bone-ache from any
cause, and chronic ringworm (?)'.

20–1 **impostume** abscess
21 **lime-kilns** burning sensations
22 **rivelled** shrivelled
fee-simple 'the most common use of "fee
simple" in drama . . . does not directly involve any land estate; but the absolute
nature of the estate is implied in a
metaphor in which any entire interest is
likened to an estate in fee simple' (Clarkson and Warren, 51). The phrase here
means that the tetter will be permanent.
23 **preposterous** unnatural (hinting at sod-
omy)
27 **butt** (a) hogshead (b) buttock
29 **exasperate** exasperated
30 **sleave-silk** 'soft floss-silk used for weav-
ing' (Schmidt)
sarcenet fine, thin soft silk
32 **waterflies** Like Osric, the affected courtier
in *Hamlet*, 5.2.
35 **Finch-egg** diminutive, gaily-coloured, in-
significant

ACHILLES

My sweet Patroclus, I am thwarted quite
From my great purpose in tomorrow's battle.
Here is a letter from Queen Hecuba,
A token from her daughter, my fair love,
Both taxing me and gaging me to keep   40
An oath that I have sworn. I will not break it.
Fall Greeks; fail fame; honour or go or stay;
My major vow lies here; this I'll obey.
Come, come, Thersites, help to trim my tent;
This night in banqueting must all be spent.
Away, Patroclus!   *Exeunt Achilles and Patroclus*

THERSITES With too much blood and too little brain, these
two may run mad; but if with too much brain and too little
blood they do, I'll be a curer of madmen. Here's Agamemnon, an honest fellow enough and one that loves quails,   50
but he has not so much brain as ear-wax; and the goodly
transformation of Jupiter there, his brother, the bull, the
primitive statue and oblique memorial of cuckolds, a
thrifty shoeing-horn in a chain, hanging at his brother's
leg – to what form but that he is, should wit larded with
malice and malice forced with wit turn him to? To an ass,
were nothing; he is both ass and ox; to an ox, were nothing; he is both ox and ass. To be a dog, a mule, a cat, a
fitchew, a toad, a lizard, an owl, a puttock, or a herring
without a roe, I would not care; but to be Menelaus, I   60
would conspire against destiny! Ask me not what I would

46 *Exeunt . . . Patroclus*] HANMER; *not in* Q; *Exit* F   52 brother] F; be Q   54 hanging] F; *not in* Q   brother's] F; bare Q   56 forced] F; faced Q   57 he is] F; her's Q   58 dog] F; day Q   mule] Q (Moyle), F   59 fitchew] F; Fichooke Q   61 not] F; *not in* Q

38 **letter** Achilles has been reading it during the exchange of abuse between Thersites and Patroclus.
40 **gaging** engaging, binding
50 **one that loves quails** whoremonger, a quail being a slang term for a prostitute – implying, presumably, that he is a very ordinary man
51–2 **the goodly . . . bull** Jupiter transformed himself into a bull to rape Europa; Menelaus is called a bull because he has the horns of a cuckold.
52 **brother** The Q reading is probably a

misreading of *br.*
53 **primitive** archetypal
54 **shoeing-horn** subservient tool; continuing the reference to cuckoldry.
in a chain Nares suggests that thrifty persons may have carried their shoe-horns hanging from a chain, but no parallel has been found.
brother's The Q reading, *bare*, is probably a misreading of *brs.*
56 **forced** stuffed
59 **fitchew** polecat
puttock kite

be, if I were not Thersites; for I care not to be the louse of
a lazar, so I were not Menelaus. Hey-day! Sprites and fires!

Enter Hector, Ajax, Troilus, Agamemnon, Ulysses,
Nestor, Menelaus, and Diomedes, with lights

AGAMEMNON
We go wrong, we go wrong.

AJAX   No, yonder 'tis;
There where we see the lights.

HECTOR   I trouble you.

AJAX
No, not a whit.

Enter Achilles

ULYSSES   Here comes himself to guide you.

ACHILLES
Welcome, brave Hector; welcome, princes all.

AGAMEMNON
So now, fair Prince of Troy, I bid good night.
Ajax commands the guard to tend on you.

HECTOR
Thanks and good night to the Greeks' general.   70

MENELAUS
Good night, my lord.

HECTOR   Good night, sweet Lord Menelaus.

THERSITES *(aside)* Sweet draught, 'sweet' quoth a! Sweet sink,
sweet sewer.

ACHILLES
Good night and welcome, both at once, to those
That go or tarry.

AGAMEMNON Good night.

Exeunt Agamemnon and Menelaus

ACHILLES
Old Nestor tarries; and you too, Diomed,
Keep Hector company an hour or two.

---

63 Hey-day! Sprites] Hoy-day spirits F   63.1 *Hector, Ajax*] F; *not in* Q   *Troilus*] THEOBALD; *not*
in QF   63.2 *Menelaus*] CAPELL; *not in* QF   *and*] *not in* F   65 lights] light F   66 *Enter Achilles*]
F; *not in* Q   68 good night] F; God night Q   73 sewer] QF (sure)   74 at once] F; *not in* Q
76.1 *Exeunt ... Menelaus*] Q (*subs.*); *not in* F

63 **lazar** leper   73 **sewer** The QF reading was merely a
    Sprites and fires (suggested by the sight   recognized phonetic spelling.
    of the approaching torches)

DIOMEDES

I cannot, lord; I have important business,

The tide whereof is now. Good night, great Hector.   80

HECTOR Give me your hand.

ULYSSES (*aside to Troilus*)

Follow his torch; he goes to Calchas' tent.

I'll keep you company.

TROILUS   Sweet sir, you honour me.

HECTOR

And so, good night.

           Exit Diomedes, followed by Ulysses and Troilus

ACHILLES   Come, come, enter my tent.

           Exeunt Achilles, Hector, Ajax, and Nestor

THERSITES That same Diomed's a false-hearted rogue, a most
unjust knave; I will no more trust him when he leers than
I will a serpent when he hisses; he will spend his mouth
and promise, like Babbler the hound; but when he per-
forms, astronomers foretell it; it is prodigious, there will
come some change; the sun borrows of the moon when   90
Diomed keeps his word. I will rather leave to see Hector
than not to dog him. They say he keeps a Trojan drab and
uses the traitor Calchas' tent. I'll after. Nothing but lechery! All incontinent varlets!   *Exit*

5.2   *Enter Diomedes*

DIOMEDES What, are you up here, ho? Speak.

CALCHAS (*within*) Who calls?

DIOMEDES Diomed. Calchas, I think. Where's your daughter?

CALCHAS (*within*) She comes to you.

84 *Exit . . . Troilus*] CAPELL (*subs.*); *not in* QF   84.1 *Exeunt . . . Nestor*] CAPELL; *Exeunt* QF   88
Babbler] WALKER (*conj.* BALDWIN); brabler QF   89 it; it]it, that it F   93 Calchas'] Chalcas his
F   94 *Exit*] HANMER; *not in* Q; *Exeunt* F
    5.2.2, 4 (*within*)] HANMER; *not in* QF   3 your] you F

88 **Babbler** a hound that gives tongue too
freely (*OED*), when he is off the scent.
Shakespeare ought to have written
Babbler, and perhaps he did. A brabbler
is a brawler.

92 **him** Diomedes

92 **They say** (another example of dramatic
telescoping)

5.2 Outside Calchas' tent.

4 **She comes to you** Calchas is acting as
pander.

Enter Troilus and Ulysses, at a distance; then Thersites

ULYSSES

Stand where the torch may not discover us.

Enter Cressida

TROILUS

Cressid comes forth to him.

DIOMEDES   How now, my charge!

CRESSIDA

Now, my sweet guardian! Hark, a word with you.

She whispers

TROILUS Yea, so familiar!

ULYSSES She will sing any man at first sight.

THERSITES And any man may sing her, if he can take her clef;   10
she's noted.

DIOMEDES Will you remember?

CRESSIDA Remember? Yes.

DIOMEDES Nay, but do then;

And let your mind be coupled with your words.

TROILUS What should she remember?

ULYSSES List.

CRESSIDA

Sweet honey Greek, tempt me no more to folly.

THERSITES Roguery!

DIOMEDES Nay, then –   20

CRESSIDA I'll tell you what –

DIOMEDES

Foh, foh! Come, tell a pin; you are forsworn.

CRESSIDA

In faith, I cannot. What would you have me do?

4.1 *Enter . . . Ulysses*] F; *not in* Q   *at . . . Thersites*] ROWE (*subs.*); *not in* QF   5.1 *Enter Cressida*]
F; *after Troilus' speech* Q   7.1 *She whispers*] ROWE (*subs.*); *not in* QF   10 sing] finde F   clef] Q
(Cliff); life F   13 CRESSIDA] F2; Cal⟨chas⟩. Q, F1   16 should] F; shall Q   22 pin; you] F
(*subs.*); pin you Q   forsworn] a forsworne. – F

4.1 **at a distance** In this complex scene, the
tent is presumably represented by the
tiring-house or inner stage, from which
Calchas and Cressida emerge; Troilus and
Ulysses could be nominally screened by
one of the pillars, and Thersites by the
other.

5 **discover** reveal

9 **sing any man at first sight** The image is

taken from sight-reading and refers to
Cressida's rapid familiarity with
Diomedes.

10–11 **clef . . . noted** Quibbling on *clef* (cliff
Q) (a) key (b) pudend (Partridge), and on
noted (a) in musical notes (b) summed up.

22 **tell a pin** tell me nothing, i.e. 'to express
impatience at trifles' (Onions)

THERSITES A juggling trick – to be secretly open.
DIOMEDES
  What did you swear you would bestow on me?
CRESSIDA
  I prithee, do not hold me to mine oath;
  Bid me do anything but that, sweet Greek.
DIOMEDES Good night.
TROILUS Hold, patience!
ULYSSES How now, Trojan!   30
CRESSIDA Diomed –
DIOMEDES
  No, no, good night; I'll be your fool no more.
TROILUS Thy better must.
CRESSIDA Hark, a word in your ear.
TROILUS O plague and madness!
ULYSSES
  You are moved, prince; let us depart, I pray,
  Lest your displeasure should enlarge itself
  To wrathful terms. This place is dangerous;
  The time right deadly; I beseech you, go.
TROILUS
  Behold, I pray you.
ULYSSES   Nay, good my lord, go off;   40
  You flow to great distraction; come, my lord.
TROILUS
  I prithee, stay.
ULYSSES   You have not patience; come.
TROILUS
  I pray you, stay; by hell and all hell's torments,
  I will not speak a word.
DIOMEDES   And so, good night.
CRESSIDA
  Nay, but you part in anger.
TROILUS   Doth that grieve thee?
  O withered truth!

27 anything] not any thing F   34 a] one F   36 pray] pray you F   40 Nay] F; Now Q   41
distraction] F; distruction Q   42 prithee] pray thee F   43 all hell's] hell F

24 **juggling trick** 'pertaining to copulation'   28–31 **Good night ... Diomed** These four
  (Partridge)   speeches could be regarded as a
  secretly open sexually open and prepared   hexameter.
  for intercourse

ULYSSES   How now, my lord!

TROILUS   By Jove,

   I will be patient.

CRESSIDA   Guardian! Why, Greek!

DIOMEDES   Foh, foh! Adieu! You palter.

CRESSIDA

   In faith, I do not. Come hither once again.

ULYSSES

   You shake, my lord, at something; will you go?   50

   You will break out.

TROILUS   She strokes his cheek!

ULYSSES   Come, come.

TROILUS

   Nay, stay; by Jove, I will not speak a word;

   There is between my will and all offences

   A guard of patience. Stay a little while.

THERSITES   How the devil Luxury, with his fat rump and

   potato-finger, tickles these two together! Fry, lechery, fry!

DIOMEDES   But will you then?

CRESSIDA

   In faith, I will, la; never trust me else.

DIOMEDES

   Give me some token for the surety of it.

CRESSIDA   I'll fetch you one.   *Exit*   60

ULYSSES

   You have sworn patience.

TROILUS   Fear me not, sweet lord;

   I will not be myself, nor have cognition

   Of what I feel. I am all patience.

       Enter Cressida

THERSITES   Now the pledge; now, now, now!

CRESSIDA   Here, Diomed, keep this sleeve.

      She gives him the sleeve

---

46 How now, my lord] why, how now Lord F   48 Adieu] F; *not in* Q   56 these two] This
edition; these F; *not in* Q   57 But will] F; Will Q   58 la] THEOBALD; lo QF   61 sweet] F; my
Q   65.1 *She . . . sleeve*] COLLIER 1853 (*subs.*); *not in* QF

55 **Luxury** lust

56 **potato** regarded as an aphrodisiac (and
   possibly referring to the phallic appearance of the finger)
   two This insertion makes a more
   forceful phrase. F probably restored

only part of the Q omission.

65–82 **keep this sleeve . . . follows it** Tannenbaum (p.80) argues for the original
   text, the sleeve changing from one to the
   other five times; but this would be difficult
   in performance.

TROILUS

O beauty, where is thy faith?

ULYSSES   My lord –

TROILUS

I will be patient; outwardly I will.

CRESSIDA

You look upon that sleeve; behold it well.

He loved me – O false wench! – Give't me again.

She takes it back

DIOMEDES Whose was't?   70

CRESSIDA

It is no matter, now I have't again.

I will not meet with you tomorrow night.

I prithee, Diomed, visit me no more.

THERSITES Now she sharpens; well said, whetstone!

DIOMEDES

I shall have it.

CRESSIDA   What, this?

DIOMEDES   Ay, that.

CRESSIDA

O, all you gods! O pretty, pretty pledge!

Thy master now lies thinking on his bed

Of thee and me, and sighs, and takes my glove,

And gives memorial dainty kisses to it,

As I kiss thee.

She kisses it; Diomedes snatches it

                        Nay, do not snatch it from me: 80

He that takes that doth take my heart withal.

DIOMEDES

I had your heart before; this follows it.

TROILUS I did swear patience.

CRESSIDA

You shall not have it, Diomed; faith you shall not;

I'll give you something else.

67–81 . . . will. | CRESSIDA] F; *not in* Q   69.1] WALKER; *not in* QF   71 have't] F; ha't Q   77 on]
in F   80 *She . . . snatches it*] This edition; *not in* QF   Nay . . . me:] *spoken by Cressida* THEOBALD
(*conj.* THIRLBY); *spoken by 'Dio⟨medes⟩.'* QF   81 doth take] rakes F   84 CRESSIDA] F; *not in* Q

78 **memorial** remembering (our love)   since they do not suit Diomedes, has been
80 **Nay . . . me** Thirlby's conjecture, that   followed by nearly all editors.
   these words should be given to Cressida,

DIOMEDES

I will have this. Whose was it?

CRESSIDA   It is no matter.

DIOMEDES Come, tell me whose it was.

CRESSIDA

'Twas one's that loved me better than you will.

But now you have it, take it.

DIOMEDES   Whose was it?

CRESSIDA

By all Diana's waiting-women yond,   90

And by herself, I will not tell you whose.

DIOMEDES

Tomorrow will I wear it on my helm,

And grieve his spirit that dares not challenge it.

TROILUS

Wert thou the devil, and wor'st it on thy horn,

It should be challenged.

CRESSIDA

Well, well, 'tis done, 'tis past – and yet it is not;

I will not keep my word.

DIOMEDES   Why then, farewell;

Thou never shalt mock Diomed again.

CRESSIDA

You shall not go; one cannot speak a word,

But it straight starts you.

DIOMEDES   I do not like this fooling.   100

TROILUS

Nor I, by Pluto; but that that likes not you,

Pleases me best.

DIOMEDES   What, shall I come? The hour?

CRESSIDA

Ay, come. O Jove! Do come. I shall be plagued.

DIOMEDES

Farewell till then.

---

88 one's] Q (on's); one F   90 By] F; And by Q   101 TROILUS] HANMER; *Ther⟨sites⟩*. QF
you] me F

86 **Whose was it?** Diomedes must know from   101–2 **Nor I . . . best** The words seem to be
4.4 that Troilus is his rival. He wants   Troilus'. He has earlier sworn by Pluto
Cressida to confess it as a token of her sur-   (4.4.125); and Thersites does not norm-
render.   ally use verse, except in satirical couplets
90 **Diana's waiting-women** the stars   (as 111–12 below).

CRESSIDA   Good night; I prithee, come.

                                              Exit Diomedes

Troilus, farewell! One eye yet looks on thee,
But with my heart the other eye doth see.
Ah, poor our sex! This fault in us I find,
The error of our eye directs our mind;
What error leads must err – O, then conclude
Minds swayed by eyes are full of turpitude.   *Exit*   110

THERSITES

A proof of strength she could not publish more,
Unless she said 'My mind is now turned whore'.

ULYSSES

All's done, my lord.

TROILUS   It is.

ULYSSES   Why stay we then?

TROILUS

To make a recordation to my soul
Of every syllable that here was spoke.
But if I tell how these two did co-act,
Shall I not lie in publishing a truth?
Sith yet there is a credence in my heart,
An esperance so obstinately strong,
That doth invert th'attest of eyes and ears;   120
As if those organs had deceptious functions,
Created only to calumniate.
Was Cressid here?

ULYSSES   I cannot conjure, Trojan.

TROILUS

She was not, sure.

ULYSSES   Most sure she was.

TROILUS

Why, my negation hath no taste of madness.

ULYSSES

Nor mine, my lord; Cressid was here but now.

104.1 *Exit Diomedes*] F (*after* 'then'); *not in* Q   112 said] say F   116 co-act] F (coact); Court
Q   120 th'attest] that test F   121 had deceptious] F; were deceptions Q

TROILUS
> Let it not be believed for womanhood!
> Think we had mothers. Do not give advantage
> To stubborn critics, apt without a theme
> Fo⸱ depravation, to square the general sex   130
> By Cressid's rule; rather think this not Cressid.

ULYSSES
> What hath she done, prince, that can soil our mothers?

TROILUS
> Nothing at all, unless that this were she.

THERSITES Will a swagger himself out on's own eyes?

TROILUS
> This she? No; this is Diomed's Cressida.
> If beauty have a soul, this is not she;
> If souls guide vows, if vows be sanctimonies,
> If sanctimony be the gods' delight,
> If there be rule in unity itself,
> This was not she. O madness of discourse,   140
> That cause sets up with and against itself!
> Bifold authority, where reason can revolt
> Without perdition, and loss assume all reason
> Without revolt! This is, and is not, Cressid.
> Within my soul there doth conduce a fight
> Of this strange nature, that a thing inseparate
> Divides more wider than the sky and earth;
> And yet the spacious breadth of this division

---

132 soil] F; spoile Q   134 a] he F   137 be sanctimonies] are sanctimonie F   140 was] is F
141 itself] thy selfe F   142 Bifold] Q (By-fould); By foule F

---

127 **for** for the sake of
130 **depravation** vilification
130-1 **square . . . rule** judge all women by
  Cressida (quibbling on a carpenter's
  ruler)
137 **sanctimonies** sacred things
138 **If sanctimony . . . delight** I. A. Richards
  (*Speculative Instruments*, 209) cites
  Socrates' question to Euthyphro in the
  dialogue of that name: 'Do the gods love
  sanctimony because it is sanctimony? Or
  is it sanctimony because the gods love it?'
  It is, however, improbable that Shakespeare had direct knowledge of this
  passage.

139 **If there . . . itself** 'If unity is bound by
  rule, so that one cannot be more than
  one' (Deighton). Baldwin shows that the
  idea is derived ultimately from Aristotle.
142 **Bifold** divided
145 **doth conduce** is gathering together,
  starting. (Not previously recorded; 'of uncertain use', *OED*; but Variorum cites
  Cooper's *Thesaurus*, 1563, '*conduco*',
  gather or assemble in one place.)
146 **inseparate** undivided. Troilus is be-
  wildered by the fact that his Cressida and
  Diomedes', though one, is apparently split
  into two utterly different persons.

Admits no orifex for a point as subtle
As Ariachne's broken woof to enter.   150
Instance, O instance, strong as Pluto's gates:
Cressid is mine, tied with the bonds of heaven.
Instance, O instance, strong as heaven itself:
The bonds of heaven are slipped, dissolved and loosed,
And with another knot, five-finger-tied,
The fractions of her faith, orts of her love,
The fragments, scraps, the bits and greasy relics
Of her o'er-eaten faith are given to Diomed.

ULYSSES

May worthy Troilus be half attached
With that which here his passion doth express?   160

TROILUS

Ay, Greek; and that shall be divulgèd well
In characters as red as Mars his heart
Inflamed with Venus. Never did young man fancy
With so eternal and so fixed a soul.
Hark, Greek. As much as I do Cressid love,
So much by weight hate I her Diomed.
That sleeve is mine that he'll bear on his helm.
Were it a casque composed by Vulcan's skill,
My sword should bite it. Not the dreadful spout
Which shipmen do the hurricano call,   170

---

150 Ariachne's] F; *Ariathna's* Q *(uncorr.)*; *Ariachna's* Q *(corr.)*   155 five-finger-tied] POPE;
finde finger tied Q; fiue finger tied F   158 given] bound F   159 half] but half DYCE 1864 *(conj.*
W. S. WALKER)   165 as I] F2; I Q, F1   Cressid] *Cressida* F   167 on] in F

149 **orifex** orifice. (Condemned by *OED* as an
     error; but Shakespeare, following the
     comparatively learned Marlowe (*2 Tam-
     burlaine*, 2.4.9), deliberately used this
     form.)
150 **Ariachne** It used to be thought that
     Shakespeare confused Arachne, who was
     changed into a spider, with Ariadne; but
     he knew his Ovid too well for such a con-
     fusion. He may have given Arachne an
     extra syllable for metrical reasons; or, as
     Richards suggests (*Speculative Instru-
     ments*, 210), the confusion is not his but
     Troilus'. 'The opposites are all before
     him . . . and yet they come together and
     are indistinguishable – as Ariadne's clue
     and Arachne's web are merged in
     "Ariachne's broken woof".'
151 **Instance** 'A case adduced in objection

to or disproof of a universal assertion'
(*OED*)
155 **five-finger-tied** Chaucer, writing of lech-
     ery in the Parson's Tale, speaks of the five
     fingers of the Devil: 'The firste finger is the
     fool lookinge of the fool woman and the
     fool man ... The seconde finger is the
     vileyns touchinge in wikkede manere . . .
     The thridde, is foule words, that fareth lyk
     fyr that right anon brenneth the herte.
     The fourthe finger is the kissing . . . The
     fifthe finger of the deviles hand is the stin-
     kinge dede of Lecherie' (T. M. Pearce, *N.
     & Q.*, 7, 1960, 18–19).
156 **orts** fragments (of food)
159 **attached** affected
162 **Mars his** Mars's
168 **casque** helmet
170 **hurricano** waterspout

Constringed in mass by the almighty sun,
Shall dizzy with more clamour Neptune's ear
In his descent, than shall my prompted sword
Falling on Diomed.

THERSITES He'll tickle it for his concupy.

TROILUS

O Cressid! O false Cressid! False, false, false!
Let all untruths stand by thy stainèd name,
And they'll seem glorious.

ULYSSES   O, contain yourself;
Your passion draws ears hither.

        Enter Aeneas

AENEAS

I have been seeking you this hour, my lord.   180
Hector by this is arming him in Troy;
Ajax your guard stays to conduct you home.

TROILUS

Have with you, prince. My courteous lord, adieu.
Farewell, revolted fair, and, Diomed,
Stand fast, and wear a castle on thy head!

ULYSSES I'll bring you to the gates.

TROILUS Accept distracted thanks.

        Exeunt Troilus, Aeneas, and Ulysses

THERSITES Would I could meet that rogue Diomed! I would
croak like a raven; I would bode, I would bode. Patroclus
will give me anything for the intelligence of this whore;   190
the parrot will not do more for an almond than he for a

---

171 sun] Fenne F

171 **Constringed** pressed together (first occurrence)
172 **dizzy** make dizzy
173 **prompted** ready and eager
175 **He'll tickle it for his concupy** Some
editors think that 'He' = Diomedes, and
that the line means 'He'll be tickled for his
concupiscence' (New Variorum). Others,
with whom I agree, suppose that 'He' =
Troilus, the line meaning 'He'll fight it out
for his concupiscence' (or 'for his concubine'). Walker, however, thinks that
'it' = Diomedes' helmet, and that Thersites is mocking at Troilus' ranting.
concupy only recorded use; 'an allusion

to lustful desire . . . and secondarily to
concubine; perhaps the word is a
blend of concubine and occupy'
(Partridge; occupy, 'have sexual intercourse with')
177 **Let all . . . name** See 3.2.181 ff.
185 **castle** an extra-strong helmet
188–9 **I would croak like a raven** Tilley R33:
'The croaking raven bodes misfortune.'
189–90 **Patroclus . . . whore** despite his
relationship with Achilles
190 **intelligence of** information about.
191 **parrot . . . for an almond** Tilley A220:
'An almond for a parrot.'

commodious drab. Lechery, lechery! Still wars and lechery! Nothing else holds fashion. A burning devil take
them!   *Exit*

5.3   *Enter Hector and Andromache*
ANDROMACHE
    When was my lord so much ungently tempered,
    To stop his ears against admonishment?
    Unarm, unarm, and do not fight today.
HECTOR
    You train me to offend you; get you in.
    By all the everlasting gods, I'll go!
ANDROMACHE
    My dreams will sure prove ominous to the day.
HECTOR
    No more, I say.
            Enter Cassandra
CASSANDRA   Where is my brother Hector?
ANDROMACHE
    Here, sister; armed, and bloody in intent.
    Consort with me in loud and dear petition;
    Pursue we him on knees; for I have dreamed   10
    Of bloody turbulence, and this whole night
    Hath nothing been but shapes and forms of slaughter.
CASSANDRA
    O, 'tis true.
HECTOR   Ho! Bid my trumpet sound!
CASSANDRA
    No notes of sally, for the heavens, sweet brother.
HECTOR
    Be gone, I say. The gods have heard me swear.
CASSANDRA
    The gods are deaf to hot and peevish vows;
    They are polluted off'rings, more abhorred
    Than spotted livers in the sacrifice.

5.3.4 in] gone F   5 all] *not in* F   14 CASSANDRA] F; *Cres⟨sida⟩*. Q

---

192 **commodious** accommodating   **5.3** The palace.
193 **burning devil** (an allusion to venereal   4 **train** teach
     disease)   9 **dear** earnest

ANDROMACHE

O, be persuaded! Do not count it holy
To hurt by being just; it is as lawful,   20
For we would countenance give to violent thefts,
And rob in the behalf of charity.

CASSANDRA

It is the purpose that makes strong the vow;
But vows to every purpose must not hold.
Unarm, sweet Hector.

HECTOR   Hold you still, I say;
Mine honour keeps the weather of my fate.
Life every man holds dear; but the dear man
Holds honour far more precious-dear than life.
        Enter Troilus
How now, young man! Mean'st thou to fight today?

ANDROMACHE

Cassandra, call my father to persuade.   *Exit Cassandra*   30

HECTOR

No, faith, young Troilus; doff thy harness, youth.
I am today i'th' vein of chivalry.
Let grow thy sinews till their knots be strong,
And tempt not yet the brushes of the war.
Unarm thee, go; and doubt thou not, brave boy,
I'll stand today for thee and me and Troy.

TROILUS

Brother, you have a vice of mercy in you,
Which better fits a lion than a man.

HECTOR

What vice is that? Good Troilus, chide me for it.

TROILUS

When many times the captive Grecian falls,   41
Even in the fan and wind of your fair sword,
You bid them rise and live.

HECTOR

O, 'tis fair play.

19–24 ANDROMACHE ... hold] *See Appendix 2d.*   29 Mean'st] F;   meanest Q

19–24 O ... hold See Appendix 2d.
26 **keeps the weather** is to windward
27 **dear man** worthy man
32 **vein of chivalry** mood for (chivalrous) combat

34 **tempt not ... war** (a curious remark in view of what we hear of Troilus from Ulysses, 4.5.96 ff.)
41 **in** within

TROILUS   Fool's play, by heaven, Hector.

HECTOR

How now! How now!

TROILUS   For th'love of all the gods,
Let's leave the hermit Pity with our mother;
And when we have our armours buckled on,
The venomed vengeance ride upon our swords,
Spur them to ruthful work, rein them from ruth.

HECTOR

Fie, savage, fie!

TROILUS   Hector, then 'tis wars.

HECTOR

Troilus, I would not have you fight today.   50

TROILUS Who should withhold me?
Not fate, obedience, nor the hand of Mars
Beck'ning with fiery truncheon my retire;
Not Priamus and Hecuba on knees,
Their eyes o'ergallèd with recourse of tears;
Nor you, my brother, with your true sword drawn,
Opposed to hinder me, should stop my way,
But by my ruin.   .

Enter Priam and Cassandra

CASSANDRA

Lay hold upon him, Priam, hold him fast;
He is thy crutch; now if thou lose thy stay,   60
Thou on him leaning, and all Troy on thee,
Fall all together.

PRIAM   Come, Hector, come, go back.
Thy wife hath dreamed; thy mother hath had visions;
Cassandra doth foresee; and I myself
Am like a prophet suddenly enrapt,
To tell thee that this day is ominous;
Therefore, come back.

HECTOR   Aeneas is afield;
And I do stand engaged to many Greeks,
Even in the faith of valour, to appear
This morning to them.

---

45 mother] Mothers F   58 But ... ruin] F; *not in* Q

53 **fiery** stock epithet for Mars applied to his   65 **enrapt** carried away (first occurrence)
truncheon (Walker)   69 **faith of valour** a warrior's honour

PRIAM   Ay, but thou shalt not go.   70
HECTOR I must not break my faith.
  You know me dutiful; therefore, dear sir,
  Let me not shame respect, but give me leave
  To take that course by your consent and voice
  Which you do here forbid me, royal Priam.
CASSANDRA
  O Priam, yield not to him!
ANDROMACHE   Do not, dear father.
HECTOR .
  Andromache, I am offended with you;
  Upon the love you bear me, get you in.
                                        Exit Andromache

TROILUS
  This foolish, dreaming, superstitious girl
  Makes all these bodements.
CASSANDRA   O, farewell, dear Hector!   80
  Look how thou diest! Look how thy eye turns pale!
  Look how thy wounds do bleed at many vents!
  Hark how Troy roars! How Hecuba cries out!
  How poor Andromache shrills her dolours forth!
  Behold, distraction, frenzy, and amazement,
  Like witless antics, one another meet,
  And all cry 'Hector! Hector's dead! O Hector!'
TROILUS Away! Away!
CASSANDRA
  Farewell – yet soft! Hector, I take my leave;
  Thou dost thyself and all our Troy deceive.   *Exit*   90
HECTOR
  You are amazed, my liege, at her exclaims.
  Go in and cheer the town; we'll forth and fight,
  Do deeds worth praise, and tell you them at night.
PRIAM
  Farewell. The gods with safety stand about thee!
                        Exeunt Priam and Hector, separately
      Alarum

82 do] doth F   84 dolours] dolour F   85 distraction] F; destruction Q   89 yet] yes F   91
exclaims] WALKER (*conj.* TANNENBAUM); exclaime QF   93 worth] of F   94.1 *Exeunt ...
separately*] MALONE (*subs.*); *not in* QF

73 **respect** i.e. due to a parent   91 **exclaims** The plural seems more natural
86 **antics** 'burlesque performers' (Onions)   here than the singular.

TROILUS

   They are at it, hark! Proud Diomed, believe
   I come to lose my arm, or win my sleeve.
         Enter Pandarus
PANDARUS Do you hear, my lord? Do you hear?
TROILUS What now?
PANDARUS Here's a letter come from yon poor girl.
TROILUS Let me read.   100
PANDARUS (*aside*) A whoreson tisick, a whoreson rascally
   tisick so troubles me, and the foolish fortune of this girl;
   and what one thing, what another, that I shall leave you
   one o'these days. And I have a rheum in mine eyes too,
   and such an ache in my bones that, unless a man were
   cursed, I cannot tell what to think on't. – What says she
   there?
TROILUS

   Words, words, mere words; no matter from the heart;
   Th'effect doth operate another way.
         He tears the letter
   Go, wind, to wind! There turn and change together.   110
   My love with words and errors still she feeds,
   But edifies another with her deeds.   *Exeunt separately*

5.4   *Alarum. Excursions. Enter Thersites*
THERSITES Now they are clapper-clawing one another; I'll
   go look on. That dissembling abominable varlet, Diomed,
   has got that same scurvy doting foolish young knave's
   sleeve of Troy there in his helm. I would fain see them
   meet; that that same young Trojan ass, that loves the
   whore there, might send that Greekish whoremasterly
   villain with the sleeve back to the dissembling luxurious

---

104 o'these] ROWE; ath's Q; oth's F   109.1 *He ... letter*] ROWE; *not in* QF   112 *Exeunt
separately*] MALONE (*subs.*); *Exeunt* Q; *Exeunt* F (*after additional passage*). *See Appendix 2e.*
   5.4.0.1 *Alarum*] F (*at end of 5.3 before 'Exeunt'*); *not in* Q   *Excursions ... Thersites*] CAPELL;
Enter Thersites: excursions Q; *Enter Thersites in excursion* F   3 *young*] F; *not in* Q

---

96 **I come** Troilus is about to leave.
101 **tisick** dialectal form of 'phthisic', loosely
   applied to various lung or throat complaints.
109 **Th'effect ... way** i.e. the letter, designed
   to soften my heart, has hardened it
112 + F adds 2½ lines. See Appendix 2e.

5.4 The battlefield is the setting for the rest
   of the play.
1 **clapper-clawing** scratching, mauling.
   The word is used in the Epistle.
3–4 **knave's sleeve of Troy** i.e. Trojan
   knave's sleeve.

drab of a sleeveless errand. O'th' tother side, the policy of
those crafty-swearing rascals, that stale old mouse-eaten
dry cheese, Nestor, and that same dog-fox, Ulysses, is   10
proved not worth a blackberry. They set me up in policy
that mongrel cur, Ajax, against that dog of as bad a kind,
Achilles; and now is the cur Ajax prouder than the cur
Achilles, and will not arm today; whereupon the Grecians
begin to proclaim barbarism, and policy grows into an ill
opinion. Soft! Here comes Sleeve, and t'other.
         Enter Diomedes, Troilus following
TROILUS
    Fly not; for shouldst thou take the river Styx,
    I would swim after.
DIOMEDES   Thou dost miscall retire;
    I do not fly; but advantageous care
    Withdrew me from the odds of multitude.   20
    Have at thee!
THERSITES Hold thy whore, Grecian! Now for thy whore,
    Trojan! Now the sleeve, now the sleeve!
                Exeunt Troilus and Diomedes, fighting
         Enter Hector
HECTOR
    What art thou, Greek? Art thou for Hector's match?
    Art thou of blood and honour?
THERSITES No, no; I am a rascal; a scurvy, railing knave; a
    very filthy rogue.
HECTOR I do believe thee. Live.   *Exit*
THERSITES God-a-mercy, that thou wilt believe me; but a
    plague break thy neck for frighting me! What's become of 30
    the wenching rogues? I think they have swallowed one

---

9 stale] stole F   11 proved not] WALKER (*conjectured anonymously,* CAMBRIDGE); not proou'd QF
15 begin] ROWE 1714; began QF   16 Sleeve] This edition; sleeue Q, F (*subs.*)   t'other] th'
other F   16.1 *Enter ... following*] CAPELL; *not in* Q; *Enter Diomed and Troylus* F   23.1-2 *Exeunt*
... Hector] MALONE; *Enter Hector* QF   24 thou, Greek] F; Greeke Q

8 **sleeveless** proverbially futile (Tilley E180),
    with a quibble on the actual sleeve.
    policy craftiness
11 **proved not** An improvement on the order
    in QF. (Such transpositions are common
    in Elizabethan texts.)
15 **proclaim barbarism** declare that they will

choose barbarism or anarchy (since
'policy' has failed to bring results)
18 **miscall retire** i.e. as flight
20 **odds of multitude** because I was greatly
    outnumbered
29 **God-a-mercy** Thank God

another. I would laugh at that miracle; yet in a sort lechery eats itself. I'll seek them.   *Exit*

5.5   *Enter Diomedes and Servant*
DIOMEDES
Go, go, my servant, take thou Troilus' horse;
Present the fair steed to my lady Cressid.
Fellow, commend my service to her beauty;
Tell her I have chastised the amorous Trojan,
And am her knight by proof.
SERVANT   I go, my lord.   *Exit*
        Enter Agamemnon
AGAMEMNON
Renew, renew! The fierce Polydamas
Hath beat down Menon; bastard Margarelon
Hath Doreus prisoner,
And stands Colossus-wise, waving his beam,
Upon the pashèd corpses of the kings,   10
Epistrophus and Cedius; Polixenes is slain;
Amphimachus and Thoas deadly hurt;
Patroclus ta'en or slain; and Palamedes
Sore hurt and bruised; the dreadful sagittary
Appals our numbers; haste we, Diomed,
To reinforcement, or we perish all.   *Exit*
        Enter Nestor and other Greeks

5.5.0.1 *Servant*] Q; *Seruants* F   5 *Exit*] HANMER; *not in* QF   **5.1** *Enter Agamemnon*] *as here* F;
after 'proof' Q   10 kings.] F3; Kings: QF   11 Epistrophus] STEEVENS; *Epistropus* QF   Cedius]
CAPELL; *Cedus* QF   16 *Exit*] WALKER (*goes*); *not in* QF   **16.1** *and other Greeks*] WALKER; *not in* QF

32–3 **lechery eats itself** A particular example
  of the anarchy described by Ulysses
  (1.3.119–24); and perhaps a reference to
  Aaron's rod, which turned into a serpent
  and devoured the others – Exodus 7: 12
  (Carter).
5.5.2 **Present . . . Cressid** Caxton, ii. 608.
  5 **by proof** not by words only
6–13 **Renew . . . Palamedes** The names are
  from Caxton (ii. 599–600), but Shakespeare does not follow the details of the
  narrative. King Epistropus and Cedus, his
  brother, were killed by Hector; King Amphimachus was slain by Aeneas; Hector
  slew Doreus and Polixenes; Polydamas
  was Antenor's son; Margareton, one of

Priam's bastards, was slain by Achilles;
Menon wounded Achilles in revenge for
the death of Hector; Palamedes was later
chosen as generalissimo and killed by
Paris.
  7 **Margarelon** (possibly a misprint for
    Margareton)
 10 **pashèd** smashed
 14 **sagittary** A 'marvellous beast' brought to
    Troy by Epistropus, 'that behinde the mid-
    dest was an horse, and before a man, this
    beast was harie, like an horse, and had his
    eyes red as a coale, and shot right well
    with a bowe' (Caxton, ii. 567); not the
    Epistropus mentioned earlier.

NESTOR

Go, bear Patroclus' body to Achilles,
And bid the snail-paced Ajax arm for shame.

                                        Exeunt some

There is a thousand Hectors in the field.
Now here he fights on Galathe his horse,   20
And there lacks work; anon he's there afoot,
And there they fly or die, like scalèd schools
Before the belching whale; then is he yonder,
And there the strawy Greeks, ripe for his edge,
Fall down before him, like a mower's swath;
Here, there, and everywhere he leaves and takes,
Dexterity so obeying appetite
That what he will he does, and does so much
That proof is called impossibility.

          Enter Ulysses

ULYSSES

O courage, courage, princes! Great Achilles   30
Is arming, weeping, cursing, vowing vengeance;
Patroclus' wounds have roused his drowsy blood,
Together with his mangled Myrmidons,
That noseless, handless, hacked and chipped, come to him,
Crying on Hector. Ajax hath lost a friend,
And foams at mouth, and he is armed and at it,
Roaring for Troilus, who hath done today
Mad and fantastic execution,
Engaging and redeeming of himself
With such a careless force and forceless care   40
As if that luck, in very spite of cunning,
Bade him win all.

          Enter Ajax

AJAX

Troilus! Thou coward Troilus!   *Exit*

18.1 *Exeunt some*] WALKER (*subs.*); *not in* QF   22 scalèd] F; scaling Q   24 strawy] straying F
25 a] the F   41 luck] F; lust Q   42.1 *Enter Ajax*] F; *in place of speech prefix* Q

18 **snail-paced** See 2.1.28–9. Tilley S579:
   'as slow as a snail'.
20 **Galathe** Mentioned as the name of Hector's horse by Caxton, ii. 580.
22 **scalèd** (a) dispersed (b) scaly
   schools 'sculls' (QF) is a variant

spelling (*OED*)
24 **edge** i.e. of his sword
29 **proof** visible fact (Seltzer)
40 **careless force and forceless care** non-
   chalant strength and effortless concern

DIOMEDES   Ay, there, there!   *Exit*
NESTOR
  So, so, we draw together.
        Enter Achilles
ACHILLES   Where is this Hector?
  Come, come, thou boy-queller, show thy face;
  Know what it is to meet Achilles angry;
  Hector! Where's Hector? I will none but Hector.

                                                    Exeunt

5.6   *Enter Ajax*
AJAX
  Troilus, thou coward Troilus, show thy head!
        Enter Diomedes
DIOMEDES
  Troilus, I say! Where's Troilus?
AJAX   What wouldst thou?
DIOMEDES I would correct him.
AJAX
  Were I the general, thou shouldst have my office
  Ere that correction. Troilus, I say! What, Troilus!
        Enter Troilus
TROILUS
  O traitor Diomed! Turn thy false face, thou traitor,
  And pay the life thou ow'st me for my horse.
DIOMEDES Ha! Art thou there?
AJAX
  I'll fight with him alone. Stand, Diomed.
DIOMEDES
  He is my prize; I will not look upon.   10
TROILUS
  Come both you cogging Greeks; have at you both!
                                      Exeunt fighting

43 [*Diomedes] Exit*] WALKER (*goes*); *after 'together', l. 44* QF   47.1 *Exeunt*] CAPELL; *Exit* QF
  5.6.0.1. *Enter Ajax*] F; *in place of speech prefix* Q   1.1 *Enter Diomedes*] F; *in place of speech prefix*
Q   7 the] CAPELL; thy QF   ow'st] CAPELL; owest QF   11.1 *Exeunt fighting*] ROWE; *Exit Troylus* F; *not in* Q

44 **draw together** overcome our divisions –   **5.6**.3 **correct** punish
  because he realizes that Achilles will   10 **look upon** act as spectator
  fight.   11 **cogging** cheating

Enter Hector

HECTOR

    Yea, Troilus! O, well fought, my youngest brother!

    Enter Achilles

ACHILLES

    Now do I see thee; ha! Have at thee, Hector!

    They fight

HECTOR Pause, if thou wilt.

ACHILLES

    I do disdain thy courtesy, proud Trojan.

    Be happy that my arms are out of use;

    My rest and negligence befriends thee now,

    But thou anon shalt hear of me again;

    Till when, go seek thy fortune.   *Exit*

HECTOR   Fare thee well.

    I would have been much more a fresher man,   20

    Had I expected thee.

    Enter Troilus

            How now, my brother!

TROILUS

    Ajax hath ta'en Aeneas. Shall it be?

    No, by the flame of yonder glorious heaven,

    He shall not carry him; I'll be ta'en too,

    Or bring him off. Fate, hear me what I say:

    I reck not though thou end my life today.   *Exit*

    Enter one in sumptuous armour

HECTOR

    Stand, stand, thou Greek; thou art a goodly mark.

    No? Wilt thou not? I like thy armour well;

    I'll frush it and unlock the rivets all,

    But I'll be master of it.   *Exit Greek*

            Wilt thou not, beast, abide?   30

    Why then, fly on; I'll hunt thee for thy hide.   *Exit*

11.2 *Enter Hector*] F; *not in* Q   12.1 *Enter Achilles*] F; *in place of speech prefix* Q   13.1 *They fight*] ROWE; *not in* QF   21 *Enter Troilus*] *as here* CAMBRIDGE; *at end of line* QF   26 thou] F; I Q 26.1 *sumptuous*] MALONE; *not in* QF   30 *Exit Greek*] WALKER (*the Greek flees*); *not in* QF

14 **Pause, if thou wilt** An example of Hector's 'fair play', he having won the first bout.

17 **My rest . . . now** (referring to the period when he kept his tent)

25 **bring him off** rescue him

29 **frush** smash

31 **I'll hunt thee for thy hide** This episode is recounted by Caxton and Lydgate, but only the latter draws the moral that Hector is guilty of covetousness: 'He hent him up afore him on his stede, | And fast

5.7   *Enter Achilles with Myrmidons*

ACHILLES

Come here about me, you my Myrmidons;
Mark what I say. Attend me where I wheel;
Strike not a stroke, but keep yourselves in breath,
And when I have the bloody Hector found,
Empale him with your weapons round about;
In fellest manner execute your arms.
Follow me, sirs, and my proceedings eye;
It is decreed, Hector the great must die.   *Exeunt*

5.7a   *Enter Menelaus and Paris, fighting, and Thersites*

THERSITES The cuckold and the cuckold-maker are at it.
   Now, bull! Now, dog! 'Loo, Paris! 'Loo now, my double-   10
   horned Spartan! 'Loo, Paris, 'loo! The bull has the game.
   Ware horns, ho!   *Exeunt Paris and Menelaus*
      Enter Margarelon

MARGARELON Turn, slave, and fight.

THERSITES What art thou?

MARGARELON A bastard son of Priam's.

THERSITES I am a bastard too; I love bastards. I am bastard
   begot, bastard instructed, bastard in mind, bastard in

5.7.1 ACHILLES] F; *not in* Q   6 arms] arme F   8 *Exeunt*] POPE; *Exit* QF   8.1 *fighting*] CAPELL;
not in QF   11 horned] ALEXANDER (*conj.* KELLNER); hen'd QF   Spartan] sparrow F   12.1 *Enter
Margarelon*] CAPELL; *Enter Bastard* QF   16–17 bastard begot] a Bastard begot F

gan wyth him for to ryde. | From the
wardes a lytell out of syde. | At good leyser
playnly if he may, | To spoyle him of his
ryche arraye, | Full glad and lyght of his
newe empryse. | But out alas of false
covetise, | Whose gredy fret the which is
great pytee, | In hertes may not lightly
staunched be' (iii. 5348 ff.). It is doubtful
whether Shakespeare meant to imply the
same moral.

5.7.1 **Myrmidons** According to Caxton, the
   Myrmidons did not enter the battle until
   long after the death of Hector. The circumstances of Hector's death are
   borrowed from Caxton's account of the
   death of Troilus.

2 **wheel** change direction, as in military
   parlance (to encircle Hector?)

8 Pope marked a new scene here; Dyce,
   followed by later editors, ignored the

division, but the stage is cleared and the
action is not continuous.

10 '**Loo** a cry to incite a dog to attack

10–11 **double-horned Spartan** The F reading, 'double hen'd sparrow', would refer
   to Paris, sparrows being proverbially
   lecherous. The Q reading, 'double hen'd
   spartan', would refer to Menelaus and
   imply that he had a double (deceitful)
   wife. Neither reading is satisfactory. As
   Thersites is treating the fight as a bull-
   baiting, with alternate references to the
   two combatants, one would expect the
   disputed reading, coming as it does between two references to Paris as a dog,
   would refer to Menelaus. The Kellner conjecture makes excellent sense: Menelaus
   is double-horned, as bull and as cuckold.
   Walker compares 5.1.52 ff.

11 **has the game** is winning

valour, in everything illegitimate. One bear will not
bite another, and wherefore should one bastard? Take
heed; the quarrel's most ominous to us; if the son of a   20
whore fight for a whore, he tempts judgement. Farewell,
bastard.   *Exit*

MARGARELON The devil take thee, coward!   *Exit*

5.8   *Enter Hector*

HECTOR

Most putrefièd core, so fair without,
Thy goodly armour thus hath cost thy life.
Now is my day's work done. I'll take good breath.
Rest, sword; thou hast thy fill of blood and death.
        He disarms.
        Enter Achilles and Myrmidons

ACHILLES

Look, Hector, how the sun begins tó set,
How ugly night comes breathing at his heels;
Even with the vail and dark'ning of the sun,
To close the day up, Hector's life is done.

HECTOR

I am unarmed; forgo this vantage, Greek.

ACHILLES

Strike, fellows, strike; this is the man I seek.   10
        They strike Hector down
So, Ilium, fall thou next! Come, Troy, sink down!
Here lies thy heart, thy sinews, and thy bone.
On, Myrmidons, and cry you all amain:
'Achilles hath the mighty Hector slain.'

---

22 *Exit*] WALKER (*goes*); *not in* QF   23 *Exit*] *Exeunt* F
5.8.3 good] F; my Q   4.1 *He disarms*] KITTREDGE; *not in* QF   7 dark'ning] darking F   10.1
They ... down] ROWE (*subs.*); *not in* QF   11 next! Come] now F   13 and cry] cry F

18–19 **One bear will not bite another** Tilley
W606

5.8.0.1 As there would be some difficulty in
removing the body, though presumably
the Myrmidons could remove it with Hector's, it is probable that Hector does not
lug on the body of the Greek he has killed.
Possibly he comes on with the armour
alone.

1 **putrefièd** S. L. Bethell, *Shakespeare and the
Popular Dramatic Tradition* (1944), 104,
remarks on 'the "outward show" which
covers an inner corruption . . . The
"sumptuous armour" with its "putrefied
core" thus becomes a symbol of all the
play presents to us'.

7 **vail** going down (Onions)

Retreat sounded
Hark! A retire upon our Grecian part.
A MYRMIDON
The Trojan trumpets sound the like, my lord.
ACHILLES
The dragon wing of night o'erspreads the earth,
And stickler-like the armies separates.
My half-supped sword that frankly would have fed,
Pleased with this dainty bait, thus goes to bed.   20
He sheathes his sword
Come, tie his body to my horse's tail;
Along the field I will the Trojan trail.

Exeunt

5.9   *Sound retreat. Shouts off. Enter Agamemnon, Ajax,*
Menelaus, Nestor, Diomedes, and the rest, marching
to the sound of drums
AGAMEMNON   Hark! Hark! What shout is that?
NESTOR   Peace, drums!
SOLDIERS   (*within*) Achilles! Achilles! Hector's slain!
Achilles!
DIOMEDES
The bruit is Hector's slain, and by Achilles.
AJAX
If it be so, yet bragless let it be;
Great Hector was as good a man as he.
AGAMEMNON
March patiently along. Let one be sent
To pray Achilles see us at our tent.
If in his death the gods have us befriended,   10
Great Troy is ours, and our sharp wars are ended.

Exeunt

14.1 *sounded*] MALONE; *not in* QF   15 retire] retreat F   part] F; prat Q   16 Trojan trumpets]
F; Troyans trumpet Q   sound] sounds F   20 bait] bed F   20.1 *He...sword*] MALONE; *not in* QF
5.9.0.1 *Sound retreat*] F; *not in* Q   *Shouts off*] CAPELL (*after 5.9.2*); *Shout* F; *not in* Q   0.3 *to*
the sound of drums] This edition; *not in* QF   1 shout] F; *not in* Q   that] F; this Q   3 (*within*)] *not*
in F   7 as good a man] a man as good F

18 **stickler-like** i.e. like a referee. 'The   19 **frankly** freely, unrestrictedly
dragon wing' is the subject of the   20 **bait** snack
sentence.   **5.9.5 bruit** rumour, report

5.10   *Enter Aeneas, Paris, Antenor, and Deiphobus*

AENEAS

Stand, ho! Yet are we masters of the field.
   Enter Troilus

TROILUS

Never go home; here starve we out the night.
Hector is slain.

ALL   Hector! The gods forbid!

TROILUS

He's dead; and at the murderer's horse's tail
In beastly sort dragged through the shameful field.
Frown on, you heavens, effect your rage with speed!
Sit, gods, upon your thrones and smile at Troy!
I say, at once let your brief plagues be mercy,
And linger not our sure destructions on!

AENEAS

My lord, you do discomfort all the host.   10

TROILUS

You understand me not that tell me so;
I do not speak of flight, of fear of death,
But dare all imminence that gods and men
Address their dangers in. Hector is gone.
Who shall tell Priam so, or Hecuba?
Let him that will a screech-owl aye be called
Go in to Troy and say there 'Hector's dead'.
There is a word will Priam turn to stone,
Make wells and Niobes of the maids and wives,
Cold statues of the youth, and, in a word,   20

5.10.0.1 *and*] F; *not in* Q   1.1 *Enter Troilus*] *as here* Q; *after l.* 2 F   2 TROILUS Never] Neuer F
7 smile] smite HANMER   8 say, at once] DYCE 1864; say at once, QF   16 screech-owl] F
(screechoule); scrich-ould Q   17 in to] F; into Q   there] F; their Q   20 Cold] Coole F

5.10.1–2 **Stand . . . night** F gives both lines
to Aeneas, but the second line, spoken by
Troilus (Q), improves the effectiveness of
his entrance. In F, he enters after l. 2.

2 **starve . . . out** endure in perishing cold
(*OED* 5b; only recorded use in this sense)

5 **sort** fashion

7 **smile** Hanmer's emendation, *smite*, has
been generally accepted, because it appeared to suit the next two lines. But
smite at is feeble; and the gods could hardly do this while sitting on their thrones.

The gods are smiling in scorn, while the
heavens, their instruments, are attacking
Troy (Upton, who cites Psalms 2: 4 and
37: 13: 'He that dwelleth in heaven shall
laugh them to scorn: the Lord shall have
them in derision').

8 **at once . . . mercy** kill us quickly, to put
us out of our misery

13 **imminence** impending evils

14 **Address . . . in** i.e. prepare to endanger me
(whatever form they take)

19 **Niobes** women weeping for their children

Scare Troy out of itself. But march away:
Hector is dead; there is no more to say.
Stay yet. You vile abominable tents,
Thus proudly pight upon our Phrygian plains,
Let Titan rise as early as he dare,
I'll through and through you! And thou great-sized
　　coward,
No space of earth shall sunder our two hates;
I'll haunt thee like a wicked conscience still,
That mouldeth goblins swift as frenzy's thoughts.
Strike a free march to Troy! With comfort go;   30
Hope of revenge shall hide our inward woe.

　　　　　　　　　　　　　　　　Exeunt all except Troilus

　　Enter Pandarus
PANDARUS　But hear you, hear you!
TROILUS
　　Hence broker-lackey! Ignomy and shame
　　Pursue thy life, and live aye with thy name!   *Exit*
PANDARUS
　　A goodly medicine for my aching bones!
　　O world, world, world! – Thus is the poor agent despised.
　　O traitors and bawds, how earnestly are you set a-work,
　　and how ill requited! Why should our endeavour be so
　　desired, and the performance so loathed? What verse for
　　it? What instance for it? Let me see.   40
　　　　Full merrily the humble-bee doth sing
　　　　Till he hath lost his honey and his sting;

21–2 But ... dead] F; *not in* Q　　23 yet. You vile] F; *yet you proud* Q　　24 pight] F; *pitcht* Q
30 march to Troy!] F (*subs.*); *march, to Troy* ∧ Q　　31.1 *Exeunt ... Troilus*] MALONE (*subs.*); *not
in* QF　　33 broker-lackey] DYCE; *broker, lacky* QF　　Ignomy and] F; *ignomyny* Q　　´34 *Exit*]
CAPELL; *Exeunt all but Pandarus* Q; *Exeunt* F　　35 my] *mine* F　　36 world, world, world] F; *world,
world* Q　　37 traitors] *traders* DEIGHTON (*conj.* CRAIG)　　39 desired] F; *lou'd* Q

24　**pight** pitched
25　**Titan** Helios, the Sun, one of the Titans.
26　**coward** (Achilles, not Diomedes)
30　**free** unregimented(?)
31　**inward woe** The play at the Globe perfor-
　　mance probably ended here. The 2½ lines
　　which follow come, with some variants,
　　at the end of 5.3 See Appendix 2*e*.
33　**broker-lackey** pander
　　Ignomy ignominy
37　**traitors** Deighton accepted Craig's con-

jecture 'traders'. But 'traders and bawds'
would be feeble, as in this context the
words are synonymous. The later mention of traders (l. 45) makes it less, not
more, likely here. The text as it stands
makes perfectly good sense. Calchas, a
traitor, is despised by the Greeks who use
his services; and when the play was first
performed there were plenty of contemporary traitors.

And being once subdued in armèd tail,
Sweet honey and sweet notes together fail.
Good traders in the flesh, set this in your painted cloths.
As many as be here of Pandar's hall,
Your eyes, half out, weep out at Pandar's fall;
Or if you cannot weep, yet give some groans,
Though not for me, yet for your aching bones.
Brethren and sisters of the hold-door trade,   50
Some two months hence my will shall here be made.
It should be now, but that my fear is this,
Some gallèd goose of Winchester would hiss.
Till then I'll sweat and seek about for eases,
And at that time bequeath you my diseases.   *Exit*

49 your] F; my Q   55 Exit] ROWE 1714; not in Q; Exeunt F

43 **armèd** i.e. with a sting (but with an allusion to impotence caused by venereal disease)

45 **painted cloths** cheap substitutes for tapestries, often with moralistic intent, and with words as well as pictures

46 **hall** Each guild of tradesmen had its own Hall (*OED sb.* 6); Pandarus addresses an imaginary fraternity of master panders.

47 **eyes, half out** Another reference to the ravages of venereal disease.
half out half blind

49 **aching bones** another result of syphilis

50 **sisters of the hold-door trade** whores who stood at the open doors of brothels to attract (or repel) customers

51 **two months hence** See Introduction, p. 8.

53 **gallèd goose of Winchester** The brothels in Southwark were under the jurisdiction of the Bishop of Winchester. A 'gallèd goose' is a person suffering from venereal disease, either a prostitute or her client. (A 'Winchester goose' can also mean a swelling in the groin, but not apparently here.)
hiss as a sign of the audience's displeasure (so that those who hissed would be identifying themselves as diseased)

54 **sweat** the standard treatment for venereal disease

APPENDIX

ON the whole it seems most likely that this epistle was written soon after the private performance of the play and before the public performance. It must have turned up during the printing of the Quarto, but may well have been written in 1602 or early 1603, at the time of the original entry in the Stationers' Register, when it was hoped to publish the play. Bonian and Walley, going by the early entry, may have genuinely believed that the play had been performed at the Globe, but then the epistle seemed to show that they and the Stationers' Register had been mistaken. Hence their attempt to put the record straight – though they did the opposite – by altering the title-page and inserting the epistle. If this account is correct, it would seem to suggest that the play was not successful enough to remain for long in the Globe repertory.

The text of the Epistle from Q^b is given below in modernized spelling.

A NEVER WRITER, TO AN EVER READER. NEWS.

Eternal reader, you have here a new play, never staled with the stage, never clapper-clawed with the palms of the vulgar, and yet passing full of the palm comical; for it is a birth of your brain that never undertook anything comical, vainly: and were but the vain names of comedies changed for the titles of commodities, or of plays for pleas, you should see all 5 those grand censors that now style them such vanities, flock to them for the main grace of their gravities – especially this author's comedies, that are so framed to the life, that they serve for the most common commentaries of all the actions of our lives, showing such a dexterity and power of wit, that the most displeased with plays are pleased with his comedies. 10 And all such dull and heavy-witted worldlings, as were never capable of the wit of a comedy, coming by report of them to his representations, have found that wit there that they never found in themselves, and have parted

A NEVER WRITER This seems to imply that the author was not a professional.

1 **a new play** This shows that the epistle was written soon after the first performance, rather than in 1609.
   never staled with the stage not performed on the public stage. Either these words were written before a public performance, or so long after that it had been forgotten. See the previous note.

2 **clapper-clawed** The usual meaning of 'clapper-clawing' (5.4.1) is thrashing, or reviling. Here it seems telescoped with

clapping. The applause of the groundlings would be regarded by the snob who wrote the epistle as an adverse recommendation.

3 **your brain** Frequently emended (e.g. by Greg, *The Shakespeare First Folio* (Oxford, 1955), 339) to 'that brain', i.e. Shakespeare. But 'your' makes reasonable sense as 'that you know of' (*OED* 5b).

5–6 **commodities . . . censors** It looks as though there had been some ill-feeling between the city and one of the Inns of Court.

better witted than they came, feeling an edge of wit set upon them, more
15 than ever they dreamed they had brain to grind it on. So much and such
savoured salt of wit is in his comedies that they seem (for their height of
pleasure) to be born in that sea that brought forth Venus. Amongst all
there is none more witty than this; and had I time I would comment upon
it, though I know it needs not (for so much as will make you think your
20 testern well bestowed) but for so much worth, as even poor I know to be
stuffed in it. It deserves such a labour, as well as the best comedy in Terence
or Plautus. And believe this, that when he is gone, and his comedies out
of sale, you will scramble for them, and set up a new English Inquisition.
Take this for a warning; and at the peril of your pleasure's loss and judge-
25 ments, refuse not, nor like this the less for not being sullied with the smoky
breath of the multitude; but thank fortune for the scape it hath made
amongst you, since by the grand possessors' wills I believe you should
have prayed for them rather than been prayed. And so I leave all such to
be prayed for (for the states of their wits' healths) that will not praise it.
30 *Vale.*

17 **born . . . Venus** Shakespeare's comedies had love as their theme, and possibly there is a suggestion that they give sexual pleasure.

20 **testern** a form of 'tester', i.e. sixpence

22–3 **out of sale** out of print

23 **English Inquisition** The phrase, not recorded in *OED*, seems to have passed without comment. It appears to be a joking allusion to the result of Archbishop Whitgift's appeal to Elizabeth 'to establish a new Commission for Causes Ecclesiastical . . . the main purpose of which . . . was to enable him to search out all unlawfully printed books and to deal with those "disordered persons (commonly called Puritans)"' (Donald J. McGinn, *John Penry and the Marprelate Controversy*, New Brunswick, 1960, p. 37). Lord Burghley disapproved of Whitgift's extreme anti-Puritanism and, in a letter of 1 July 1584, complained that the 'instrument of twenty-four articles, of great length and curiosity formed in a Romish style . . .' was 'so curiously penned, so full of branches and circumstance, as I think the Inquisitors of Spain use not so many questions to comprehend and to trap their prey' (cited in Conyers Read's *Lord Burghley and Queen Elizabeth*, 1960, repr. 1966, p. 295). (S.W.)

25–6 **not being . . . multitude** Another attempt to excuse the lack of a public performance.

26 **scape** escape into print

27 **grand possessors** Possibly the owner of the manuscript, but more likely the actors who did not like to release any of Shakespeare's comedies.

28 **prayed . . . prayed** prayed for them to be released for publication, rather than prayed to buy copies.

28 **them** Sometimes emended to 'it', but it refers to the comedies as a whole.

2. TEXTUAL NOTES

(a) 2.1.36–42

QUARTO:

> Ther. Thou shouldst strike him, *Aiax Cobloafe*,
> Hee would punne thee into shiuers with his fist, as a saylet
> breakes a bisket, you horson curre. Do? do?
> *Aiax:* Thou stoole for a witch:
> Ther. I, Do? do? thou sodden witted Lord, thou hast

FOLIO:

> *Ther.* Thou should'st strike him.
> *Aia.* Cobloafe.
> *Ther.* He would pun thee into shiuers with his fist, as
> a Sailor breakes a bisket.
> *Aia.* You horson Curre.   *Ther.* Do,do.
> *Aia.* Thou stoole for a Witch.
> *Ther.* I, do,do,thou sodden-witted Lord: thou hast

The Q compositor did not realize that *Aiax* in the first of these lines was a speech prefix; and he left out the speech prefix (*Ther.*) in the next line, and two other speech prefixes (*Aiax., Ther.*) in the third of these lines. F corrects these four errors. Walker argues convincingly that, in view of the hoary pun on *Ajax/a jakes*, 'Thou stoole for a witch' should be spoken to Ajax, not by him. The *Aia* is probably a vocative. Riverside concurs. It may be added that 'Cobloaf' interrupts Thersites' remark, and 'strike him' should therefore be followed by a dash. Pope adds the obvious direction '*Beating him*' at l. 40.

(b) 2.3.124–7

QUARTO:

> yea watch
>
> His course, and time, his ebbs and flowes, and if
> The passage, and whole streame of his commencement,
> Rode on his tide.

FOLIO:

> yea watch
>
> His pettish lines, his ebs, his flowes, as if
> The passage and whole carriage of this action
> Rode on his tyde.

It seems probable that Shakespeare himself was responsible for both

versions of this passage. The third *his* (125) in F may be a misprint or a first
shot, corrected to *and*, or even a legitimate correction. In the same line F
as is clearly right, Q *and* being repeated by mistake. Most editors accept
Hanmer's *lunes*, which is supported by *Winter's Tale* 2.2.30. It has, however, been suggested that this was a misprint for *lines*, which in both
contexts makes good sense as 'course of action or conduct' (*OED* line *sb.*[2]
27, 29). In the next line, as Deighton suggests, the words 'streame of his
commencement' (which Walker would emend to *commercement*) were
altered to avoid 'such a figure as a stream riding upon a tide, and perhaps
also because of "the stream of his dispose" (173)'. In the F version, which
we follow with Hanmer's emendation, 'this action' refers to the expedition
to Troy.

(c) 2.3.208–16

QUARTO:

> *Agam.* Hee wilbe the phisition, that should bee the paci-
> ent.   *Aiax.* And all men were of my minde.
> *Vliss.* Wit would bee out of fashion.
> *Aiax:* A should not beare it so, a should eate swords first?
> shall pride carry it?
> *Nest.* And two o'od yow'd carry halfe.
> *Aiax.* A would haue ten shares. I will kneade him, Ile
> make him supple he's not yet through warme?
> *Nest.* Force him with praiers poure in, poure, his ambition
> is die.

FOLIO:

> *Ag.* He will be the Phyfitian that should be the pa-
> tient.
> *Aia.* And all men were a my minde.
> *Vlif.* Wit would be out of fashion.
> *Aia.* A should not beare it so, a should eate Swords
> first: shall pride carry it?
> *Nest.* And 'twould, you'ld carry halfe.
> *Vlif.* A would haue ten shares.
> *Aia.* I will knede him, Ile make him supple, hee's not
> yet through warme.
> *Nest.* Force him with praifes, poure in, poure in; his am-
> bition is dry.

Apart from an obvious misprint in Q (*praiers*) and one omission, the two
texts closely correspond. But there is considerable disagreement about the

allocation of speeches. As Nestor and Ulysses exchange satirical remarks about Ajax, F is right to give 'A would haue ten shares' to Ulysses (meaning that Ajax would get all). There remains the question of the rest of the speech ascribed to Ajax. If Ajax is really the speaker, he must be referring to Achilles, and must be interpreted to mean that he will somehow bring down his pride. But this surely is a forced interpretation of the massaging metaphor. Nestor's next speech apparently refers to their buttering up of Ajax, and it seems to be a natural continuation of 'He's not yet through warme'. It would therefore seem that the speech ('A would . . . warme') should all be spoken by Ulysses and refer to Ajax. This is the conclusion of Riverside and is here followed.

(d) 5.3.19–24

QUARTO:

> *A*nd. O be perſwaded, do not count it holy,
> It is the purpoſe that makes ſtrong the vow,
> But vowes to euery purpoſe muſt not hold.

FOLIO:

> *And.* O be perſwaded, doe not count it holy,
> To hurt by being iuſt; it is as lawfull:
> For we would count giue much to as violent thefts,
> And rob in the behalfe of charitie.
> *Caſſ.* It is the purpoſe that makes ſtrong the vowe;
> But vowes to euery purpoſe muſt not hold:

Q omits three lines and ascribes two of Cassandra's lines to Andromache. Either Shakespeare himself omitted them or, since the two speeches of Cassandra which sandwich Andromache's lines make 'a logically complete unit' (New Variorum), he may have written some partially legible lines in the margin, which the Q compositor failed to decipher. The F compositor spoilt his attempt to decipher the lines by copying *count* from the first of Andromache's lines, and *as* from the second. The meaning seems to be that to steal for charity is as lawful as hurting people by keeping a vow. Collier's conjecture ('For he would countenance give to violent thefts') would explain the second *count*, but would be improved if it were preceded by a line 'To commit ill that good may come of it' or some similar words. Most modern editors, however, with varying degrees of reluctance, accept Tyrwhitt's conjecture 'For we would give much, to use violent thefts'. Riverside paraphrases the first half of the line 'For we would like to give generously'. It seems unlikely that Shakespeare wrote this; but Dyce quoted appositely from Middleton, *Women Beware Women* (4.3.36), 'to use adulterous thefts'.

(e) 5.3.112+

FOLIO:

> *Pand.* Why, but heare you?
> *Troy.* Hence brother lackie ; ignomie and ſhame
> Purſue thy life, and liue aye with thy name.
>   *A Larum.*   *Exeunt.*

These lines, which are omitted at this point in Q but printed in 5.10 both in Q and (with variants) in F, belong to a version of the play in which Pandarus did not reappear. If the epilogue was added, Shakespeare borrowed these lines as a connecting link between Troilus' last speech on the battlefield and the epilogue. They should have been deleted in 5.3, as their absence in Q shows. But if the epilogue belonged only to the first version of the play, then Shakespeare, in meaning to delete it, inserted the lines in 5.3.

3. ALTERATIONS TO LINEATION

1.1.32–3	Well . . . else] *as verse, breaking after* 'Well', 'looke', 'else' F
1.2.15–16	They . . . alone] *as here* CAPELL; *as prose* QF
65–6	Then . . . Hector] *as here* This edition; *as prose* Q; *lines ending* 'say', 'Hector' F
1.3.1	Princes . . . cheeks?] Princes:	What . . . cheekes? F
123	And . . . Agamemnon] *as here* ROWE; *as two lines, breaking after* 'himself' QF
226–7	Modest . . . Phoebus] *as here* F; *as one line* Q
326–7	Ay . . . him] *as here* F; *as one line* Q
359–60]	*as here* F; *as prose* Q
2.2.50–1	Brother . . . keeping] *as here* THEOBALD; *as prose* Q; *as two lines, breaking after* 'worth' F
2.3.187–8	As . . . to Achilles] *as here* JOHNSON; *as one line* QF
196–7	If . . . face] *as here* ROWE 1714; *as prose* QF
221–2	Here . . . silent] *as here* F; *as prose* Q
225–6]	*as here* POPE; *as prose* QF
3.1.63–4]	*as prose* CAPELL; *as verse, breaking after* 'Queen, go to – ' QF
65–6]	*as prose* HANMER; *as verse, breaking after* 'melody' QF
118–9]	*as two lines* F; *as one line* Q
120–1]	*as two lines* POPE; *as one line* QF
3.2.69–70]	*as prose* POPE; *as verse, breaking after* 'fear' QF
116–8]	*as here* ROWE; *as prose* QF
3.3.73–4	To come . . . altars] *as here* ROWE 1714; *as one line* QF
86–7	Doth . . . fall] *as here* F; *as one line* Q
125–6]	*as here* Q; *breaking after* 'Ajax', 'horse', 'are' F
142–4]	*as here* JOHNSON AND STEEVENS 1778; *lines ending* 'it', 'beggars', 'look', 'forgot' QF
148–50]	*as here* JOHNSON AND STEEVENS; *lines ending* 'past', 'made', 'lord' QF
170–1]	*as here* POPE; *as one line* QF
4.1.34–5]	*as here* F; *line-break after* 'business' Q
45–6	With . . . unwelcome] *as here* F; *line-break after* 'wherefore' Q
46–8	That . . . Troy] *as here* F; *as prose* Q
49–50	The . . . so] *as here* POPE; *as one line* QF
79–80]	*as here* F; *as prose* Q
4.2.15	Prithee, tarry] *as here* CAPELL; *as part of next line* QF
23–4]	*as prose* POPE; *as verse, breaking after* 'maidenheads' QF
27–8]	*as prose* POPE; *as verse, breaking after* 'say what' QF
29–30]	*as verse* CAPELL; *as prose* QF
45–6]	*as verse* POPE; *as prose* QF
73–5]	*as verse* This edition; *as prose* QF
78–9]	*as here* SISSON; *as prose* QF
4.4.15–19]	*as here* POPE (*subs.*); *as consecutive prose* QF
53–4]	*as verse* CAPELL; *as prose* QF
65–6]	*as here* F; *as prose* Q
72–3	To . . . true] *as here* F; *as one line* Q
4.5.5–6	May . . . hither] *as here* F; *as one line* Q
20–3]	*as verse* POPE; *as prose* QF
38–9]	*as here* POPE; *as one line* QF
70–1	By . . . ask] *as here* ROWE 1714; *as one line* QF
75–6	If . . . name] *as here* POPE 1728; *as one line* QF
224–5	And . . . it] *as here* F; *as one line* Q

231–2	I . . . by joint] *as here* F; *as one line* Q
266–7	We . . . cause] *as here* F; *as one line* Q
268–9	Tomorrow . . . friends] *as here* F; *as one line* Q
5.1.45–6]	*as here* F; *as one line* Q
64–5	No . . . lights] *as here* CAPELL; *as one line* QF
74–5]	*as verse* THEOBALD; *as prose* QF
5.2.14–15]	*as here* CAPELL; *as prose* QF
45–6	Doth . . . truth] *as here* CAPELL; *as prose* QF
50–1]	*as here* F2; *as prose* Q, F1
97–100	Why . . . you] *as here* F; *as prose* Q
101–2]	*as here* HANMER; *as prose* QF
122–3	Created . . . here?] *as here* F; *as one line* Q
172–4]	*as here* F; *as two lines, breaking after* 'descent' Q
5.3.92]	*as here* F; *as two lines, breaking after* 'town' Q
5.4.17–18	Fly . . . after] *as here* F; *as prose* Q
20–1	Withdrew . . . thee] *as here* F; *as one line* Q
22–3]	*as prose* F; *as verse, breaking after* 'Trojan' Q
5.5.41–2]	*as here* ROWE 1714; *as one line* QF

INDEX TO THE COMMENTARY

BIBLICAL parallels and proverbial expressions are grouped together. As *Troilus and Cressida*'s vocabulary is of exceptional interest, an asterisk is used to indicate that this is the first recorded occurrence of a word as well as for words used in a sense not recorded in *OED*.

.

	Women's Writing 1778–1838
WILLIAM BECKFORD	**Vathek**
JAMES BOSWELL	**Life of Johnson**
FRANCES BURNEY	**Camilla**
	Cecilia
	Evelina
	The Wanderer
LORD CHESTERFIELD	**Lord Chesterfield's Letters**
JOHN CLELAND	**Memoirs of a Woman of Pleasure**
DANIEL DEFOE	**A Journal of the Plague Year**
	Moll Flanders
	Robinson Crusoe
	Roxana
HENRY FIELDING	**Joseph Andrews and Shamela**
	A Journey from This World to the Next and
	The Journal of a Voyage to Lisbon
	Tom Jones
WILLIAM GODWIN	**Caleb Williams**
OLIVER GOLDSMITH	**The Vicar of Wakefield**
MARY HAYS	**Memoirs of Emma Courtney**
ELIZABETH HAYWOOD	**The History of Miss Betsy Thoughtless**
ELIZABETH INCHBALD	**A Simple Story**
SAMUEL JOHNSON	**The History of Rasselas**
	The Major Works
CHARLOTTE LENNOX	**The Female Quixote**
MATTHEW LEWIS	**Journal of a West India Proprietor**
	The Monk
HENRY MACKENZIE	**The Man of Feeling**
ALEXANDER POPE	**Selected Poetry**

The Oxford World's Classics Website

www.worldsclassics.co.uk

- Information about new titles
- Explore the full range of Oxford World's Classics
- Links to other literary sites and the main OUP webpage
- Imaginative competitions, with bookish prizes
- Peruse the Oxford World's Classics Magazine
- Articles by editors
- Extracts from Introductions
- A forum for discussion and feedback on the series
- Special information for teachers and lecturers

www.worldsclassics.co.uk

American Literature

British and Irish Literature

Children's Literature

Classics and Ancient Literature

Colonial Literature

Eastern Literature

European Literature

History

Medieval Literature

Oxford English Drama

Poetry

Philosophy

Politics

Religion

The Oxford Shakespeare

A complete list of Oxford Paperbacks, including Oxford World's Classics, OPUS, Past Masters, Oxford Authors, Oxford Shakespeare, Oxford Drama, and Oxford Paperback Reference, is available in the UK from the Academic Division Publicity Department, Oxford University Press, Great Clarendon Street, Oxford OX2 6DP.

In the USA, complete lists are available from the Paperbacks Marketing Manager, Oxford University Press, 198 Madison Avenue, New York, NY 10016.

Oxford Paperbacks are available from all good bookshops. In case of difficulty, customers in the UK can order direct from Oxford University Press Bookshop, Freepost, 116 High Street, Oxford OX1 4BR, enclosing full payment. Please add 10 per cent of published price for postage and packing.